POSTRACIAL RESISTANCE

CRITICAL CULTURAL COMMUNICATION

General Editors: Jonathan Gray, Aswin Punathambekar, Nina Huntemann
Founding Editors: Sarah Banet-Weiser and Kent A. Ono

Postracial Resistance

Black Women, Media, and the
Uses of Strategic Ambiguity

Ralina L. Joseph

March 4, 2019

Dear Havana,
I hope you see yourself in these pages! You are an inspirational young woman who is shooting to the stars. I am blessed to know you!

Love,
R.

NEW YORK UNIVERSITY PRESS
New York

NEW YORK UNIVERSITY PRESS
New York
www.nyupress.org

References to Internet websites (URLs) were accurate at the time of writing. Neither the author nor New York University Press is responsible for URLs that may have expired or changed since the manuscript was prepared.

Library of Congress Cataloging-in-Publication Data
Names: Joseph, Ralina L. (Ralina Landwehr), 1974–   author.
Title: Postracial resistance : Black women, media, and the uses of strategic ambiguity / Ralina L. Joseph.
Description: New York : New York University Press, [2018] | Series: Critical cultural communication | Includes bibliographical references and index.
Identifiers: LCCN 2017060990 | ISBN 9781479862825 (cl : alk. paper) | ISBN 9781479886371 (pb : alk. paper)
Subjects: LCSH: African Americans and mass media. | Mass media and women. | African American women—Social conditions.
Classification: LCC P94.5.A37 J67 2018 | DDC 305.48/896073—dc23
LC record available at https://lccn.loc.gov/2017060990

New York University Press books are printed on acid-free paper, and their binding materials are chosen for strength and durability. We strive to use environmentally responsible suppliers and materials to the greatest extent possible in publishing our books.

Manufactured in the United States of America

10 9 8 7 6 5 4 3 2 1

Also available as an ebook

Forever, for always: JJ, NV, TJ

CONTENTS

In their very first conversation, a college student's new roommate shifts the conversation from pleasantries about home towns and class schedules to hair, first complementing her roommate's "cool style," and then moving closer, saying, "I just want to see what it feels like." Just before her roommate's hand grazes her locs, the student gently catches and removes it. She feels her stomach, her cheeks, and her hands constrict with indignation but she doesn't slap her hand away; she doesn't yell; she doesn't lecture. She takes a breath, permits a tired smile, and says, with a measured tone, "please don't touch my hair." Later she will journal about this experience, describe it in her request letter to transfer into a single, and share it with faculty, students, staff, and community members at her campus's #BlackLivesMatter protest.

The morning after another widely-televised murder of a Black man goes viral, the woman heads back to her job as a television writer. She takes a deep breath at the threshold of the writers' room, pausing to re-balance her coffee, laptop, and script bursting with a rainbow of sticky notes. She hears raucous laughter and feels relieved at the promised distraction, but as soon as she walks in the conversation stops and her colleagues' eyes dart to their phone screens. Busying herself with setting up her space, and giving herself a pep talk to pitch her first idea, she smiles and enthuses, "you all ready to start?" Later she will channel her emotions from this moment into her own spec script.

On the first day of classes, a lecture hall full of students wanting add codes for an oversubscribed course parade past the woman shuffling through papers and outfitted in a tweed blazer and slacks. They line up behind a bearded man in bike commuter attire, sitting on stage, legs dangling. The students address the man reverently as "professor," and ask him for the honor of joining the class. The woman assesses the students in line in front of her flattered and smiling graduate student teaching assistant. She takes the podium and warmly addresses the crowd, "welcome to communication 389! I am your professor, and I will answer all questions about add codes after class." Later she will narrate this experience for her students in her lecture on stereotyping.

In spaces of privilege such as a college dormitory, a writers' room, or a lecture hall, twenty-first century racism and sexism rarely register as blatant or bald. Instead, gendered and racialized discrimination functions as a frequently ignored, allegedly well-intentioned, often-excused phenomenon. Such moments of racialized sexism are textbook examples of microaggressions, what psychologist Derald Wing Sue describes as "brief, everyday exchanges that send denigrating messages to certain individuals because of their group membership."[1] Microaggressions thrive in spaces where racism remains unacknowledged, and where people believe in the fallacy that our world is now postracial, or that we are beyond racialized inequality, and perhaps race itself. But racialized identity is better understood through the matrix of domination, to use sociologist Patricia Hill Collins's famous phrase[2]—the imbricated connections of race, gender, sexuality, and class that construct intersectional identity. Postracial ideologies hide that matrix, denying that it even exists.

This book developed in part from my own everyday experience of negotiating resistance to microaggressions in a world where racism and sexism continue to be a given for some, and a fantasy for others. It emerged from my life as a professional (and privileged) woman of color. Within a month of being a new assistant professor, I learned a word that I would come to hear virtually every time I was given advice by a well-meaning colleague: strategic. I needed to be strategic. Being strategic meant not simply writing and publishing steadily as I climbed the tenure hill. It meant choosing my battles, meting out my words, and conducting myself in a quieter, less obtrusive, and less radical way. It meant not making people uncomfortable. While my White, male colleagues might have received the same advice, such words registered differently with me. I heard that my research, which pushed on the boundaries of communication scholarship, was dangerous and illegitimate; I learned that I myself, a woman of color faculty member, was dangerous and illegitimate.

So I held my nose, swallowed my pill, and learned how to become strategic. The words of my advisor Jane Rhodes rang clear in my head: if you don't earn tenure, you don't just lose your job, you lose your career. That wasn't going to be me. As I became more deeply inculcated into the ways of a large research university, I learned how to hold on to my core critique and perform in the respectably calculated ways that the university demanded: I learned how to be strategically ambiguous. I learned how to foster my own communities; I learned how to bite my tongue in certain spaces, and sing freely in others. I learned how to think of my carefully controlled speech in particular places as an exercise in delayed gratification; I learned how to play the long game. This book emerged from my lived experience of strategic ambiguity. It began as a side project when I was finishing my first book, *Transcending Blackness: From the New Millennium Mulatta to the Exceptional Multiracial* (Duke University Press, 2013). As I shared pieces of it at conferences and in journal articles, the identity negotiations I came to understand as strategic ambiguity registered as something not exclusive to me, but emblematic of privileged minoritized subjects' constraints and resistance in the so-called postracial era. This book is for all of my people who perform strategic ambiguity with a wink, a sigh, a nod, and a determination to not just exist, but resist.

Introduction

When morning news show host Robin Roberts interviewed TV star and media darling Kerry Washington on the 2016 Oscars Red Carpet, the two glamorous Black women celebrities,[1] replete in sleeveless floor-length gowns, dipped their toes into the topic of the day, #OscarsSoWhite. While the hashtag swirled across social media to critique the total absence of actors of color on the award list, Washington spoke without ever naming race, or using the words "Black" or "White":

> I mean I felt like a lot of people have asked me why I'm here tonight and the thing I've been thinking about is that when you think about the history of movements, the history of change, a lot of voices are needed at the table so I really respect and actually admire some of the people who are not here tonight—I really get it. But for me I felt like my voice and my heart, my voice is best used at the table. As a new member of the academy, I joined the academy about three years ago, I really want to be part of the conversation to make sure that there's institutional change so that we never have a year like this again, so that we can be as inclusive as possible.

With few, controlled gestures and a welcoming smile, Washington graciously supported Black celebrities, like Jada Pinkett Smith, who took a very different approach to the topic of Black exclusion in Hollywood by boycotting the event. Washington nodded towards herself as a change-maker in a movement and stressed that her role was to claim a spot "at the table." To underscore this idea, Washington explained, "we need everybody's feelings. We need all those voices at the table." She concluded her "inclusive" statement by asserting that the issue was "about women, it's about people of color, it's about age, it's about making sure that our films and the awards that we give for films represent humanity." In that quick two-minute interview, Washington coyly, and in a

Figure I.1. The look of strategic ambiguity. Screenshot from "2016 Oscars: Kerry Washington Explains Why She Is Presenting Amid Diversity Protests," The Hollywood Reporter, March 28, 2016. Viewed June 12, 2017. www.hollywoodreporter.com/.

postracial manner, did not name Black representation; she did not name racism; she did not name #OscarsSoWhite or #BlackLivesMatter. What she did instead was speak through code as Blackness emerged through the inclusive term "people of color." Invoking other underrepresented groups, she created equivalences between gender, age, and race to soften the prickly issue of White-perpetrated, anti-Black racism.

Washington tied up her ideas with the ultimate postracial bow of "inclusivity" and "humanity." Her demure, ladylike performance contrasted sharply with Oscar host and comedian Chris Rock's skewering of anti-Black racism, which uplifted Black men by stepping on Black women and other people of color; it also diverged from Pinkett Smith's direct, speak (Twitter) truth to power boycott, pilloried by Rock and others as ineffectual, outmoded, and the stereotypical act of an Angry Black Woman. Washington's equivocation ensured both that a large, diverse audience heard her intersectional suggestion for inclusion, and that neither #AllLivesMatter nor #BlackLivesMatter supporters changed the channel. It was an Oscar-worthy performance of what this book calls *postracial resistance* through the use of *strategic ambiguity*.

In the recent, but what feels like long-ago moment, the *Michelle* Obama era, Black women redefined what it meant to be an icon in our celebrity-obsessed world. They enjoyed some of the most prestigious and most visible positions in U.S. popular culture and yet still could not speak in a forthright manner about racialized and gendered discrimination in mainstream spaces without retribution. Strategic ambiguity is a way of pushing back against that discrimination anyway through a coded resistance to postracial ideologies. It entails foregrounding crossover appeal, courting multiple publics, speaking in coded language, and smoothing and soothing fears of difference as simply an incidental sidenote. Strategic ambiguity comes about when a privileged minoritized person—in the first half of this book, a Black woman celebrity—and in the second half—a Black woman audience member or Hollywood cultural worker—gauges microaggressions in a room and uses the failure to *name* racism—one of the primary tools of postrace—in order to, as Washington puts it, claim a seat at the table.

Strategic ambiguity registers to postracial racists (i.e., those who hold deeply racist beliefs—both acknowledged and unacknowledged—but know better than to iterate them in public) as a safe response to twenty-first century gendered racism because it does not appear to upend the space; strategic ambiguity does not attack racialized sexism through walk-outs, pickets, or sit-ins. At the same time, strategic ambiguity is not simply the safe choice. It's a different, necessarily subtle form of resistance and risk that balances on an escape hatch of deniability. Any race/gender talk by Black women is risky, even if that risk is insulated by the extreme privilege of celebrity, the conflicting codes of postrace, and the deniability of strategic ambiguity. As media consumers, we watch our favorite (or most hated) celebrities negotiating microaggressive forms of postracial racism, and we see our own strategies of resistance mirrored or rejected, which enables us to form new strategies for everyday life that align or diverge from their performances.

As Washington's performance on the Red Carpet demonstrates, Black women's inclusion—to use her word—in elite arenas such as celebrity culture was contingent upon their performance of strategic ambiguity. Washington was not the only celebrity whose success was contingent upon such a performance, and television was not the only cultural medium to deliver such a message. Because she showcased herself as a connoisseur of glamour and fitness, fashion blogs extolled the stylistic virtues of our First Lady, Michelle Obama, and lifestyle blogs fetishized her exercise routine and healthy diet. Because she "transcended race," in her own words, media mogul Oprah Winfrey remained *Forbes'* number one most powerful celebrity in the world year after year.[2] Because she exuberantly promoted "colorblind casting," entertainment magazines proclaimed that African American woman writer/producer/director (i.e. *showrunner*) Shonda Rhimes cracked the code of television (melo) drama, churning out the hits *Private Practice* (2007–2013), *Grey's Anatomy* (2005–present), *Scandal* (2012–2018), and *How to Get Away with Murder* (2014–present). Because she sold her "African American, Native American, French" heritage as purchasable through the L'Oréal makeup True Match color called "soft sable," Queen Bey—superstar singer Beyoncé Knowles—garnered crossover fans; her earlier strategic ambiguity laid the groundwork for her to transform to a Black feminist heroine of wokeness whose "Negro/Creole" background became an unapologetic articulation of radical Southern Blackness.[3]

Postracial Resistance: Black Women, Media, and the Uses of Strategic Ambiguity looks at how, in the first Black First Lady era, African American women celebrities, cultural producers, and audiences subversively used the tools of postracial discourse—the media-propagated notion that race and race-based discrimination are over, and that race and racism no longer affect the everyday lives of both Whites and people of color—in order to resist its very tenets. "The postracial discourse," communication scholar Manoucheka Celeste argues, "seeks to keep power structures intact by making them almost impossible to critique."[4] This is a key part of the ambiguity in strategic ambiguity. Black women's resistance to disenfranchisement has a long history in the U.S., including struggles for emancipation, suffrage, and *de jure* and *de facto* civil rights. In the Michelle Obama era, some minoritized subjects used a different, more individual form of resistance by negotiating through strategic ambiguity. I listen to and watch Black women in three different places in media culture: I use textual analysis to read the strategies of the Black women celebrities themselves; I use production analysis to harvest insights from my interviews with Black women writers, producers, and studio lawyers; and I use audience ethnography to engage Black women viewers negotiating through the limited representations available to them.

The book arcs from case study analyses that document the individual successes that strategic ambiguity enables and the limitations it creates for Black women celebrities, to a conscientious critique of the way performing strategic ambiguity can (perhaps) unintentionally devolve into playing into racism from the perspective of Black women television professionals and younger viewers. In the first half of the book, I analyze three examples of Black female icons—Michelle Obama, Oprah Winfrey, and Shonda Rhimes—who, in different ways, have experienced a racialized sexism specific to Black women. Each woman's anti-racist, anti-sexist critique enacts postracial resistance by utilizing strategic ambiguity. In the second half of the book, I analyze the words of Black women audiences and industry executives who sometimes perform, sometimes negotiate, and sometimes flout strategic ambiguity in their own resistance to postracial racism.

For many media consumers, the ubiquity of strategically ambiguous Black women on our screens is evidence that we have now, finally, arrived at equality, a world where race and gender are irrelevant in life chances or choices. And yet, such images on our screens—our televisions, phones, computers, tablets, and watches—function as fabricated fantasies that conceal very real intersectional disparities, at once racialized, gendered, sexualized, and classed. A quick snapshot of health statistics shows that African American women have greater rates of high blood pressure than any other group of women,[5] the highest mortality rates from breast cancer,[6] and are four times as likely to die from pregnancy-related causes or have premature births.[7] In the realm of education, African American women's college graduation rate has failed to rise with the rates of White women, Latinas, or Asian American women. Even college degrees do not level the playing field as statistically White women make more than Black women *regardless of* their degrees.[8] Economic statistics tell us that Black women make 64 cents to every 78.1 cents White women make on every White man's dollar.[9] From 1980–2002, the median Black-White wage gap grew among women workers from eight to eighteen percent, while the median Black-White wage gap remained fairly constant for men.[10]

This economic gap persists in the realm of entertainment media, where the median income of Black women writers, who make up only 1.9% of the membership of the Writers Guild of America, is far below other demographic groups.[11] Although during the Michelle Obama era Black women's images on screen were enjoying a surge in popularity,[12]

Black women's representation behind the scenes has yet to experience such a boom. In another subset of representations, the images on social media and mainstream news of seemingly state-sanctioned violence, Black women face similar disproportionality. Media portray that violence as exclusively targeting Black men and boys. For example, 2014 marked the killings of rallied-for names like Mike Brown, Eric Garner, and Tamir Rice at the hands of police, but few know the names of similarly murdered Gabriella Navarez, Aura Rosser, Michelle Cussaux, and Tanisha Anderson.[13] Black cis- and transwomen are systematically murdered in much the same ways Black men are killed: they are caught "driving while Black," and are casualties of the "war on drugs." Like Black men, they receive insufficient services for mental health crises and die in police custody. In addition, Black women also experience a particular form of intersectional oppression. Black women are called criminals after surviving domestic and sexual abuse, are policed because of their gender and/or sexuality, and face excessive force when pregnant and caring for young children. However, these women remain invisible in the media. The activist scholars in the "#SayHerName" project explain: "neither these killings of Black women, nor the lack of accountability for them, have been widely lifted up as exemplars of the systemic police brutality that is currently the focal point of mass protest and policy reform."[14]

Indeed, "the erasure of Black women is not purely a matter of missing facts"—it's also a media framing problem. Media simply do not show *all* Black women—alive or dead—and that means that the greater public does not register the importance of all Black women's lives. The #BlackLivesMatter movement was begun by three Black women—Alicia Garza, Patrisse Cullors, and Opal Tometi—but critics and fans represent the movement online and in protests with an almost exclusive focus on Black men, often through visual registers.[15] The prominent placement of a few Black women celebrities and the erasure of so many others in discursive spaces and representational practices shows up postracial discourse—or the idea that racism is now over—as an empty and dangerous lie.

Postracial Resistance asks what happened when the media spotlighted Michelle Obama, Oprah Winfrey, and the women in Shondaland, but shrouded the nameless, faceless Black women victims of police brutality, the women who did not become the rallying cries of the media's version of #BlackLivesMatter protests or past presidential addresses. This book can help us understand how the United States transitioned from the Obama to the Trump eras; I contend that the lie of postracialism, with its failure to expose how racism lay in wait beneath its façade, helped lull some 2016 Trump voters into the mythology that racism thus no longer existed, and the racial bile Trump spewed was inconsequential. *Postracial Resistance* documents a moment when the media's racial progress narrative of our first Black First Family subsumed discourses of racialized violence against other Black people, and fomented desire for Black celebrity women. This book comes out of the Michelle Obama-Oprah-Beyoncé moment when individual Black women set standards for beauty, talent, and fame for *all* Americans, while structures of racism and sexism remained largely unchanged for large groups of Black women. Media texts can open or foreclose intersectional nuance; media can capture or erase the imbricated nature of race, gender, class, sexuality, and of racism, misogyny, classism, and homophobia. *Postracial Resistance* examines how, in the midst of the discursive foreclosures on racism and sexism at the heart of postracial ideologies, prominent Black women positioned themselves as strategically ambiguous, to what effect, and how cultural producers and audiences rejected such strategic ambiguity.

So What Exactly Is the Postrace in Postracial Resistance?

This book examines performances of Michelle Obama-era strategic ambiguity in the face of *postracial* racism. But what exactly is postrace? "Postrace" is a term used by race commentators to sometimes describe, sometimes decry, and sometimes imagine another racialized world. Postrace is far from neutral; indeed, as a racial ideology, it is so loaded and powerful that it delimited the iterative space for race critics in the Obama era. Commentators of all political stripes and academics in a variety of disciplines encased it in quotation marks, and punctuated the sentences it populated with question marks. Its existence, or lack thereof, was debated and celebrated. For some, it was something to aspire towards; for others, it was something to dismiss. Postrace can be seductive to a wide and diverse swath of race thinkers. One of the more strident embraces of postrace comes from postcolonial theorist

Paul Gilroy who challenges the "crisis of raciology," claiming that hold-ing onto "race thinking," even—or perhaps especially—by anti-racist activists and critical race scholars, fosters "specious ontologies" and "lazy essentialisms."[16] "Postrace" is a term chosen by authors to denote or critique some moment after the importance of race. I use "postrace" to name the ideology—skeptically—and to point out the continued centrality of race in this ideology where race is ostensibly immaterial. I contend that in its very denial of the uses of race, postraciality remains embroiled in precisely what it claims not to be. In other words, postrace is an ideology that cannot escape racialization, complete with control-ling images or racialized stereotypes.

Despite its ubiquity in the 21st century media landscape, postracial lacks a clear definition. Like many post words, postracial is far from self-explanatory. To chase the etymological roots of the word, the first part appears to be self-evident: post is Latin for after, but it also sometimes is translated as behind.[17] Postrace means after race, in an evolutionary, next-stage-of-humanity fashion, as well as behind race, in a hiding-in-plain-sight, out-of-sight-out-of-mind fashion. And how about the second part, the "racial"? Race itself remains an open signifier, something un-tethered from biology, but bound to our everyday and institutionalized lives. Race scholars trip over ourselves to painstakingly point out that we *understand* that race is constructed, but that we must also *document* its very real existence in our world. Put another way, race is something "imagined but not imaginary."[18] With this definition, after race could mean after biological, essentialized definitions of race, after racialism or racial particularity, or, in other words, after racialized primordial attach-ments. After race could mean after estimations of racial difference, lead-ing to an assumed equality of culture, biology, and intelligence. Taken a step further, after race could mean after structural and interpersonal prejudice, or after racism or race-based inequality and injustice. Postrace could also mean against race—again, in the words of Gilroy, where we decry how "ideas of racial particularity . . . provide sources of pride rather than shame and humiliation . . . [and] become difficult to relinquish."[19]

And yet, postrace doesn't mean any of these things alone: context is key. The openness of race further muddies the openness of post. Phi-losopher Kwame Anthony Appiah tracks down the open signifier of two other posts—postcolonial and postmodern—noting that "the *post-* in postcolonial, like the *post-* in postmodern, is the *post-* of the space-clearing gesture ... what has come to be theorized as popular culture, in particular—[is] not in this way concerned with transcending, with going beyond, coloniality."[20] Sociologist Mike Featherstone writes that, with regards to postmodernism, "the prefix 'post' signifies that which comes after, a break or rupture with the modern which is defined in counter-distinction to it." But, Featherstone goes on to argue, this particular post also means "a negation of the modern, a perceived abandonment, break with or shift away from the definitive features of the modern, with the emphasis firmly on the sense of the relational move away."[21] Similarly, postfeminist does not mean "after second wave feminism" to feminist media studies scholars like Angela McRobbie; postfeminism does not denote the egalitarian rewards produced by feminism, but rather a de-clared after moment that ironically conjures pre-feminist ideals.[22]

Another post—post-Black—appears, according to Nicole Fleetwood, to mean not after Black but rather to "register a profound frustration with normative ways of understanding black representation, aesthetic practice, and reception."[23] Curator Thelma Gordon in conversation with artist Glenn Lignon coined post-Black in the 1990s to differentiate a new generation of African American artists, who were, in Gordon's words to journalist Touré, not "labelled Black" but "steeped in Black-ness."[24] Touré describes twenty-first century American post-Blackness as "individual Blackness" as opposed to group consciousness.[25] To Touré, post-Blackness means that "the number of ways of being Black is infinite."[26] Interestingly, in Touré's formulation of post-Blackness, which he riffs off of Michael Eric Dyson's "three primary dimensions of Blackness," Black women barely register. Touré exemplifies his "extro-verted" (Dyson's intentional) Blackness through Malcolm X, Dr. King, Jim Brown, and Jay-Z; his ambiverted/Dyson's incidental Blackness means Barack Obama, Colin Powell, and Will Smith; finally, Touré's "introverted" (Dyson's accidental) Blackness means Clarence Thomas or, in his only example of a woman, Condoleeza Rice. Although Touré interviews some prominent African American women in *Who's Afraid of Post-Blackness?* and indeed acknowledges that the author of the term is herself a woman, in his explication, despite his assertion that post-Blackness comprises a state of "Black multilinguality,"[27] Black women aren't the primary speakers of the language. All of these theoretical post terms—postmodern, postfeminism, postrace, and post-Black—are not simply markings of after, but are instead, in the words of Appiah, "space clearing gestures" that ostensibly make way new ways of expression and being, such as strategic ambiguity.

As is befitting strategic ambiguity, postracial is a similarly not an as-it-appears-to-be term. Instead of the post in postracial meaning after, it means later and quieter. Strategic ambiguity reflects the postracial label where race is inevitably and perpetually postponed or silenced only to be trotted out in delayed and more coded forms. Just as Stuart Hall reads Derrida's definition of *différance* as pivoting between its two meanings of "to differ" and "to defer," postrace means both immediate awareness of different race and eventual acknowledgment of that race.[28] "Different race" in this case is akin to different racialization, or different ways of reading Blackness, through, for example, the lens of "hope and change." This is certainly the way in which postrace was deployed during the 2008 election, with its utopian, post-first Black president, "yes we can" euphoria that overtook many liberal and progressive circles. But hope and change remained slogans and not precursors to a new Black enfranchisement in the Obama era. Postrace was not a new way of understanding race, but instead a slippery escape from race talk under the guise of a new phenomenon; strategic ambiguity made use of this slippage. In this book, strategic ambiguity is offered up as an affective iteration of and speaking back to postracial resistance that, like hope and change, doesn't always move the needle on racial progress.

The meaning(s) of postrace come not just from its etymology and its mode of pronouncement but from its ideological genealogy. While the popularity of the term postrace is relatively recent, the philosophy behind it is not. Colorblindness, a topic on which critical race scholars have written for decades, is one of the most prominent predecessors to postrace. In his critique of colorblind constitutionalism, Neil Gotanda draws upon fellow critical race theorist Kimberlé Williams Crenshaw's writings about a certain "perspectivelessness" or a "colorless" positionality that legal analysts of color are expected to enact.[29] Gotanda describes colorblindness as akin to assimilation whereby "race should have no real significance, but instead be limited to the formal categories of white and black, unconnected to any social, economic or cultural practice."[30] Media studies scholars Sarah Nilsen and Sarah E. Turner utilize the term "colorblind" to denote "an ideological rhetorical stance that serves to distort the goals of the civil rights movement by claiming that the movement's objective was the eradication of racial considerations."[31] Sociologist Eduardo Bonilla-Silva names this phenomenon "colorblind racism," and education scholar Mica Pollock calls this same ideology "colormute," whereby "*deleting* race words can actually help *make race matter more*."[32] To denote postracial racism anthropologist John Jackson uses the phrase *de cardio* racism to describe "a kind of hidden or cloaked racism, a racism of euphemism and innuendo, not heels-dug-in pronouncements of innate black inferiority."[33] Critical rhetorician Anjali Vats looks at the appropriation of race in high fashion to demonstrate how racism hides inside postracial ideologies in "racechange."[34] Whether called perspectiveless, colorless, colorblindness, colormute, colorblind racism, *de cardio* racism, racechange, or postrace, these ideologies share the deleterious effect of silencing race talk while ignoring—and perhaps even fomenting—racialized discrimination.

Postrace thus remains slippery. One way to pin down such slipperiness is to describe postrace through the way in which sighted humans understand evidence: a visual image, a look. In other words, who, exactly, can be postracial? I've posed this question to groups of undergraduates by showing them a variety of photographs of our last few presidents and having them shout out whether they believe each president to be postracial or not. I explain that this is an unquestionably problematic exercise that falls back on the very binaries I exhort them to move beyond . . . and yet, in class, we all admit that we cannot help but default to the position that we "know" race by "seeing" it. I've found that the students assess the images of presidents as "postracial" or "not postracial" according to the degree to which the presidents appear to "enact otherness," as art historian Cherise Smith has described racialized identity play.[35] Audiences remain split about Bill Clinton, who enacted various signifiers of Black cool (such as playing the saxophone in sunglasses on a 1992 election campaign episode of *The Arsenio Hall Show*) while also legislating policies disproportionately disenfranchising African Americans (such as the 1996 Personal Responsibility and Work Opportunity Reconciliation Act, i.e., welfare reform). Without fail they agree that George W. Bush, who enacted White populism (signified through his strong Texas drawl and "charming" garbling of language) while being the heir to a White,

Connecticut-bred political dynasty (with a grandfather as senator, father as Vice President, and brother as governor), is not postracial. Not only is Bush not postracial, but he's also not raced; as a White male subject, he has the luxury of occupying a neutral, unracialized, normative (i.e., White) space.

Barack Obama, who students read as phenotypically Black, enacts racial flexibility harder to pin down as he fluidly switched codes with different audiences during his presidential campaigns and presidency. At times he was sneered at for his "mom jeans"—what could signify as less cool, hence "less Black" and less threatening—and, at other times, he was fetishized for his swagger, read by audiences to be particularly African American and male. Students most overwhelmingly vote Obama to embody the postracial, and they seem to agree that the postracial label means not simply "enacting otherness," but also "having [minoritized] race." By popular race logic, iterated by Whiteness studies scholars such as Ruth Frankenberg, Toni Morrison, and George Lipsitz, White people—as traditionally constructed—are raceless; as normative racialized bodies, Whites are rhetorically absent from race.[36] Thus, Whites cannot be postracial but people of color who "have race" can. But not all people of color signify as postracial. Postracial people succeed in White settings, or more specifically, garner mainstream power and privilege across demographic groups, but especially with Whites. Such postracial people of color must also be seen by Whites as nonthreatening and safe. Black women who are read as postracial, are subjects positioned to successfully enact strategic ambiguity.

My choice to show students pictures of presidents is not a random one. Much mediated discourse on postrace has focused on African American male politicians, and, in particular, Barack Obama. Communication scholar Catherine Squires tracks the rise of the term from a one-off mention in a 1976 Newsweek article on Jimmy Carter's egalitarian Southern politics (a far cry from the "Southern strategy" of race-baiting politicians) to the near-constant application of the term to the "new generation" of Black politicians, including Barack Obama, who "were heralded as proof of racial progress since the 1960s."[37] However, the Obama era, in which the fiction of meritocracy became hegemonic and restricted, and enabled the space for minoritized subjects. Such restriction emerged from the refusal of race and racism to be named because of postracial discourse, and such enabling occurred when Black women learned from and used this very refusal.

As I examine in this book, Black women who succeed in mixed spaces—whether public figures like our former First Lady, a talk show host, a showrunner, television writers, producers, and executives, or "regular folk" like college students at a predominantly White institution—perform strategic ambiguity. These women's public performances, in the words of literary scholar Daphne Brooks, illuminate not the invisible but, rather, "the politics of Black female hypervisibility in the American cultural imaginary."[38] In a climate in which frank discussions of difference can be impossible, many hypervisible Black women carefully couch and code their sentiments on race and gender. In other words, postrace succeeds not at silencing powerful African American women, but in generating new iterations of resistant speech through strategic ambiguity.

Despite daily reports and videos of race-based violence across the country, a postracial ethos remains deeply entrenched in U.S. culture, including U.S. media culture. This book identifies how minoritized subjects respond when those invested in the myth of postrace dismiss mere reference to race and gender, much less racialized or gendered discrimination or pride, as outmoded, irrelevant, or even racist and sexist. *Postracial Resistance* examines what such individual struggles against racism and sexism look like when viewed through the screens of media representations, audiences, and creatives in the very recent past. Such ideologies gain their strength from their everyday and everywhere quality. Repeated, truncated, postracial soundbites on all of our screens told us that Michelle Obama was "racist" because she identified the existence of racism or that Oprah was "crying racism" because she made public an experience of discrimination.

Black women, and particularly powerful Black women, could (and can) not speak in a forthright manner about racialized sexism or indeed anti-Black violence because they were always seen as driven by bias and agenda. But they did speak back. They resisted in ways that didn't always look like traditional resistance, with strategic ambiguity. Such individual resistance, coded through the politics and performances of Black women's respectability politics, meshed well with postrace. To elucidate the contours of this resistance, *Postracial Resistance* uncovers different responses-to-postrace strategies, and centers different media studies methodologies. I use what media studies scholars such as Toby Miller and Douglas Kellner describe as the tripartite methodologies of textual analysis, political economy, and, in Miller's words, audience ethnography or, in Kellner's, audience reception.[39]

This book illuminates the promises and perils of the postracial resistance of strategic ambiguity through my examination of not simply mediated events and the entertainment industry, but also audiences and media executives. Popular culture cannot be understood fully without incorporating the voices of audiences; as media scholar John Fiske notes, "popular culture [is] a site of struggle, but while accepting the power of the forces of dominance, [effective audience analysis] focuses rather upon the popular tactics by which these forces are coped with, are evaded or are resisted." Fiske's ideas point to the multiple cultural studies approaches to incorporating audiences. Communication scholar Robin Means Coleman explains: "Reception studies (variously termed 'reception theory,' 'reception analysis,' and 'reception aesthetics') are distinguished by an examination of the nexus between a medium and its audience." While all forms of reception studies focus on meaning-making, Means Coleman articulates a number of central and guiding questions for scholars of audiences. She questions: "What is the nature of reality as perceived by the audience during reception? What do these acts of decoding and interpretation mean? What knowledge can be derived from understanding the reception process? How should these realities, meanings, and knowledge be explored?"[40] Means Coleman's research questions illustrate how she celebrates the knowledge of individuals, instead of, in an alternate media studies approach, simply "envisaging the audience as a *construct*" [emphasis in original], and in particular how readers are positioned by a commercial nexus.[41] Means Coleman's approach—like Stuart Hall's, Jacqueline Bobo's, and John Fiske's, which I emulate in this book—imbues more agency in individuals as the "active audience" than circumscribing viewers as constructs.

Strategic Ambiguity

The subtitle of this book draws upon revered rhetorician Kenneth Burke's phrase to denote the flexible analytic frame a listener or watcher must deploy to understand a rhetor's motives in constructing a speech or action. To lay out the terms of his "grammar of motives," Burke states, "what we want is *not terms that avoid ambiguity, but terms that clearly reveal* [to rhetorical critics] *the strategic spots at which ambiguities necessarily arise*" (italics in original).[42] In other words, we can't rely upon seemingly clear language if we want to understand complex motivation. Burke's phrase has been taken up by scholars and practitioners in a wide variety of arenas. Strategic ambiguity is commonly known as a military policy utilizing doublespeak for sensitive and often explosive issues of national security, such as weapons of mass destruction.[43] Organizational communication scholars have adapted Burke's phrase to describe how elites protect their privilege and manage potential conflict among underlings.[44] Economists describe strategic ambiguity as a feature of successful contracts that allows for pragmatic flexibility.[45] Anthropologists and sociolinguists also document such flexibility in their discussions of code-switching, where strategic ambiguity is deployed by an outsider speaker who seeks to decrease potential conflicts with both outsider and insider groups.[46]

While my definition of strategic ambiguity draws upon aspects of doublespeak, conflict-management, pragmatism, and code-switching as elements of the performance, I use the term more in the way rhetorician Leah Ceccarelli describes it, as something that can "result in two or more otherwise conflicting groups of readers converging in praise of a text."[47] Ceccarelli draws upon John Fiske's reading of Madonna as a polysemous text to provide the example of how 1980s and '90s era Madonna can be read by certain audiences as "sex kitten" and by others as the assumed opposite, "feminist." As a strategically ambiguous agent, Madonna enables "subordinate and dominant social groups [to] gain pleasure from their support of the text (even though that support derives from different interpretations of the text's meaning), and the 'author' of the text [i.e., Madonna] benefits from the increased popularity."[48] Ceccarelli describes strategic ambiguity as a tool that the powerful can use to shore up hegemony but also that the powerless can use to chip away at that hegemony. On the one hand, powerful groups use strategic ambiguity to consolidate their power by "appealing to the powerful while placating the marginal just enough to keep them from openly rebelling against the discourse and the system it supports." On the other hand, disempowered groups use strategic ambiguity to "insert . . . a hidden, subversive text" that "critique[s] an oppressive regime without inviting suppression, imprisonment, or death." I am interested in the uses of strategic ambiguity by elite Black women who, in Ceccarelli's formulation, are simultaneously powerful and disempowered.

Ceccarelli also notes that, regardless of political impact, strategic ambiguity is "an effective way to increase the popularity of a text."[49] Because of these divergent political ends to the means of strategic ambiguity, polysemic texts should neither be "universally praise[ed] . . . as subversive of hegemonic power, [n]or . . . universally condemn[ed] . . . as an example of miscommunication."[50] Indeed, polysemy is the very stuff of media studies—as Stuart Hall famously documents, some viewers will decode the dominant messages encoded in the text, others will decode entirely oppositional messages, while a third group will enact a negotiated positionality.[51] For example, in the realm of reality TV, media studies scholar Racquel Gates writes that media "texts [are] intrinsically polysemic, laden with meanings and significance that are activated by a variety of factors."[52] This book is concerned with precisely these polysemic, negotiated, grey areas.

The phrase "strategic ambiguity" also speaks to Gayatri Spivak's notion of "strategic essentialism" whereby groups consisting of similarly-identified members can set differences aside to work together for a specific political end; it is "a strategic use of positive essentialism in a scrupulously visible political interest."[53] The two phrases differ as they contain elements that are near inverses of each other: where ambiguity is soft, undefined, and connected, essentialism is hard, defined, and oppositional. Essentialism is easily pinned down where ambiguity is slippery. As opposed to strategic ambiguity, which individuals enact for the purposes of *individual* success, strategic essentialism happens through groups for the purposes of *group* betterment. Strategic essentialism remains in a time-and-issue bound political realm, and not, as in strategic ambiguity, the non-temporally-bound realm of identity construction. In other words, strategic essentialism is what coalitions of the weak engage in to garner strength by partnering with each other, while strategic ambiguity is how individuals who are disempowered by their minoritized identity status, and yet often privileged by class, garner strength by individual action. Ambiguity and essentialism are, in fact, polar opposites: ambiguous performances embrace the grey spaces, whereas essentialized ones rely upon black and white delineations.

While theories of strategic ambiguity might well apply to other minoritized groups, in this book, strategic ambiguity functions as an articulation of a sometimes conflicted, sometimes confounding, and always postracial twenty-first century iteration of Black feminist resistance, which must be considered in the grey spaces Ceccarelli shades and the means-for-an-end motivation Spivak iterates. Indeed, while—in the words of Carole Boyce Davies—"the Black female subject refus[es] to be subjugated," reading such refusal is not a straightforward process. Instead, again with Davies's insight, we must understand that "Black female subjectivity . . . can be conceived not primarily in terms of domination, subordination, or 'subalternization,' but in terms of slipperiness, elsewhereness." This "slipperiness" means that Black women are "constantly eluding the terms of the discussion."[54] Such slipperiness, the strategic ambiguity of the Michelle Obama era, is the tool that minoritized subjects use to resist intersectional oppression when, in a postracial moment, those around them ignore oppression, explain it away, or acknowledge it only in a single register.

Why Do We Care So Much About Media Representations?

Representation matters. Media representations inform political representations, and political representations feed media representations, as Stuart Hall and his colleagues at the Birmingham School describe in their model of the endless circuit of culture.[55] All representations are more than simply images, sounds, and writing on a screen; they are more than entertainment or distractions. In what media studies scholar Douglas Kellner calls "media culture," "a culture of the image" provides "the materials out of which people forge their very identities."[56] Representations of Black women, like representations of most minoritized groups, are particularly meaning-laden. Black women both in front of and behind the screens bear a heavy burden of representation—what historian Kevin Gaines documents as the philosophy of "uplifting the race."[57] For all audiences, regardless of racialized identification, images of African American women are either affirmations or denials of Black women's very humanity. They are primers on and cautionary tales about respectable or inappropriate actions, dress, speech, and demeanor.

Audiences place an undue burden on representations of Black women as both hypervisible—objects of desire and scorn—and invisible entities who fail to register as significant. Indeed, as visual culture scholar WJT Mitchell notes: "Hypervisibility—being remarked, noticed, stared at—can only be understood if it is placed in some relation to its dialectical twin: invisibility."[58] Such hypervisibility and invisibility are racialized and gendered. Hypervisiblity—such as the omnipresent showcasing of Black women celebrities in our media—is, as digital media studies scholar Safiya Noble puts it, "a means of rendering Black women and girls invisible,"[59] or failing to show how intersectional discrimination affects everyday Black girls and women. We see a few famous Black women's bodies, but we don't hear multiple, complex narrations of Black women's lives. Such representations bear particular weight because Black women are still underrepresented in popular culture, especially on television. In 1976, George Gerbner and Larry Gross described TV as "the central cultural arm of American society," and "an agency of the established order" that "as such serves primarily to extend and maintain rather than to alter, threaten, or weaken conventional conceptions, beliefs and behaviors . . . Its function is, in a word, enculturation."[60]

Race/gender framing in the invisible/hypervisible dialectic means that minoritized audiences can castigate less-than-"respectable" images of the group(s) with which we identify and wring our hands in dismay. We highlight the representations that make us look "the best," pinning them, liking them, and re-tweeting them in pride. In short, we imbue representations with our hopes and our dreams, our fears, and our anxieties. While representations most certainly perform a disciplining role of interpellating or hailing subjects into being, our interactions with mediated images are far from straightforward or cause-and-effect.[61] Because representations of *us* are so pregnant with meaning, we sometimes struggle to see representations as politicized tools, or performative events, that are conscribed by the burden of representation, what cultural studies scholar Kobena Mercer describes as a "moment of 'corrective inclusion' to counteract . . . historical exclusion."[62]

However, this doesn't mean that minoritized audiences mindlessly consume our representations, becoming the "dupes" Max Horkheimer and Theodor Adorno feared the "culture industry" would create.[63] Sometimes, for example, consuming popular images of Black women on television prompts us to, as author Morgan Parker writes, "move out of Shondaland," and boycott beautiful, seductive, and also troubling racialized and gendered images despite our hunger to see ourselves.[64] Thought of another way, minoritized audiences experience what Judith Butler calls disidentification when we encounter problematic images of ourselves.[65] Jose Estaban Muñoz describes disidentification as what happens when audiences confront stereotypical representations of themselves but instead of accepting such stereotypes as truth, they "scramble[e] and reconstruct . . . the . . . message of a cultural text." This scrambling allows minoritized audiences to "recircuit" its meanings. Muñoz explains: "disidentification is a step further than cracking open the code of the majority; it proceeds to use this code as raw material for representing a disempowered politics or positionality that has been rendered unthinkable by the dominant culture."[66] In other words, individual media consumers resist the constant pressure from media texts to believe that we are the stereotypes on screen. Many minoritized viewers, instead, maintain a strategically ambiguous relationship to our images on our screens in small moments of postracial resistance. This book illustrates that the postracial resistance of strategic ambiguity is an approach that not only celebrities employ, but that all audiences enact as well.

The Power of Screens

Our ever-present screens enable 21st century Black women's strategic ambiguity. In the Michelle Obama era, any given speech event or performance might, at any given time, have been recorded, taken out of context, excerpted, and highlighted. Savvy 21st century media consumers, producers, and critics, who are often one and the same person, are ultimately aware that screens, and the surveillance technologies behind them, will influence if not infiltrate every moment. Truly, as communication scholar Amanda Lotz notes, "the new technologies available to us require new rituals of use. Not so long ago, television use typically involved walking into a room, turning on the set, and either turning to specific content or channel surfing."[67] Today, not only is our watching not bound to a particular physical location, but it is also not bound to a particular temporal moment; as Lotz asserts, "the control over the television experience that various technologies offer has ruptured the norm of simultaneity in television experience and enabled audiences to capture television on their own terms."[68] Audiences' viewing habits "on their own terms" has only increased the impact of televisual imagery in all of our lives.

The representations I consider in this book have, by essence of their popularity, been celebrated by audiences as screen-worthy and as such must be understood through the logic of their digital capture for the ages. Such representations never simply go away; they live on in echoes. The moments of both resonance and cacophony created by these mediated echoes are the phenomena with which *Postracial Resistance* is concerned. Representations acquire meaning because they are not, in Stuart Hall's words, "isolated and separate concepts" but rather connected through "the articulation of different elements into a distinctive set or chain of meanings."[69] Mediated images are never floating in isolation; they always function in relation to each other. Furthermore, representations, even those that seem ephemeral, exist as links in a chain sutured together with our omnipresent social, digital media. Although ideologies weld the links of the chain, the chain is not unbreakable; as Hall notes, "one of the ways in which ideological struggle takes place and ideologies are transformed is by articulating the elements differently, thereby producing a different meaning."[70] This book considers such ideological struggle through performances of postracial resistance and strategic ambiguity on a variety of screens. Because of digital technologies, audiences will always be able to read Oprah's strategic ambiguity emerging through her tweets about being shut out of a fancy Swiss store just as her press tour for her film *The Butler* begins (chapter 2). We will re-experience Michelle Obama's strategic ambiguity bubbling up as she charms *The View* audiences so successfully that the entire country temporarily sublimates its racism to obsess about her fashion iconicity (chapter 1). We will follow, once again, Shonda Rhimes' tweets that manage to skirt racial specificity while signifying racial critiques (chapter 3).

Women of color audiences will benefit from such endless access to images of other women of color, as they castigate or adore such representations (chapters 4 and 5). Black women television workers will negotiate this loop of imagery as they fight against racist and sexist Hollywood systems in order to include their voices (chapter 6).

Postracial Resistance suggests that mediated images do not produce, reflect, or create unidirectional iterations of audience desires but instead provide insight into complex and co-constitutive performances of race, class, gender, and sexuality. Reading the performances of prominent Black women in media as strategically ambiguous means understanding how they can use rhetorical tools of postrace to resist its very ideological tenets. Reading the responses of audiences and executives as skeptical, reluctant, or resistant uses of strategic ambiguity means understanding how Black women perform racialized and gendered identities in myriad ways. Strategic ambiguity is a way to speak back to controlling images. It's an acknowledgement that women of color's access to privilege and power in mainstream or ostensibly egalitarian, meritocratic spaces is contingent upon the tricky dance of postracial resistance or performing the codes of postrace to resist racist ideologies. Strategic ambiguity means fomenting a certain desire for Black women celebrities across all of America or, as film scholar Michael DeAngelis writes in his work on Hollywood stars' self-construction as sexually ambiguous, developing the means to "operate as fantasy."[71] Strategic ambiguity, as a co-constitutive performance of Black feminist resistance, is key to naming and fighting against racialized sexism without appearing aggressive or angry; strategic ambiguity means avoiding being pinned down as oversensitive or delusional in a so-called postracial moment.

Black Feminist Resistance and Strategic Ambiguity

While *Postracial Resistance* documents postracial resistance in 21st century media culture, Black women's resistance is far from a new phenomenon, as historians and literary critics have thoroughly documented. Historian Deborah Gray White notes that, for African American women, "resistance in the United States was seldom politically oriented, consciously collective, or violently revolutionary. [I]t was generally individualistic and . . . aimed at maintaining what seemed to all concerned to be the status quo."[72] Historian Stephanie M. H. Camp describes enslaved Africans' "everyday resistance," a phrase she draws from political scientist James Scott, as "the wide terrain between consent, on one hand, and open, organized opposition, on the other."[73] Historians Darlene Clark Hine and Kathleen Thompson write that "the extraordinary achievements of black women in the nineteenth and twentieth centuries did not grow out of degradation but out of a legacy of courage, resourcefulness, initiative, and dignity that goes back to 1619,"[74] the moment when enslaved Africans encountered first contact with Europeans and Native Americans in North America. Hine and Thompson detail the resistance of enslaved women "by refusing to work, by engaging in sabotage, even by running away . . . Some committed suicide, which was not necessarily an act of despair and defeat . . . [as] most enslaved Africans believed that death would return them to their families and countries."[75] For enslaved people, Hine and Thompson point out, "resistance was a way of life . . . Survival itself was a form of resistance."[76] Both overt and covert, individualistic and collective, Black women's opposition formed, in the words of Patricia Hill Collins, a "culture of resistance."[77]

In the post-bellum period, some Black feminist resistance also took the particular form of performing, in the words of Lisa B. Thompson, as a "Black lady." Thompson argues,

> Acting like a black lady became a highly conscious performance developed in part as a response to social codes and ideals of propriety dictated by nineteenth- and twentieth-century reformers who strategized for more humane treatment of African Americans . . . circulating ideologies such as the Cult of True Womanhood and the Cult of Domesticity, which emphasized piety, purity, and submissiveness, held promise for revising notions about black people as immoral.[78]

Such enactments of the "politics of respectability," in the words of Evelyn Brooks Higginbotham, "disavowed, in often repressive ways, much of the expressive culture of the 'folk,' for example, sexual behavior, dress style, leisure activity, music, speech patterns, and religious worship patterns."[79]

The nineteenth-century club women's movement showcased such "Black lady" performance. The leaders of Black middle-class club women's movement and in particular the National Association of Colored Women (NACW), explain Cindy L. White and Catherine A. Dobris, "were acutely aware that prevailing racist ideologies made no distinctions among Black women; all would be judged by the worst." The NACW took the motto "Lifting as We Climb," which meant, in the words of White and Dobris, that their organization "address[ed] the condemnation of any Black women by elevating all Black Women."[80] While social uplift was the primary goal of the NACW, White and Dobris argue the notion of "elevation" was not a conservative idea because Black women were not afforded the privileges of humanity granted to White women. In fact, Lisa B. Thompson describes such women as *activists*; their performances of a Black lady brand of "domesticity, chastity, and propriety" exemplifies, to these scholars, a form of Black feminist resistance couched in respectability politics.

Respectability politics also created, in Hine's phrase, a "culture of dissemblance," a particular silence around Black women's private lives so that they might "protect the sanctity of inner aspects of their lives."[81] The idea of minoritized subjects' silence as resistance is not one that simply applies to the past. Anthropologist Signithia Fordham writes of silence as resistance in her landmark studies of African American girls' educational experience. Fordham observes: "silence among the high achieving females at . . . school is an act of defiance, a refusal on the part of the high-achieving females to consume the image of 'nothingness' so essential to the conception of African-American women. This intentional silence is also critical to the rejection and deflection of the attendant downward expectations."[82] As Fordham illustrates, the history of Black feminist resistance-that-might-not-look-like-resistance lives in the present. Visual culture scholar Nicole Fleetwood puts it this way: "In the early twenty-first century, black women continue to be marked by blackness rooted in a legacy of a racial past and their bodies continue to bear these psychic and corporeal scars in dominant visual culture."[83] This violence is not simply metaphorical. Representational violence—or images of Black women as less-than-fully-human—helps justify real-life violence against Black women. Media representations of racialized gender both inform and are informed by constructions of race and gender in U.S. culture.[84]

From Celebrities to Consumers to Producers of Celebrities: Chapter Setup

Postracial Resistance looks at how, in the Michelle Obama era, the media positioned highly visible and successful African American icons, such as our former First Lady, as having transcended race, to use Oprah Winfrey's words; this permitted the media to ignore issues of Black female disenfranchisement. I show how Black women, including icons such as Winfrey herself, strategically negotiated such positioning with postracial resistance. The first half of the book—chapters 1 through 3—uses textual analysis to uncover how Michelle Obama, Oprah Winfrey, and Shonda Rhimes echoed media framing, employing the language and styles of postrace, while fighting against its ideologies. Like film scholar Mia Mask, in the first half of the book, I aim to "push the discussion of African American celebrity beyond the 'good, politically progressive role model' versus 'bad, regressive black stereotype' binary that stifles dialogue and divides scholars."[85]

Chapter 1—"'Of Course I'm Proud of My Country': Michelle Obama's Postracial Wink"—scrutinizes the First Lady's response to her racist and sexist treatment in mainstream media in the 2008 presidential election campaign. Michelle Obama faced many attacks from the McCain-Palin campaign and the conservative media in the 2007–8 election campaign season, including ridicule over her "fist bump" with Barack Obama at a St. Paul, Minnesota, campaign rally and the parody of her as a Black Panther on the cover of the *New Yorker*. But no attack was as brutal and sustained as the one that came after her "pride" comments during a stump speech in early 2008. In this chapter, I analyze Obama's response: coming out as a postracial, postfeminist glamour goddess on *The View*. How did such a strategically ambiguous performance allow Obama to speak back to negative popular media representations without incurring additional racist and sexist wrath? Why did Obama's reframes, redefinitions, and coded language work so effectively in this particular case?

As no book on Black women in media would be complete without at least a mention of Oprah Winfrey, chapter 2—"'Because Often It's Both': Racism, Sexism, and Oprah's Handbags"—takes us straight to the Queen of All Media. Winfrey has always occupied a unique, exceptional, and almost superhuman position in the American cultural imaginary. From the advent of her national talk show in 1986, Winfrey quickly ascended the pop culture mountain, partially by strategically positioning herself as a figure who can at times supersede the pesky bodily, cultural, and historical instantiations of identity, the trifecta of race, gender, and class, and partially by strategically signifying in particularly raced, gendered, and classed manners. Winfrey has long since abandoned the status of mere mortal in the eyes of fans and foes alike. In her ubiquity, Winfrey did much to not only shore up her own brand, but also configure the representational space of a particular brand of celebrity African American womanhood. That particular brand was strategic ambiguity, and Oprah Winfrey was the ultimate magician who transformed a racialized space into one safe for Whiteness. But what happened when the magic trick stopped working, or when Winfrey's postracial, strategically ambiguous negotiations of race and gender weren't successful? What happened when Winfrey experienced a gendered racism that was far from coded and polite? In this chapter, I analyze the limits of Winfrey's so-called racial transcendence, considering a telling moment when she used strategic ambiguity but was still pilloried in the press as a race-baiting, uppity, Angry Black Woman.

Chapter 3—"'I Just Wanted a World That Looked Like the One I Know': The Strategically Ambiguous Respectability of a Black Woman Showrunner"—examines Shonda Rhimes' twenty-first century Black respectability politics through the form of strategic ambiguity. I trace Rhimes' performance of strategic ambiguity in the press, first in the pre-Obama era and at the beginning of her first show, *Grey's Anatomy,* when she stuck to a script of colorblindness, and a second in the #BlackLivesMatter moment and after a string of hits, when she called out racialized sexism and redefined Black female respectability. In the first moment, when *Grey's Anatomy* just got its legs and the press celebrated her and her new show as a success, Rhimes appeared to have a clenched-teeth approach to all aspects of self-disclosure and, in particular, to talking about race and gender. Then, in the second moment, and after a racialized and gendered attack, Rhimes spoke back with an unambiguous critique. In the shift from the pre-Obama era to the #BlackLivesMatter era, how did Rhimes' careful negotiation of the press demonstrate that, in the former moment, to be a respectable Black woman was to perform strategic ambiguity, or not speak frankly about race, while in the latter, respectable Black women could and must engage in racialized self-expression, and thus redefine the bounds of respectability?

The second half of the book, chapters 4 to 6, analyzes the words of Black women who are behind and speaking back to their screens, and postulates about what happens when postracial resistance and strategic ambiguity are not available as strategies for success. Companion chapters 4 and 5 consider the vernacular—but no less powerful—responses of a woman of color audience responding to representations of women of color on television who perform strategic ambiguity. These two chapters use ethnographic and audience reception research to analyze how a group of young women of color form their community in opposition to televisual claims of the postracial and of strategic ambiguity. I look at how non-mediated, "real-life" Black women speak back to controlling media images.

I met once a week for thirteen weeks with a group of young women who gathered weekly to watch a full season of their favorite television program, *America's Next Top Model*. In their flow of commentary before, during, and after the show, the women used the televisual representations of Black women to deconstruct the ethos of postraciality and to negotiate their multifaceted racialized and gendered personae in a White-dominant city and university. These young women claimed agency in the face of what they interpreted to be racist and sexist media representations, and they subsequently produced counternarratives to strategic ambiguity. They identified themselves against what they read to be limited scripts of Black womanhood featured on their TV screens, and did so by centering their community of women of color. Chapter 4—"'No, But I'm Still Black': Women of Color Community, Hate-Watching, and Racialized Resistance"—focuses on how the young women constructed their community through identifying against strategic ambiguity. Chapter 5—"'They Got Rid of the Naps, That's All They Did': Women of Color Critiques of Respectability Politics, Strategic Ambiguity, and Race Hazing"—looks at how the young women rejected the corporate notion of the management of difference in their viewing community.

The final and sixth chapter—"Do Not Run Away from Your Blackness": Black Women Television Writers and the Flouting of Strategic Ambiguity"—focuses on television production economies and relies upon interview data in order to illustrate how Black female television writers, studios' in-house legal counsel, and producers skirt and tease notions of postrace in constructing their own brands of resistance. This chapter investigates how a coded, more polite, and postracial form of racialized sexism affects those who work in the industry as much as infiltrates the entertainment products that make their way to audiences. Additionally, because of the preponderance of *narrowcasting* (or niche marketing) today, Black women television writers, who largely fail to receive the interracial sponsorship necessary to work outside of their niche, are consigned to Black shows. This chapter draws upon interview data with prolific Black women television professionals in Hollywood in order to understand the ways in which twenty-first century representations of African Americans on television are shaped by segregated spaces. What possibilities do segregated writers' rooms foreclose? What do they open up? How do television executives produce certain images of African Americans? What happens when discussions of race arise in interracial writers' rooms and interracial production meetings? By investigating these questions, this chapter illustrates the ways in which television workers negotiate through strategic ambiguity in segregated Hollywood of the Michelle Obama era.

Postracial Resistance is a critical, cultural communication studies book in both methods and content, because visual media are ever more the vehicle by which people make sense of their racialized and gendered world. I chose each moment of postracial resistance in front of, behind, and on screen for its representativeness and popularity, and for challenging postracial ideologies in a different and powerful manner. Each woman picks up on anti-Black woman themes common in discourse throughout U.S. culture. The impact of strategic ambiguity is emphatic: media examples are not just isolated cultural texts but resonate within a broader framework that oddly, persistently, and blatantly stigmatize Black women while arguing that their race and gender are irrelevant. Inequality is propagated in the United States of the new millennium through postracial ideology, driven by mainstream media narratives that all Americans live in an egalitarian, meritorious society. The postracial inflection of this ideology has gone from being the buzzword of the 2008 U.S. presidential election season to the idea at the center of U.S. discourse on difference to, in the Trump era, seeming almost quaint.

Audiences construct their self-images in conversation with their screens. At the same time, if our media—whether in the long-established and venerable *New York Times* or more newly-formed and community-mobilized Black Twitter—are the means by which we assess humanity, Black women's representations are forever upheld by our media as should-be role models; they are trapped in the intractable frame of respectability. While I never want to essentialize Black female experiences and take my students to task for deploying such flattening expressions such as "*the* Black experience" or "*the* Black community," I also acknowledge that, for audiences who identify as or with Black women, such mediated images are especially weighty. Black female media representations provide audiences with fantasies of when and how Black women should speak, and when and how Black women should remain silent.

Black women's bodies and behaviors are scrutinized in public because of the media's use of racial priming, what political scientist Tali Mendelberg describes as how "racial cues . . . racialize opinion" as "cues in the formation environment activate or deactivate citizens' racial predispositions."[86] Popular representations and responses of iconic and everyday Black women, such as the ones I analyze in this book, can also serve another, perhaps unexpected purpose: they are lessons about how to navigate a twenty-first century world that propagates intersectional discrimination while denying the reality of such discrimination and, indeed, intersectionality itself. Black women are rarely interpellated as raced *and* gendered *and* classed *and* sexed *and* bodied; as a result, scholars, critics, cultural workers, and audiences do not always represent discrimination against Black women as existing across multiple axes. In contrast, understanding performances of postracial resistance and strategic ambiguity allows us to make such intersectional interventions.

This book encourages audiences to move our reading strategies of Black women in media to outside of the frame, to read past the representation, considering not simply text but also contexts, as well as audiences and media executives. Black women's mediated images, just like all mediated images, are best understood as representations that function for a whole range of specific ends, not singular iterations of "the community." Freeing Black women's representations from a limited and limiting frame also frees audiences to understand the intersectional identities that are at stake in representation. Changing reading strategies helps us to understand why certain Black or female bodies are deemed worthy of representation while others are simply erased. Changing reading strategies helps answer media sociologist Herman Gray's question as to what happens when representation is not enough in our struggle to create change.[87] Changing reading strategies helps audiences not only understand Black women's representations as the "mirror moments" communication scholar Beretta Smith-Shomade—in a Black feminist riffing-off of Lacan—smartly reminds us that such representations are,[88] but also as strategic performances of ambiguity, carefully created constructions designed to wink at certain audiences and smile blandly in the face of others. Strategic ambiguity provides space to resist both facets of postracialism: the myth that racism doesn't exist, and racism itself.

1

"Of Course I'm Proud of My Country!"

Michelle Obama's Postracial Wink

In the months leading up to the selection of the 2008 Democratic nominee, Michelle Obama was widely considered to be a liability to her husband's campaign. In both anonymous online spaces and mainstream media outlets, journalists and lay-commentators alike attacked Ms. Obama with astoundingly racist, sexist vitriol. Black feminist theorist Brittney Cooper summed up these comments as focusing on Obama as "unpatriotic, unfeminine, emasculating, and untrustworthy,"[1] while sociologist Natasha Gordon described how Obama "has been charged with epithets ranging from being 'ape-like' to a 'terrorist' to a 'bitter, angry Black woman' to President Obama's 'baby mama.'"[2] If online comments were crude and explicit, mainstream press sentiments circulated barely sublimated racialized codes that amounted to one underlying assumption: Michelle Obama simply wasn't the image of a First Lady.

Then, within a matter of months, the First-Lady-to-be's popularity surged. While she would continue to dodge barbs from the extreme racist fringes of the country, her quickly climbing ratings demonstrated that the country was falling in love with Michelle Obama, mom-in-chief, down-to-earth fashionista. She was still an Ivy League-educated attorney, like her husband, but she didn't make a big deal about it. Alongside Laura Bush, Michelle Obama enjoyed higher favorability ratings than any First Lady since Pat Nixon.[3] What happened to precipitate such a flip? Did the country somehow magically become less racist and sexist, or did Michelle Obama do something to win the hearts and minds of America? This chapter explores one specific media event that helped create this shift, in which Michelle Obama played the ultimate magic trick: postracial resistance through strategic ambiguity.

* * *

Imagine that it is November 5, 2008, and you are Michelle Obama, on the cusp of potentially becoming the first Black First Lady of the United States.[4] Along with the virtues of femininity, strength, maternity, humility, and grace, you must perform constant restraint. You must be cognizant that each and every one of your words is being scrutinized, taken out of context, and magnified for the world to dissect. You are in the midst of a constant media circus of neither your own creation nor desire. You must not only grin and bear the media's obsession with you, but present yourself as happy to be in the midst of such a spectacle. How do you face open, unbridled hostility? And not just any type of hostility, but a particularly virulent, racist, misogynistic, anti-Black woman brand. What do you do?

This conundrum—how, as a minoritized subject, to negotiate a metaphoric straitjacketing in response to racist, misogynistic verbal attacks—is, of course, not just an issue for a potential First Lady. Ironically, because of her success, those "of difference," whether race, gender, sexuality, class, or ability, received arguably fewer options to respond to the vitriol targeting our bodies in the Michelle Obama, first Black First Lady era. "We" were ostensibly past discrimination and even past identity.[5] The mainstream media presented the ubiquitous cultural assumption that all Americans reached a moment "after" or "post" oppression that defaulted to "after" or "post" race.[6] Scholarship exposing the danger of these posts has exploded in the past decade, illuminating, as communication scholar Catherine Squires, puts it, "the material stakes of so-called identity politics and how the rhetorical shenanigans of the post create another layer of difficulty in decoding and detecting regressive, oppressive tactics."[7]

Postrace has been interdisciplinarily deconstructed by sociologists, critical race scholars, critical theorists, and communication scholars.[8] Under the rubric of postrace scholarship, some authors such as geographer Anoop Nayak, building on the work of Paul Gilroy, celebrate how "post-race ideas offer an opportunity to experiment, to re-imagine and to think outside the category of race";[9] but others such as sociologist Brett St. Louis warn against "putative post-racial attempts to dismantle the meaningful symbolism and materiality of race."[10] Crucially, race/gender media studies scholars, from Mary Beltran, to Julietta Hua, to Kimberly Springer, have centered representations of women of color in their conjoined critique of race and gender and postrace and postfeminism, connecting illuminating yet largely single axis debates—race *or* gender—in postrace and postfeminism.[11]

To read Michelle Obama's strategic ambiguity, and how effectively she resisted the ideology of postrace by using the tropes of postrace against themselves, I investigate two of her speaking events that were heavily hyped by the media: a before and after picture, if you will. In the first, Michelle Obama was verbally attacked for her line at a February 2008 campaign rally: "for the first time in my adult lifetime, I'm really proud of my country." In the second event, four months later on the daytime talk show *The View*, Obama used strategic ambiguity to address criticism of these comments.

To make sense of the landscape of talk about and talk by Michelle Obama, I did an initial Lexis-Nexis search of the major U.S. newspapers using the terms "Michelle Obama" and "race," from January 1, 2008, when Michelle Obama began to occupy the national consciousness after Barack Obama became a viable candidate following his January 2008 win at the Iowa caucus, to September 24, 2009, the date of my first search. This search produced a total of 959 articles, of which I found 84 to be particularly relevant because they showed sustained engagement with issues of Obama and racialization. From these eighty-four articles, I found that the "pride" event (in February 2008) and its reframing (in June 2008) was the most comprehensive "media spectacle," to borrow media studies scholar Douglas Kellner's phrase, because it encapsulated a number of the newspaper articles' themes.[12] These included Michelle Obama's providing "Black authenticity" to Barack (negatively spun in this event, equating Blackness with bitterness); the obsession with her body (through the constant refrain of her height, described as "5'11" or "just shy of 6 feet," and descriptions of her "fit" and "athletic" body); and, most importantly for my purposes, her Americanness, patriotism, and the American Dream. (Choosing an event with clear beginning and ending dates also helped me avoid, in the words of Gilbert Rodman, "one of the occupational hazards of studying contemporary culture . . . It's a constantly moving target."[13]) Michelle Obama affords minoritized subjects a model of how to resist the assumption that we are in a postracial culture, or how, to flip Audre Lorde's famous phrase, to dismantle the master's house with his tools in our new era of sanctioned racialized misogyny.

If, as sociologist Patricia Hill Collins writes, "in the post-civil rights era, the power relations that administer the theater of race in America are now far more hidden,"[14] minoritized postcivil rights subjects need new ways to become powerful actors. Michelle Obama's postracial resistance through strategic ambiguity provided us with this new model. Although the intentions behind her scripting are impossible to determine, I do believe that, as communication scholar Mary Kahl argues, Michelle Obama's public statements exhibited an "awareness of the persona she is fashioning for herself."[15] Through her reframings, redefinitions, and coded language, Obama demonstrated her refusal to accept when anti-Black, anti-woman controlling images were superimposed by hateful conservative and fetishizing liberal media culture onto her body.

Situating Postrace

To make sense of Michelle Obama's strategic refutation of postrace, and build on the previous chapter's discussion of the theory and its uses, I briefly historicize some of the metatheoretical moves that have enabled twenty-first century post ideologies. The idea of being past identity is not new, although in this historical moment the popular media often presents it as such. Postracial ideology, reflecting both neoconservative and neoliberal leanings, can be traced not only to reactionary political thought but also to what were largely understood to be liberatory political and academic movements, at least in their time. I read central tenets of postrace against three landmark movements of thought and activism: postmodernism, civil rights and feminism, and women of color theory's interrogations of identity. To answer how Michelle Obama resists postrace, I investigate how we have arrived at a moment in which postrace conscribed the landscape of talk by and around Obama.

In the Obama era, the media presented postrace, intended to mean post-bias, somewhere along the spectrum from fact to aspiration. In reality, the discourse and concomitant ideology of postrace dictated a contemporary, media-fueled moment in which "different" racialized and gendered identities (those of color and those female) were somehow magically granted equal status and were therefore expected to agree that historic, structural, interpersonal, and institutional discrimination were exclusively in the past. Those who merely referenced race or gender, much less racialized or gendered discrimination or racialized or gendered "pride," got dismissed or attacked by the popular media as outmoded, irrelevant, paranoid, or even themselves "racist" and "sexist." Racialized and gendered disparities that abounded and dictated life chances were simply not allowed to enter into the ideological space of postrace. Scholarship that deploys the term postrace has a tendency to quickly breeze past both identity categories and structures of discrimination, to think through the "possibilities" inherent in leaving behind identity, as opposed to thinking through the possibilities inherent in leaving behind minoritized people or ignoring inequities. I argue here that postrace was a fabricated realm where race-blind fiction supplanted racialized fact. As differential outcomes and structural inequalities were silenced in postracial ideology, they were, in effect, allowed to continue, unfettered. Interestingly, the body did not disappear in the ideology of postrace. Instead, the body of color was symbolically important as its freedoms and successes, despite its markers of racialized difference, were used to measure progress from the civil rights era.

Postracial ideologies, while present for decades, emerged on a large-scale in the 2008 election campaign, when Barack Obama and Hillary Clinton became the top two Democratic Party contenders for U.S. president; they crescendoed after Obama's election. These two firsts were offered up in the popular media as evidence of the United States emerging as a truly meritocratic state. This new millennium moment of postrace, in which the fiction of meritocracy became hegemonic, defined the incredibly restrictive landscape in which Michelle Obama, an African American female icon and then potential First Lady, was allowed to speak. When frank discussions of difference were verboten, hypervisible Obama had to couch her words as she carefully fought off her verbal attacks. With help from her media team, Michelle Obama skillfully used strategic ambiguity to create a counternarrative to controlling images of Black women. Ideologies, including what Stuart Hall called the formulation of identities, are never complete but always in flux; counterhegemonic narratives like Obama's speak back.[16]

Michelle Obama deployed strategic ambiguity specifically in reframing and redefining ideologies such as "American" and "patriotism" and in speaking of race, class, and gender in code.[17] In *resisting, reframing, redefining, and coding*, Obama used the tactics articulated in women of color theory, also known as the U.S. third-world feminism. Cultural studies scholar Michelle Habell-Pallán illustrates that, for more than 30 years, "women of color [have been] initiating and advancing a politics of difference . . . in response to liberal essentialist notions embedded in the women's movement and scholarship as well as to ethnic nationalism."[18] Women of color theory does not refer to the scholarship produced by a demographic group but to a particular way of reading or of what literary theorist Valerie Smith calls a "strategy of reading simultaneity."[19] Smith builds on critical race theorist Crenshaw's ideas of intersectionality, where "ideologies of race, gender . . . class, and sexuality . . . are reciprocally constitutive categories of experience and analysis."[20] These are the instruments with which Obama and, following her, we ourselves can cut through both her racist marking as a Black bestial body and her postrace framing as an exemplar of Black achievement and the sign of the end of racism.[21]

Postrace is the culmination of a narrative of progress from a past notion of identity categories as biased, discriminated against, and particular, to a current notion of identity categories as unbiased, discrimination-free, and universal. Postrace has clear resonance with postmodern scholarship, particularly that which is associated with fragmentation, pastiche, and a play of identity—with the denial of any fixed meaning. One node of postmodernism originated with Jean-Francois Lyotard, who expressed a certain "incredulity [toward] metanarratives," whereby he questions the previously assumed-to-be-sacred teleologies of Enlightenment progress. In poststructuralism, too, an "identity" lost much of its integrity.[22] For example, Jacques Derrida's critique of the so-called scientific nature and objectivity of language in *Writing and Difference* assessed the "logocentrism" of structuralism and argued that language is ambiguous, unstable, full of "slippage," constantly changing, and open in meanings, and that the self is not separate or singular but is rather a construct. Poststructuralist scholarship celebrated the fluidity of linguistic meanings. Similarly, today, postracial ideology champions the ostensible fluidity of racialized meanings;[23] new millennium postrace culture claims that there is no singular essence to a racialized identity.

However, as the Michelle Obama case will demonstrate, in practice, post ideologies can lead to media and politics representing and sometimes even spotlighting different bodies, whether queer, disabled, of color, or working-class—but also rhetorically erasing them. In other words, when differences are visually present but disempowered and un-remarked on they are devalued. Indeed, although bodies of color are often featured prominently in postracial culture, they can function as mere multicultural decoration or, in the words of media scholar Brenda Weber, operate as "a discourse of style as substance."[24]

What does it mean for race and gender to have these same types of open meanings? Can changing our definition of race mean that we elim-inate racialized and gendered stereotypes? Theorizing race and gender through a postmodern framework means that racialized and gendered identity remains unhistoricized and thus not recognized as the effect of historic processes of racialization or gendering? Postmodernism and twenty-first century postracial ideology—like neoliberalism—present identity as ambiguous, unstable, changing, open, fragmented, and, per-haps most importantly, the result of *choice*. Mainstream media repre-sentations play on many of these tropes in their coverage of Michelle Obama. Through postmodern notions of identity play, the dynamics of race—as well as gender—can become, in effect, elements of style. In her media representations, Michelle Obama's gendered image signified ele-ments of "girl power" culture: she was portrayed as a "strong woman" who could still be interested in ostensible frivolities (as a penchant for fashion is understood to be un-, anti-, or postfeminist) and yet not be dismissed as frivolous. At the same time, postmodernism could not only be spotted in talk *about* Michelle Obama: postmodernism guided talk and action *by* Obama and her media team. For example, during the elec-tion campaign, Obama often wore oversized pearls and her hair in a flip reminiscent of Jacqueline Kennedy, a lighthearted nod to what *Vogue* editor-at-large Andre Leon Talley called "a black Camelot moment."[25] Playing to a mediatized embrace of her fashion choices, Obama directed audiences away from her inside (as in second-wave feminism) and in-vited us to celebrate her outside (as in postfeminism).

Postmodern challenges to conventional iterations of identity must also be seen alongside 1960s and 1970s era civil rights and feminist ac-tivists' articulation of identity. Both movements held explicit goals of exposing and challenging material, social inequality. Importantly, the media frequently represented Michelle Obama as the beneficiary of the civil rights and second-wave feminist movements: the press and Obama's own media team focused on her "American Dream" story whereby, as the narrative goes, her working-class African American family produced two children who overcame the barriers of their neighborhood, their race, and their socioeconomic background to attend Princeton University and "make it." This narrative was one of moving from lack of economic opportunity and racialized specificity to wealth and postracial universalism. This narrative wasn't false; it was partial and it had an agenda. Obama's story was contingent upon silences and exclusions as she omitted the realities of structural, institutional, and historical racism affecting the South Side of Chicago.

This example is of Michelle Obama controlling racialized narratives through postracial resistance and strategic ambiguity. In addition, scholars such as Crenshaw have illustrated how, in the service of political efficacy, civil rights and feminist movements scripted "authentic" Black and female subjects.[26] The mainstream of both movements aligned themselves with the most empowered members of their respective communities: middle-class, straight White women in the feminist movement and middle-class, straight Black men in the civil rights movement. Thus, the leadership of the civil rights and the second-wave feminist movements was often reliant on singular, essential, bodily instantiations of identity. Forgotten were those with multiple marginalized or intersectional identities who crossed and fell out of categories, such as women of color. Identity was not at all "post" in such activist movements—*un*ambiguous, *un*changing, authentic, bodily, status regulated inclusion.

Michelle Obama's public statements and actions illustrated that she sought to challenge discrimination, even though she had to speak of materiality and inequities in code, particularly when discussing those dynamics as racialized or gendered. To be clear, however, post ideology relies on the narratives of the civil rights and second-wave feminist movements as the moments in which America already conquered inequality. Cementing discrimination firmly in the past helps prove that the twenty-first century is about the unequivocal success of the movements. We have now arrived at the "after" moment when inequality is over. Postrace as an ideology assumes that structural inequities, too, are relics of the past. In this vein, for example, a popular newspaper piece investigated Michelle Obama's family tree all the way back to her last enslaved relative[27]—not to illustrate the legacy of enslavement's effects on structural and institutional racism today but rather to note that we have so profoundly over-come a dehumanizing system that an individual with an enslaved relative ascended to the White House. For some who believed deeply in postra-cial ideologies, these pieces functioned as racism's death knell.

But postrace is slippery. Although diametrically opposite in the realm of politics, women of color theory, along with scholarship by and about other minoritized and historically forgotten people, is yet another influ-ence on postrace. Women of color theory was born out of a moment in which the identity fluidity and play inspired by postmodernism met the materialist, racialized, gendered, and most certainly identity-based concerns of liberation movements. Cultural studies scholar Michael Millner characterizes this scholarly moment as "a rich and sophisticated reconceptualization of identity—as performative, mobile, strategically essential, intersectional, incomplete, in-process, provisional, hybrid, partial, fragmentary, fluid, transitional, transnational, cosmopolitan, counterpublic, and, above all, cultural."[28] Millner describes authors such as Homi Bhabha, Judith Butler, Rey Chow, Paul Gilroy, Jose Esteban Munoz, and Eve Sedgwick as expressing "exhaustion around the whole project of identity."

But the exhaustion, at least as it pertains to women of color theory, has been centered on the project of *essentialism* (a limiting litmus test of authenticity) and not the projec*ts* of identi*ties* (de-essentialized, open, multiple, and hybrid entities).[29] Essentialism and identity are, of course, not one and the same. In many spheres of discussions of "difference" in arenas as varied as the popular press and communication scholarship, the slippage between identity and essentialism flourishes. Writings on identity, in and of themselves, are not necessarily stultifying. Although Millner describes certain critics as writing "past" identity in the 1990s, not all scholars are in agreement. For example, literary scholar Farah Jasmine Griffin, identifies that same decade as "one of the most intel-lectually exciting and fruitful developments" for Black feminist studies. Griffin points out that "it is quite likely that the latter critique of es-sentialism was made possible by the very terms and successes of Black feminist literary critics who were among the first to call attention to the constructed nature of racial and gender identity."[30] Grounded in the Combahee River Collective's articulations of simultaneity, women of color theorists in the 1990s built on the work of sociologists Michael

Omi and Howard Winant, specifically their classic formulation of race as materially, institutionally, and structurally constrained as well as fluid, performative, and mobile.[31]

Reformulating racial formation theory in light of women of color theorizing, we can see that acknowledging the constructed and the conscribed results in a denial of *the either/or* formulation and a celebration of *the both/and*, to borrow the language of Patricia Hill Collins.[32] The body, although not the sole determinant of life chances or life choices, is essential and cannot be disregarded. Identity is, by these meanings, not essentially defined. The identity/essentialism slippage, as it flourished in popular discourse, helped produce the post era. Michelle Obama navigated this slippage by resisting racialized, gendered verbal attacks through redefining and reframing "traditional" ideologies. Her invocation of a highly feminized performance of postrace to fight against the racist/misogynistic effects of postrace is enabled by postmodernism, the civil rights and second-wave feminist movements, and women of color theory.

The reading tools of women of color theory help us see that Michelle Obama entered a public sphere in which, as Black feminist theorist Joy James writes, "commercial and stereotypical portrayals of Black females center on fetishized and animalized sexual imagery; consequently Blacks, females, and politics become effaced or distorted. Racial and sexual caricatures corseting the black female body have a strong historical legacy."[33] These caricatures are contradictory, ranging from diminished humanity, as James notes, and super-humanness, which is equally limiting in nature. bell hooks explains,

> Racist stereotypes of the strong, superhuman black woman are operative myths in the minds of many White women, allowing them to ignore the extent to which Black women are likely to be victimized in this society and the role White women may play in the maintenance and perpetuation of that victimization.[34]

The "fragility of Whiteness," to use education scholar Robin DiAngelo's phrase, and White womanhood, in particular, silence discussions of Black stereotyping, and force figures like Michelle Obama to rely upon strategic ambiguity in order to make her interventions. Public refutations of postrace thrive in our media culture even as they must enter under the cover of postracial discourse, that is, by way of strategic ambiguity. Valerie Smith writes that "unacknowledged cultural narratives such as those which link racial and gender oppression structure our lives as social subjects; the ability of some to maintain dominance over others depends upon these narratives remaining pervasive but unarticulated."[35] To fight oppression, we need to articulate these cultural narratives. For women of color like Obama, explicit, uncoded speech on race and gender was simply not possible. But coded speech was still available. When she and others named minoritized and marginalized identities in code, code protected the message from outsiders' scrutiny while making it available to insiders to decipher. Here is a material postmodernism: Texts are open enough to enable, in the words of rhetorician Leah Ceccarelli, a polysemy, "a bounded multiplicity, a circumscribed opening of the text in which we acknowledge diverse but finite meanings."[36] Thus, the performance of strategic ambiguity, twenty-first century postracial resistance by an iconic figure like Michelle Obama reinvigorates late twentieth century women of color theory.

The postracial resistance Michelle Obama performed, which the popular media at least did not read as resistance, is markedly different from opposition to "traditional" racism or sexism. The game has changed: There is no room for such conventional responses. When "old-school" civil rights and second-wave feminist responses explicitly naming racism and sexism erupt, critics dismissed them as irrelevant and even laughable, as in the public parodying of Al Sharpton and Hillary Clinton for being, respectively, too old-school civil rights or old-school feminist to speak to a twenty-first century Democratic party. Their insistence on seemingly conventional antiracist or feminist politics is portrayed as out of time and out of touch with twenty-first century America. Communication scholar Robin Means Coleman notes that Sharpton, for example, faced a "'race card' dismissal . . . in favor of the perceived 'race in moderation' political discourses of Barack Obama."[37] Michelle Obama should not be evaluated in the old binary framework of either "selling out" (in other words, *not* acting appropriately Black and female by failing to prove her race/gender credentials) or "being real" (in other words, acting authentically Black and female by proving her race/gender credibility). Instead, to resist postracial ideology, Michelle Obama deployed particularly feminized elements of postracial culture in her presentation of strategic ambiguity—she performed and subverted the hyper-feminized postrace that was available to her.

Pride Attacked

There were numerous events where the McCain campaign and the conservative media pilloried Michelle Obama in the 2007–2008 presidential election campaign season; she spoke back to each of them, deploying a sophisticated resistance to postrace. These included the ridicule directed at her because of a "fist bump" with Barack Obama at a campaign rally in St. Paul, Minnesota, in June 2008, and the parody of her as a Black Panther a month later on the July 21, 2008, issue of the The *New Yorker*. But perhaps the most attacked of all of Michelle Obama's statements was her "pride" comment during a stump speech in early 2008. Carefully and critically examining Obama's words helps to reclaim her humanity,

Figure 1.1. Michelle Obama's "pride" comments. Screenshot from "Michelle Obama: First Time proud of USA," C-SPAN, February 8, 2008. Viewed October 6, 2017. www .youtube.com.

which as legal scholar Adrienne Davis writes erupts through language, from the claws of the media.[38]

Michelle Obama made her "pride" comments during a campaign speech on February 19, 2008, first in Milwaukee and then in Madison, Wisconsin (Figure 1.1).[39] In the television networks' coverage of the speech, only Obama's head and shoulders were visible in the frame; the rest of her body was concealed by a podium. She wore a crew-necked light gray sweater that accentuated her muscular lats, small pearl earrings, and a very thin gold necklace. Complementing this dressed-down look was her minimal makeup and no-nonsense bob. Obama spoke in a self-assured, even-toned voice. She was intent and focused and smiled infrequently during her remarks. In essence, her words, not her outfit, hairstyle, or personality, were the focus of this speech. She stated,

> What we've learned over this year is that hope is making a comeback. It is making a comeback and let me tell you something, for the first time in my adult lifetime, I'm really proud of my country. And not just because Barack has done well, but because I think people are hungry for change.

Obama underscored her talk of "hope" by a vision of collective and not individual success: Her investment was not just in her personal family's or her husband's success, but in the usually overlooked folks, the "people hungry for change," who were now being given hope that they were not going to be forgotten forever. She continued,

> And I have been desperate to see our country moving in that direction and just not feeling so alone in my frustration and disappointment. I've seen people who are hungry to be unified around some basic common issues, and it's made me proud. And I feel privileged to be a part of even witnessing this, traveling around states all over this country and being reminded that there is more that unites us than divides us.

In her insertion of "I" statements, Obama did not isolate herself from the people she rhetorically conjured but instead put herself in the category of the disregarded, those who have felt alone, frustrated, and disappointed. This functioned as code for minoritized people. But, also in

code, Obama was clear to illustrate that the dispossessed were not simply racialized minorities; she inserted an intersectional critique, noting
that class dispossesses people as well. In the final section of her remarks,
Obama stated that the crowd must keep in mind,

> That the struggles of a farmer in Iowa are no different than what's hap-
> pening on the South Side of Chicago. That people are feeling the same
> pain and wanting the same things for their families.[40]

Hence, working-class Whites, such as the "farmer in Iowa," were cast
out by the then-current Republican regime just as were working-class
African Americans, such as those "on the South Side of Chicago." What
her message amounted to was that we, the cast out, needed to stand together in cross-racial unity to create change. The major news networks
did not cover the last part of Obama's remarks and, indeed, I only found
Obama's full speech on a C-SPAN feed.

Although Obama named race and class only in code, a clear element of postracial discourse, Obama's call for collectivity spoke directly against the individualism inherent in postracial ideologies. She
articulated a theory that Michelle Habell-Pallán credits women of color
scholars with: "illuminat[ing] . . . the linkages . . . of economic exploi-
tation and racialization."[41] Obama refused to be seen as a token or as
an exceptional individual who has made it. Indeed, minoritized subjects who attain a degree of success are often portrayed as singularly
exceptional and therefore apart from their communities. Black feminist scholar Carol Boyce Davies examines such a case in her analysis
of former president George W. Bush's Secretary of State, Condoleezza
Rice. Davies describes the focus on individual success as "Con-di-fi-
cation," the political tactic of "exceptionalism as strategy." The "media
construction" of elite minoritized public figures such as Rice, Davies
notes, involves "a typical singling out of one member of a subordinated
group as many others with similar talents are erased."[42] Obama's use
of coded language allowed her to argue against such a singling out, an
expression of anti-Con-di-fi-cation.

In this speech, Michelle Obama also reframed hegemonic conceptions of patriotism: It was not just the purview of those who were en-
franchised but those who were disenfranchised, who were victims of

racialized, economic abuse propagated by the very political structure of this country. For Obama, patriotism was, in the words of performance studies scholar D. Soyini Madison, "the ability to both love and critique, to both honor and re-imagine, to both recognize the noble possibilities of this country while interrogating its wrongs."[43] Obama provided us with an open enough text that insider readers accustomed to strategically ambiguous race/gender winks could indeed identify an intersectional, anti-racist message imbedded in it. There was inclusivity at the very core of this message, through Obama's paralleling the similar plights of working-class Whites and Blacks.

But, despite what could have been acknowledged as a benignly multicultural moment to rhetorically unite the races, an amazingly ferocious media attack followed her remarks. I contend that her tone and appearance, which might be described by some viewers as more traditionally "feminist," made some room for it. While the message Obama gave used major tropes of postrace—reframing, redefining, and coding—her more "feminist" look didn't match, so postrace didn't fly. As feminist, Obama is imaged as strong enough to take mediatized attacks, while as glam goddess, which she will soon after this event emerge as, she is framed as needing protection from such attacks. Michelle Obama only stopped being beaten up by the media later, when she created a hyperfeminized look and persona.

Conservative commentators (most prominently television news personalities Joe Scarborough and Sean Hannity) and the McCain campaign quickly picked up on a single portion of these comments, taken out of context: "for the first time in my adult lifetime, I'm really proud of my country." Twenty-four hour cable news networks featured these comments around the clock as proof that Ms. Obama was bitter and un-American. They caricatured her, one cultural commentator said, as "emasculating, sarcastic, and bossy."[44] This is a type of "framing by foil,"[45] to use rhetorician Dana Cloud's phrase, whereby verbally denigrating one's adversary produces the attacker's image of him- or herself as all manner of positive attributes that are in direct opposition to the object of hate.

Cindy McCain, the very picture of a traditional (read: White) First Lady, picked up on Michelle Obama's line that same day, saying at a campaign rally as she introduced her husband: "I'm proud of my country. I don't know if you heard those words earlier. I'm very proud of my country."[46] Through attack, the Republicans portrayed Obama as unpatriotic. The very tone and tenor of this attack was intended to demonstrate their own so-called uber-patriotism. The Republicans' slogan for the September 2008 Republican National Convention (RNC) was "country first"; they came out with "pride in country" merchandise immediately following Michelle Obama's remark.

And, of course, the Republicans' claim to the flag is legendary. Because of Republican policing of "authentic" patriotism, for example, Democratic candidates and their spouses, including Barack and Michelle Obama, were constantly scrutinized to see if they were performing patriotism appropriately. The signifiers of patriotism included the positioning of hands over hearts for the recitation of the "Pledge of Allegiance," the prominent featuring of flag pins on jacket lapels, and the positioning of multiple flags in the background during public events and press conferences. Patriotism meant waving flags, not invoking images of the union of Blacks and Whites, as Michelle Obama conjured in her February 2008 speech. Strategic ambiguity also had a look in this particular case: it was not crewneck sweaters and minimal makeup.

The Glam Makeover: Success through Strategic Ambiguity

Obama's positioning as disgruntled, upset, and unpatriotic throughout media coverage referenced the "Angry Black woman" stereotype, and one I will go into greater depth about in the next chapter on Oprah Winfrey. Media theorist Kimberly Springer points out that, in framing figures into this controlling image, the media fails to address one basic question: why she might be angry.[47] Women of color theorizing, however, provides such an explanation. In the classic essay "The Uses of Anger: Women Responding to Racism," Audre Lorde explains,

> Women of Color in America have grown up with a symphony of anger
> at being silenced, at being unchosen, at knowing that when we survive,
> it is in spite of a world that takes for granted our lack of humanness, and
> which hates our very existence outside of its service . . . We have had to
> learn to move through [our anger] because we have had to learn to or-
> chestrate those furies so that they do not tear us apart.[48]

Part of the way in which Obama "orchestrat[ed] those furies," how she moved through what undoubtedly was anger at her attacks, was by deploying resistant postracial tactics through strategic ambiguity. In the aftermath of the media attack, Michelle Obama was forced to reframe, explain, and defend. She did so by choosing a certain type of media coverage—what media industries designate as women's television programs and magazines—in which she used coded language to redefine and expand the limits of who is American. Women, and particularly White women, were a vital demographic for Barack Obama given the challenge by Hillary Clinton. Obama's message was, in fact, the same as in the full text of the attacked comments, although the tone and venue of her comments, and her physical appearance, were different. Obama's reframing of patriotism directly spoke back to Republicans, who used "love of country" to separate "us" (White, conservative Americans) from "them" (people of color, feminists, liberals, and other assorted malcontents). The Michelle Obama media blitz reached its peak on June 18, 2008, when she appeared on the daytime talk show *The View*, described by critic Daphne Brooks as "the kaffeeklatch gossip bowl,"[49] as a "guest co-host" for the day. In accordance with the conventions of *The View*, as co-host, Obama was positioned as an insider member of the "us" of the show and not the "them" of featured guests. The change in venue, from a gender-neutral site of a political speech to a feminized location of women's television, supported Obama's transformation from "feminist" to "postfeminist."

Obama entered *The View* stage to thunderous applause and a standing ovation from the audience. *The View* was complicit in the reframe of her image, demonstrating that not all had swallowed the negative media messages circulated by the Republicans. The hosts ranged from friendly (conservative personality Elisabeth Hasselback) to giddy (panel moderator Whoopi Goldberg). Obama's appearance was drastically different from her February remarks. She wore a sleeveless black-and white floral dress accented with a floral pin on one shoulder, an off-the-rack number that sold out immediately after the show.[50] Her jewelry consisted of First Lady appropriate simple pearl earrings and a wedding ring, while her skin, enhanced by bronzer, glowed. Her hair, while still a bob, was bigger, bouncier, and shinier; a bang subtly swooped towards her left eye. Her makeup was vivid and sparkling. Her physical image, of a vibrant

Figure 1.2. Michelle Obama looking glamorous. Screenshot from "Michelle Obama on *The View*," *The View*, June 18, 2008. Viewed 6 October 2017. www.youtube.com.

fashionista, played in stark contrast to her more muted affect and dressed-down appearance during her February "pride" remarks (Figure 1.2).

After quoting the famous line, co-host Barbara Walters asked Obama, "What is your answer to all of these attacks?" to which Obama responded,

Well, you know, I take them in stride. It's a part of this process. We're not new to politics. But just let me tell you of course I'm proud of my country. Nowhere but in America could my story be possible.

As opposed to Obama's February remarks where she deployed some signifiers of postrace, on *The View* her transformation to highly feminized, postracial subject appeared complete. She used the tropes of girlishness in contrast to her Wisconsin speech: here her sentences were shorter and her tone was more intimate, friendlier, and conversational. Smiles punctuated her statements. This was not a seriously delivered speech, but a perky monologue peppered with interjections from the cohosts.

Obama's makeover provided a blueprint for how women of color could perform a postracial image transformation. Although Hortense Spillers wrote with "dismay" how Obama "had to be rechoreographed into a more palatable routine; . . . . 'handled,' 'softened' in tone and image,"[51] I respectfully disagree that her makeover was cause for alarm and that she herself wasn't a co-conspirator. Indeed, Obama's strategically ambiguous resistance remained constant even while she performed as a postracial subject. A White woman telling this story (such as Hillary Clinton or Sarah Palin) iterated a normative American rags-to-riches narrative; the intersectionality of a *Black* woman telling presented a critique of racist assumptions of African American success.

Obama continued, calling herself "a girl" twice in quick succession: "I'm a girl that grew up [Barbara Walters: Give people a little bit] I'm a girl that grew up on the South Side of Chicago." In this media appearance, Obama spoke, for the most part, on personal, individual matters and not collective ones. In utilizing the tropes of postrace, Obama named her Blackness through the code "the South Side of Chicago," which, like in the first speech, was meant to connote both Black and working class. But here it is not used alongside a conjuring of an "Iowa farmer" to foster interracial, working-class unity, a possible allusion to cultural miscegenation or shared oppression, but to signify the point from which she departed, the place she moved beyond. The South Side of Chicago became the place Michelle Obama made it out of and not a place in which people currently reside. Obama also brought together her intersectional identity here by describing herself as "Black girl from the South Side of Chicago." She continued,

My father was a working-class guy who worked a shift all his life. And because of his hard work he sent not just me but my brother to Princeton [BW: he's now the coach]. He's now the coach of Oregon State. Go Beavers!

> I tell people just imagine the pride that my parents, who didn't go to col-
> lege, felt. That they could through their own hard work and sacrifice have
> us achieve things that they could never imagine. And so I am proud of
> my country without a doubt. I think when I talked about it in my speech
> I think what I was talking about was having pride in the political process.

Obama employed the language of postrace by using no racialized
descriptor, in code or otherwise, for her father, as he was a "working-
class guy." She used the language of meritocracy, another element of
postrace, where "hard work and sacrifice" trumped structural, institutional, and historic discrimination and provided entrance to the elite,
of which the Ivy League and Princeton University were the ultimate
signifiers. Michelle Obama's utilization of postracial tropes, her strategic
ambiguity, was necessary for her voice to be heard by the mainstream
of the country.

However, focusing on Black success was far from just a pander to postrace. As part of her redefinition of Americanness, Obama paused on her
parents' "hard work and sacrifice"—two ideas that might sound like con-
servatively tinged—"all American notions," but which resonated quite
differently in lieu of the anti-Black racism in which African Americans
have been historically and contemporarily pathologized. In such a context, Obama's comments resounded far differently than Joe Biden's recounting of his kitchen-table chats with his working-class father, Hillary
Clinton's recalling her down-home roots in Scranton, or Sarah Palin's
many significations of her "real" American identity. The race and gender
of the speaker cannot be dismissed. Even though her rhetoric did not
necessarily sound remarkably different from Biden, Clinton, or Palin
here, the context of the racist and sexist nature of the previous attacks
on Michelle Obama made her remarks extremely different. She was negotiating racist, misogynistic postracial culture and must respond in a
safe, mainstream, and recognizable (read: White-friendly) manner: with
strategic ambiguity. Yet Obama did not abandon a vision of collectivi-
ties, as she finished her remarks,

> People are just engaged in this election in a way that we haven't seen in a
> long time and I think that everybody has agreed with that, that people are
> focused [Joy Behar: they're coming out]. They're coming out.

Obama narrated her own family as classically American and reframed pride and patriotism as not merely the purview of White, conservative Americans. On *The View*, Michelle Obama worked to create a space in which she could reclaim her own humanity by presenting herself as having common goals with the White mainstream of the country. In a similar vein, the popular media obsessed over her self-applied moniker of "mom in chief," a major part of this new Michelle Obama effort. But I do not think of this as pandering, as her harsher critics did. Michelle Obama's appearance on *The View*, where she *performed some* signifiers of postrace, could not be dismissed as only postracial. Instead, Michelle Obama's reframing must be seen in the context of a material history in which African American women have never had the luxury to be the most esteemed "lady" in the world. Indeed, a Black woman naming and claiming motherhood through the cutesy phrase "mom-in-chief" must also be seen in the historical context whereby Black women did not have the luxury of being stay-at-home mothers. This material history is reflected not merely in representation but also in areas of life as differential as income and mortality; in 2016, the median income of Black households was almost half of the median income of White households and, in 2014, infants born to Black mothers perished at more than twice the rate of infants born to White mothers.[52]

By recognizing this material history and taking it into account, we then understand why Obama's "playful" words are actually resistant. We could not read Obama's words as resistant if we were to look at them only in terms of race or only in terms of gender, as feminist philosopher Maria Lugones explains: "the logic of categorical separation distorts what exists at the intersection . . . [T]he intersection misconstrues women of color."[53] Reading Michelle Obama at the intersection enables an understanding of her use of, and resistance to, postrace—her strategic ambiguity. Black women's claims to humanity using the language of mainstream goals is radical given the long history, and continued present, of dehumanizing Black women. Michelle Obama's public statements illustrate that she is a Black woman voicing a collective rehumanization that is so powerful for some and so vexing for others. The key visual marker makes the difference in *The View* event as opposed to the February stump speech. Visually marked as feminist, she could not use postracial framing to resistively insert a critique of postracial assumptions about meritocracy; visually marked as hyper-feminized, she offers much of the same content without the backlash. Obama's visual code of a stylistic mask allows her to get away with such resistant content. Strategic ambiguity is successful when it comes with matched set of look and message.

From Postracial Performance to Postracial Resistance

The conventional media coverage stated that Michelle Obama went from being almost universally hated because of her unveiled racial animosity (e.g., being dubbed Mrs. Grievance on the cover of the *National Review*;[54] to being almost universally adored because of her accessibility (e.g., topping *People Magazine*'s "best dressed" list).[55] I have argued here that this mediated "makeover" is achieved by her strategic ambiguity: deploying less-coded to more-coded ideologies of postrace. Her "makeover" is achieved by her performance of visual and linguistic postracial codes in the second event. Michelle Obama's presentation of her accessible fashionista *View*-self matches the highly feminized, postracial tools she used, even while she continued to offer content that subverted the racism and misogyny that remains even in our purportedly postracial nation.

For Obama, majority–minority settings provided a safe space to name systemic and discursive racialized and gendered inequality. For example, at a 2009 campaign fundraising event with prominent African Americans, Obama used "our" and "us" to refer to African Americans, stating: "I am committed, as well as my husband, to ensuring that more kids like us and kids around this country, regardless of their race, their income, their status, the property values in their neighborhoods, get access to an outstanding education."[56] To this same group, she stated: "I know that the life I'm living is still out of the reach of too many women. Too many little Black girls. I don't have to tell you this. We know the disparities that exist across this country, in our schools, in our hospitals, at our jobs and on our streets."[57] When she became First Lady, Obama presided over a ceremony at which a bronze bust of Sojourner Truth was unveiled. There she stated: "Now many young boys and girls like my own daughters will come to Emancipation Hall and see the face of a woman who looks like them." She told the gathering: "I hope that Sojourner Truth would be proud to see me, a descendant of slaves, serving as the First

Lady of the United States of America." Such frank language illustrated that Obama saw herself as a racialized, gendered member of a larger African American community in a racist, sexist world. These statements demonstrated a clear challenge to postrace that was appropriate for the occasion and the audience. Obama crafted a public identity that allowed her to slip in critiques of the inequality still embedded in our nation, while still garnering fans who might object to such critiques if they were made explicit.

Thus, as First Lady, Michelle Obama reframed and redefined traditional ideologies in the service of refuting racism and sexism. She refused to let her body be used against her community. She resisted postrace through what Chela Sandoval calls differential consciousness, a strategy in women of color feminism "of oppositional ideology that functions on an altogether different register . . . Differential consciousness is the expression of the new subject position called for by Althusser—it permits functioning within, yet beyond, the demands of dominant ideology."[58] Sandoval sees women of color differential consciousness as a type of "differential praxis," a theory that operates through real-life practice as decolonial strategy.

Obama's strategic ambiguity can continue to be evaluated as resistant in a variety of ways. She used racialized and gendered euphemisms as a rhetorical strategy, for example, in the way that rhetorician Edward Schiappa describes the manner in which euphemisms are used to domesticate an otherwise fearful nuclear arsenal for an American public.[59] Michelle Obama's careful choice of terms could be considered a euphemism that domesticated an otherwise fearful racial arsenal for the American public. Obama's coded language could also be an attempt at resistant passing, akin to the queer rhetorics analyzed by critical rhetorician Charles E. Morris III. Performing euphemisms as rhetorical strategy and passing through coding herself as (an exceptionally glamorous) "everymom" has the effect of winking at the insider audience (of women of color) while fostering acceptance and even adoration from the outsider audience (of White women). The surge of positive feelings toward the United States' first African American First-Lady-to-be bucked a culture that still frequently reviled African American women.

In her public statements speaking back to verbal attacks, Obama performed strategic ambiguity, deploying its very tenets by speaking

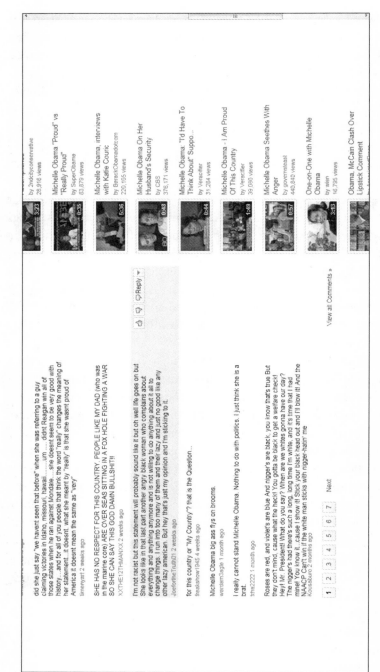

Figure 1.3. A sampling of anonymous hatred towards Michelle Obama online. Screenshot from comments underneath YouTube clip "Michelle Obama Clarifies 'Proud' Remark." Viewed May 13, 2011. www.youtube.com.

about race, class, and gender in code, and by reframing and redefining ideas such as American and patriotism. I want to be clear that all of the American public did not meet Obama's performance on *The View* with the thunderous applause of that studio audience. In fact, for a number of years I have followed the comments that are posted online below clips of her *View* appearance, and they are almost always chock-full of hate. The cropped screen shot in Figure 1.3 from 2011 demonstrates just one moment of one day of such hatred. From the nearly all caps entry, second in the image, that decried Michelle Obama's alleged lack of "RESPECT FOR THIS COUNTRY" as "GOD DAMN BULLSHIT," to the "poem," last in the image, that ends with the threat—"Stick your black head out and I'll blow it [off]!"—the anti-Black racism knew no bounds. In anonymous online commentaries, as in other mediated spaces, our Ivy League-educated First Lady/First-Lady-to-be experienced what critic Natasha Gordon-Chimpembere calls a "metaphorical lynching."[60]

I also want to be clear that this moment on *The View* happened alongside many other similar moments, from her gracing a vast array of magazine covers to her celebrated remarks at the 2008 Democratic National Convention (DNC). At that convention, as critic Caroline Brown notes, Obama combined "God and motherhood, national pride and a devotion to the military" in a successful speech that "struck a chord that has resonated with the American public."[61] Critical race scholar Verna Williams notes that Michelle Obama opened the convention by affirming, "I stand at the crosscurrents . . . of history"—not her husband, not Hillary Clinton, but Michelle Obama.[62] At that speech, as on *The View*, Obama's discussions of race had to remain coded. After 2008, Obama enjoyed much praise as First Lady.

In her 2016 DNC convention speech, Michelle Obama emerged again as the star. Wearing a cap-sleeved, fitted dress with sweetheart seaming that could only be described as deep Democrat blue, Obama's grace and poise ruled the stage. With the platform adorned in a similar blue, Obama became the physical embodiment of the 2016 Democratic party. Her hair dusted her shoulders, her bangs swooped over one eye, and her earrings appeared to be the marriage of hoops and pearls; her skin glowed while her beautifully lined eyes glimmered, and her words emerged from lips shining with a neutral color. Obama began her speech by broadly narrating the family's entrance into the White House as one of concern for their daughters. She named Trump in code, iterating the family response to negativity: "When they go low, we go high" (Figure 1.4). Continuing broadly—her speech punctuated at times by audience yells of "We love you, Michelle!"—Obama said "we know that our words and actions matter," before moving on to racial specificity. Such words mattered for all, yes, but especially for "Kids like the little Black boy who looked up at my husband, his eyes wide with hope and he wondered 'is my hair like yours?'"

Obama continued, "the story of this country," the one that "brought me to the stage tonight," was one of "generations of people that felt the lash of bondage, the shame of servitude, the sting of segregation." The next part of the speech went viral: "I wake up every morning in a house that was built by slaves." She paused with assurance for thunderous applause. Her eyes appeared to be slightly welling up with tears as she continued, "I watch my daughters [touched her chest], two beautiful, intelligent Black young women, playing with their dogs on the White House lawn." This statement was capped off by more roaring approval from the crowd. Obama refuted postrace by underscoring her daughters'

Figure 1.4. Michelle Obama rousing the crowd at the 2016 DNC. Digital image. Getty Images. July 25, 2016. www.gettyimages.com.

race and gender, calling the teens, in a feminist manner, "young women" (and not girls). In this moment, Michelle Obama's movement from post-racial resistance through strategic ambiguity to Black feminist resistance through forthright critique was complete.

In this chapter, taking Michelle Obama's lead, I have used women of color theorizing to unpack her comments at a rally and read them against her later reframing on *The View*, to show that strategic ambiguity enabled her shift in popularity. Michelle Obama's sophisticated strategic ambiguity, how she spoke back to postracial ideology, helps minoritized twenty-first century subjects understand how power, privilege, racial-ized and gendered discrimination, *and* resistance function in our pres-ent moment. She showed us when we can speak through code and when we can abandon code as we take our seats at the table. As the next chap-ter will show, not all Black women celebrities, including the Queen of All Media Oprah Winfrey, were able to perform strategic ambiguity as successfully and seamlessly as our former First Lady.

2

"Because Often It's Both"

Racism, Sexism, and Oprah's Handbags

No book on Black women in media would be complete without at least a mention of Oprah Winfrey. Winfrey has always occupied a unique position in the American cultural imaginary. Media scholar Beretta Smith-Shomade explains how monumental Winfrey's ascension has been for Black women and for Black female representation: "Over the history of visual culture, Black women's imagery has teetered between disgust and adulation, depravity and excess, objectification and agency. This pendulum has significantly impacted the lives of sentient African-American women, but *then came Winfrey*"[1] [my emphasis]. From the advent of her talk show in 1986, Winfrey climbed—and quickly topped—the popular culture mountain. Winfrey's success has been, and indeed still is, predicated upon her climbing that mountain through strategic ambiguity. She has positioned herself as a figure who can at times supersede the trifecta of race, gender, and class—the pesky bodily, cultural, and historical instantiations of identity—*and* who can signify in particularly raced and gendered manners. Winfrey's racialized performance is thus supremely postracial in its quality of picking and choosing race. She enacts racialized signifiers at particular moments, but largely ignores the historical, structural, and even interpersonal components of race and racism.

Winfrey, like Michelle Obama, has, to her fans and foes alike, long since abandoned status as mere mortal. She is superhuman, an icon, even a religious figure, as religious studies scholar Kathryn Lofton writes, capable of scripting her own doctrine and inspiring the zeal of her own pilgrims. Lofton notes that Winfrey's success comes through her many platforms and products: she is "an insignia, supplying a stylized economy that included multiple print cultures (magazine, literary, cookbook, self-help, medical, and inspirational), multimedia programming (podcasts, weekly and daily electronic updates, weekly and daily television programs, radio shows, television networks, movies, movies of the week, and stage productions), educational philosophies, international philan-thropies, interpersonal counseling, self-care workshops, and product plugs."[2] In her ubiquity, Winfrey has done much to not only shore up her own brand, but also configure the representational space of a particular brand of celebrity for African American women.

That particular brand is strategic ambiguity. Oprah Winfrey is the ultimate magician who has transformed spaces racialized as Black by es-sence of Winfrey's own race, into one safe for Whiteness, and specifically White women, by essence of her speaking about race largely in code. In-deed, strategic ambiguity in the hands of powerful Black women celebri-ties such as Michelle Obama, Oprah Winfrey, and Shonda Rhimes has the ability to perform the trick of the so-called "Magic Negro," whose performance, cultural critic Krin Gabbard explains, sates and soothes White fears.[3] Her tremendous success across platforms illustrates that she knows how to bring in multiple audiences, in particular African Americans and Whites. Literary scholar Habiba Ibrahim notes that in her first major platform, the *Oprah Winfrey Show*, Winfrey enacted "conflict control" when addressing race issues on camera, which "just as viably serve[d] an imagined black community as . . . placate[d] an over-whelmingly white viewership."[4] Such a magic trick happened through the gendering of Winfrey's genre: she made her fame through a genre oriented towards women (talk shows) and she aimed her legion of prod-ucts squarely at the very women who tuned in daily. Winfrey's strategic embrace of sisterhood, made manifest through her commercial empire, was—and is—a key component of her magic.

A silencing or coding of race-talk has functioned in tandem with gender and class in Winfrey's postracial performance of strategic am-biguity. As media studies scholar Timothy Havens notes, "*The Oprah Winfrey Show* largely downplays issues of racial difference in the inter-est of shared feminine interests and female viewership."[5] This difference was erased by Winfrey's pushing of conspicuous consumption; women of all racial backgrounds could purchase Winfrey's "favorite things" to commune in sisterhood. Winfrey's positioning as a postracial figure, communication scholar Janice Peck argues, was key to her White fe-male adulation.[6] Using strategic ambiguity, she created safe spaces to nurture White women, to absolve them of their racism, to stoke their spiritual and consumerist desires, and to help them become "their best selves." Importantly, while Winfrey enacted a postracial posture, relying on racialized codes to demonstrate movement beyond race, she did not embody a colorblind one, or rhetorically erase racialized differentiation or distinction itself. For example, Winfrey brought the phrase "Black don't crack"—one that comes from African American Vernacular English (AAVE)—to her interracial audiences on her television show, using it in such a way that gave White women permission to use a racially-specific phrase in the spirit of postracialism. If Winfrey were to embody colorblindness, she would refuse to point out racialized difference at all, not make it visible only to sell it for the purposes of appropriation.

In other words, strategic ambiguity is an analytical frame that brought together Winfrey's racialized and gendered personae. Winfrey played a postracial and not colorblind game because her own racialization and gendering as an African American woman is key to her success (and indeed to postrace discourse): she must remind White audiences of her Black womanhood in order to ask them to identify her—and themselves—as beyond race. Meanwhile, Black women audiences also flocked to Winfrey, but I believe they understood that they were not the major planets in Winfrey's orbit. Black audiences witnessed her racialized machinations, and chose to join or leave the magic show as guests who were allowed to slip through the door, but weren't actually invited to the party.

But what happened when the party was shut down, or when Winfrey's postracial, strategically ambiguous negotiation of race and gender wasn't successful? What happened when Winfrey experienced a gendered racism that was far from coded and polite? In this chapter, I analyze an incident like that of Michelle Obama in the previous chapter in which Winfrey was both attacked by and responded to a racism and sexism that was coded and covered by postrace and strategic ambiguity. Here is the timeline: a fancy Swiss store refused Winfrey entry, seeing her as any old Black woman and not superstar Oprah Winfrey. Following her usual M.O., Winfrey performed strategic ambiguity in her response to the racist action—she acknowledged and deflected it with the softened language of postrace in an *Entertainment Tonight* interview. However, this time her postracial resistance didn't work: the press exploded in disbelief of her reading of the event as racialized and attacked her with their own (barely coded) racism. In this chapter, I first do a close reading of the *Entertainment Tonight* interview where Winfrey broke the story, and the ways in which Winfrey used strategic ambiguity to safely and softly point out the existence of intersectional, historical, and contemporary racism. Then I examine the media backlash to Winfrey's story in the newspapers and blogs. I examined over 100 newspaper articles and an additional 100 blog posts on the incident from the story's crest in popularity, August 9–18, 2013. The story circulated where Winfrey's own reach is most prevalent around the world: the U.S., Canada, Western Europe, South Africa, New Zealand, Singapore, and Australia. In this media backlash, Winfrey was framed along three lines: she cried racism, she was uppity, and she was an Angry Black Woman.

This particular example demonstrates that, even though Oprah Winfrey deployed strategic ambiguity in her postracial response to racialized sexism, the press still pilloried her as a race-baiting, uppity, Angry Black Woman; her magic trick didn't work. Building on last chapter's look at what occurred when Michelle Obama performed her own magic trick of strategic ambiguity on *The View*, the Winfrey incident gives us new questions to think with:[7] can we consider Winfrey's strategically ambiguous negotiations of racialized gender to be, if not liberatory, then resistant? What happened when racism and sexism overtook the postracial narrative of strategic ambiguity as Winfrey didn't "win" like Michelle Obama did? Did becoming a victim of gendered racism, even in the midst of performing, reveal the problems with strategic ambiguity that emerged when a Black woman got too comfortable with performing postracial resistance?

Controlling the Narrative

After a twenty-five-year run, the *Oprah Winfrey Show* aired its finale in January of 2011, but Winfrey's life in the American public was far from over. She had simultaneously launched her eponymous OWN network, a testament to the survival of her brand in the uber-competitive cable network universe. Two years into this show-to-network change, the Winfrey "scandal" broke. In August of 2013, the infotainment world briefly centered its short attention span on a story about Winfrey not being allowed to see a certain designer handbag at a high-end retailer in Switzerland, a déjà vu twin incident to a 2005 story when she was denied entry to a tony Parisian retailer. The 2013 story titled "Oprah on Being a Recent Victim of Racism" by the entertainment news show that broke the story, *Entertainment Tonight* (ET), came to me, and indeed, I suspect, most viewers, not through the means by which I would have consumed my celebrity gossip a decade ago—television or print—but instead through social media headlines with links to a segmented and highlighted story on ET's website.[8] The story's insertion into an Internet landscape positioned it as ripe for re-telling in countless ways and countless times.

The website situated clips of the six-minute-long story above the splashy headline and a teaser summary of the sit-down interview TV personality Nancy O'Dell had conducted with Winfrey as part of a press junket for her 2013 film *The Butler*. If the viewer ventured beyond the teaser to the clips, one would uncover the connections the interview makes between film, Winfrey, and incident: as the film examined racial issues throughout the second half of the twentieth century, O'Dell and Winfrey's interview centered questions of race and discrimination. Winfrey's position here, at least as most audiences are accustomed to seeing, is flipped: she is the interviewee and not interviewer, and she looks the glamourous, celebrity part. With her shoulder-length hair loose, curly, and full, and her gorgeously arched brows, Winfrey wore bold gold hoops and a fiery red, notched collar tunic contrasting with her flattering lipstick and smoky eye makeup (Figure 2.1). Foreboding music played softly in the background, alerting the viewer to the fact that this was a serious conversation.

After breezing through what O'Dell names as the big race issue of the summer, Food Network television star Paula Deen's use of "the n-word" (but ignoring the summer's bigger race story of George Zimmerman's trial and subsequent acquittal for the murder of Trayvon Martin), O'Dell faced Winfrey not with an expansive invitation to address her own experiences of discrimination, but instead a confrontation with what the media often posits as the ultimate litmus test to prove the continued existence of anti-Black racism, a query as to whether she had been called "the n-word." Winfrey responded: "I would have to say that racism for me doesn't show itself that way." Winfrey went on to say that outside of "Twitter thugs" on anonymous social media sites, "nobody in their

Figure 2.1. Winfrey masterfully controlling her ET interview. Screenshot from "Oprah on Being a Recent Victim of Racism," *Entertainment Tonight*. August 5, 2013. Viewed October 31, 2013. www.etonline.com/.

right mind is going to do that to my face or in that way." Winfrey capped this particular discussion by saying that she was immune to "true racism," which she described as "being able to have power over somebody else." Winfrey implied that her celebrity and sheer economic power shielded her. Her superstar status and wealth were not the only things that shielded her from old-school racism in the form of racist epithets; Obama-era twenty-first century mores dictated that the word itself was so verboten that it could even be iterated in polite *multiracial* company more than in the euphemism "the n-word."

It is here that the seasoned and savvy Winfrey subtly took charge of the interview. The "Queen of All Media" gave an exemplary performance of negotiated speaking back, a strategically ambiguous postracial dance. Changing tack, she provided an addendum to her denial of facing "true racism" by turning to discuss the ways in which race- and gender-based discrimination did affect her life. She told O'Dell:

It shows up for me this way. It shows up for me that sometimes I'm in a boardroom or I'm in situations where I'm the only woman, I'm the only African American person within a hundred-mile radius, and I can see in the energy of the people there. They're, they don't sense that I should be holding one of those seats. I can sense that.

[Nancy [*incredulously*]: you?]

Yeah! Of course I can sense it. But I can never tell—is it racism; is it sexism? Because often it's both.

Winfrey described power-laden, interracial spaces of privilege as ones where the conjoined forces of racism and sexism could, and did, still penetrate her world. Although she denied being affected by "true racism," she named the brand of discrimination she faced as "energy," a more subtle, more ephemeral, and more nebulous brand of inequality befitting a woman who brought pop spirituality to the masses. She inserted gender into the space that O'Dell attempted to delimit as just race-specific, illustrating how power maneuvered through multiple, intersecting prisms. Winfrey finished this discussion of the ways in which discrimination functioned in her life saying: "So I don't have it the way some other people are used to having it." But this statement, like her denial of suffering from "true racism" in lieu of an assertion of a racialized/gendered "energy," was ambiguous. Were the "other people" here other African Americans or other people of color who did not have the privilege of sitting in Winfrey's boardrooms? Or were the "other people" privileged Whites who were not looked at askance as a Black woman occupying the most elite spaces of privilege would be?

Winfrey's strategic ambiguity allowed her to critique even the most exclusive areas without, as she says later in the interview, "throw[ing] down the Black card" or, in anthropologist John Jackson's formulation, exhibiting "racial paranoia," which Jackson describes as "distrustful conjecture about purposeful race-based maliciousness."[9] Furthermore, Winfrey's statements amounted to a testimonial about what were admittedly harder to nail down and often intuited experiences of gendered racism. The particular "energy" Winfrey described sounded like a microaggression, what psychologist Derald Wing Sue identifies as "the everyday slights, insults, indignities, and invalidations delivered toward people of color because of their visible racial/ethnic minority characteristics."[10] At this point in the interview, postracial resistance through strategic ambiguity remained Winfrey's tool of choice to speak back to microaggressions.

Immediately after these statements, Winfrey segued to a story that, in the context of the interview proving "Oprah being a victim of racism" as the title of the segment promised, would substantiate her experience of discrimination, in a more concrete way than the bad "energy" circulating in a board meeting. Leaning forward conspiratorially and smiling slightly, Winfrey told O'Dell: "but I will tell you this." She proceeded to narrate her experience at a high-end store in Zurich in which she was not allowed to see a handbag: the woman working in the store said, in Winfrey's recounting, putting on a slight Swiss-French accent: "no, it is too expensive." Refusing to name the store, Winfrey continued, saying that she insisted three more times that she did indeed want to see the bag, and was rebuffed each time. If in the beginning of the interview Winfrey shut down facile questions about "the n-word," and in the middle of the interview she pointed to more ephemeral experiences of racialized sexism, here Winfrey moved the discussion to a more explicit, concrete, and perhaps persuasive incident of discrimination, in which (Winfrey implies or suggests but does not explicitly state) she was denied access on the basis of race. In this incident, unlike the one in the boardroom, Winfrey was not recognized as her media mogul self; she was read by the person working in the shop as any Black American woman insisting on perusing an exclusive shop's most expensive merchandise.

Although O'Dell appeared to not accept "racism" in Winfrey's discussions of "the n-word" or racialized sexism as "energy," this incident registered with her as a real, tangible example. O'Dell stated, "it still exists," and Winfrey echoed, "it still exists." The "it" clearly means racism or sexism or, in Winfrey's words, both, but the words were not verbalized by either woman. The silencing of the loaded words "racism" and "sexism" served a softening purpose suitable for strategic ambiguity. The space remained safe and hospitable to White people and to men as neither O'Dell nor Winfrey took power and privilege to task. But despite Winfrey's careful dance through her example of interpersonal racism, O'Dell could not let go of her singular focus on "the n-word," which itself smacked of racism: Dell's insistence on Winfrey's vulnerability to the word amounted to her practically using the word itself on Winfrey. Immediately after Winfrey told this story, O'Dell, without segue, asked Winfrey *again* if she was ever called "the n-word," and Winfrey *again* deflected that question from her own personal experience. She extricated herself from O'Dell's implication that "true racism" simply meant that word by connecting discrimination to history. Winfrey stated:

> I do not run in the circle of people who use the word loosely or use the word. Because for me it's out of respect for people for whom that's the last word they heard while they were being hung. It's the last word they heard when they were being fired. It's the last word they heard when their house was being burned. It's the last word they—it's the word they heard every day when they had to step off the sidewalk and let other people pass. I just, I, I have had a sense of not just being, living this life for myself but having this life created by other people. Maya Angelou says, "I come as one but I stand as ten thousand," from that poem. I have had that sense for as long as I can remember.

Winfrey's conjuring of the historical violence and daily aggressions of anti-Black racism sutured her own experiences to those of her ancestors. As this statement came directly after Winfrey's two personal examples of gendered racism—in the boardroom and in the shop—it served the purpose of proving that discrimination functioned through a historical trajectory that continued into our present moment. Winfrey's proclamation danced through strategic ambiguity by not naming herself (a postracial move that allowed her to not seem racially touchy) but by clearly and unambiguously affirming historical, contemporary, group, and individual iterations of racism by Black men and women (an equally postracially resistant move that slid in anti-racist critique).

While O'Dell appeared to have as her mandate nailing Winfrey down to a simplistic "yes" or "no" about being called "the n-word" (perhaps because such an admission would result in a splashy headline, or perhaps because there are no other scripts with which to signal racism to viewers), seasoned interviewee Winfrey didn't take the bait and deftly negotiated around O'Dell's questions, refusing to be targeted in such a manner. She refused to let an interview on race and racism devolve into a discussion of the politics of "the n-word," and reshaped the agenda into a discussion of the realities of identity-based discrimination and racialized violence, in part by unpacking the toxicity of the word itself. She introduced race and gender as inextricable and conjoined processes through which discrimination occurred for women of color. In this six-minute segment, Winfrey masterfully steered the interview from dismissing "the n-word" to intersectional and discriminatory "energy" to racial profiling and finally to the history of anti-Black violence. Here Winfrey illustrated a form of strategic ambiguity that allowed her to critique the historical and intersectional nature of racism in a mainstream media world dismissive of racism unless it came in the forms of hate-speech and especially the "n-word."

Even Oprah Doesn't Have the Last Word: Spins on "the Incident"

Winfrey's appearance on *Entertainment Tonight* exemplified a strategically ambiguous positionality that highlighted the saturation of racism in the historic and current everyday lives of African Americans. Responses such as Winfrey's on *ET* positioned insider readers to see a wink, a sign of solidarity for the collective as well as pushback for the individual. Rhetorician Charles E. Morris III describes the "textual wink" as a message designated through "an ideology of difference." Writing of gay male passing, Morris explains that a wink is at least partially constituted by silence. However, he says, "instead of a silence that negates and excludes . . . silence functions constructively as the medium of collusive exchange. What is not said is nonetheless performative, a speech act that can be read by certain audiences, and calls those audience members into being as abettors."[11] Winfrey's African American audiences, as inside abettors, might seize upon her fairly frank discussions of racism and sexism as the moment they were invited to the party. This moment of validation could prompt Black audiences to exclaim to White skeptics: "See, even Oprah experiences racism! Now do you believe it's real!?!" But even with the most generous interpretation, such coding barely eroded postracial racism, precisely because its ambiguity allowed racism both to hide behind postracial ethos and subsequently to thrive. Some might even argue that coded postracial resistance cannot ever trigger structural change.

But my read of Oprah Winfrey's appearance on *Entertainment Tonight*, and speculation about its effectiveness as an anti-racist intervention, is just one way of examining the strategic ambiguity imbued in Black women's twenty-first century race and gender talk; centering her words emphasizes only the first layer of the multi-layered media screen. Africana studies scholar Carole Boyce Davies points out that "speech . . .

is as much an issue of audience receptivity, the fundamentals of listening, as it is of articulation."[12] As the story circulated, this first layer of Winfrey's mediated speech lost focus because of the way in which it was heard and reinterpreted by media outlets—a way, we shall see, entirely different from my interpretation. After appearing on the ET website, the story laid dormant in the news cycle for four days, an eternity in the warp-speed of infotainment news, until the tabloid-esque rag *The London Evening Standard* covered the story in an article entitled "'That bag is too expensive for you': Oprah Winfrey says 'racist' assistant refused to serve her in Zurich."[13] By putting *racist* in quotes the journalist implied, first, that Winfrey actually used the word and, second, that racism was impossible in this context. The story's title directed readers to follow how the media would spin the story: a Black American woman's hypersensitivity about race- and gender-based discrimination. Notably, as she relied upon strategic ambiguity, Winfrey never actually uttered the word "racist" in her ET interview.

She did not use the "r" word in her two comments on Twitter, referring to the incident as a "handbag diss"[14] (Figure 2.2); she also failed to provide further details or ruminate about the incident. In our tweeting and re-tweeting world today, hot-button stories such as these seldom remained a single moment on a single screen; a speaker pointing out the existence of discrimination, even in as seemingly innocuous and coded a manner as Winfrey did, rarely had the last word. The Obama-era, twenty-first century filter came into play in 140 character spins and Facebook-posted headlines, the new version of front-page news for so many Americans. Soon after the story went viral, the Swiss Tourism office released a statement through a spokesperson, saying: "We are very sorry for what happened to her," and later tweeted that the salesperson Winfrey encountered "acted terribly wrong."[15] On a red-carpet appearance, Winfrey responded to a reporter's questions, still not using the word *racist*: "I think that incident in Switzerland was really just an incident in Switzerland. I'm really sorry that it got blown up. I purposely did not mention the name of the store. I'm sorry that it was Switzerland. I was just referencing it as an example of being in a place where people don't expect that *you* [my emphasis] would be able to be there . . . No apology is necessary from the country of Switzerland!"[16] While the "you" was coded for Black and female, Winfrey carefully neither named

Figure 2.2. Oprah's tweets on "the incident." Screenshot from Oprah Winfrey's Twitter account. August 9, 2013. Viewed June 13, 2017. www.twitter.com/.

race nor gender, just as she did not name gendered racism. But the one newspaper story, Winfrey's two tweets, and her red carpet response were all that were needed for the media's version of "the incident" to explode across the popular press.

In Winfrey's case, as in so many news stories today, the story's re-reporting circulated in greater numbers than the ET interview itself. Winfrey's own remarks took a back seat to the mediated spin. How did the mainstream media, with social media riding in its wake and occasionally accelerating to take the lead, drive Winfrey's story from her nuanced, intersectional analysis to the dismissal of a Black woman's illegitimate "racism cry"?[17] The trope of "crying racism" is a riff off of one of Aesop's Fables, "The Shepherd's Boy and the Wolf" (more popularly known as "The Boy Who Cried Wolf") where a little shepherd boy tricks the nearby villagers too many times pretending that a wolf is attacking his sheep. When the wolf does arrive and he calls out for help, the villagers ignore him because their trust has been eroded; the sheep end up being killed. The boy's earlier lies desensitize the villagers: they are sick of getting themselves all worked up only to get tricked into believing yet another lie.[18] In this analogy, racism becomes the ultimate trick.

In order to pull apart the various layers of the media screen, I examined newspaper articles and blog posts where the incident circulated most prominently at the height of the incident. The media provides particular frames, what journalism scholar Michael Brüggemann—drawing upon Robert Entman, among other media scholars—describes as "*patterns of interpretation* rooted in culture and articulated by the individual" [emphasis in the original].[19] The newspapers set up the story's dominant tropes: Winfrey reluctantly admitted fault (frame: she cried racism), the whole situation was a joke (frame: she was uppity), and Winfrey was angry and a liar (frame: she was an Angry Black Woman). Blogs picked up on the newspaper stories as soon as they appeared, following the same general tropes without the pretense of objectivity. Where Winfrey successfully deployed postracial resistance to re-center racism and sexism in her *ET* interview, here in the re-reporting familiar racist tropes boxed out alternative readings and re-centered structures of racism that were anything but postracial.

Frame One: Winfrey Cried Racism

The majority of the headlines spun the story into Winfrey's reluctant admission of her fault. She was "sorry,"[20] "apologizes"[21] and had "regrets."[22] In these stories, Winfrey was performing contrition; she grudgingly exhibited remorse. The media titan was humbled and put in her place. But about what, precisely, was she sorry? While some headlines simply stopped with "Oprah says sorry,"[23] leaving the headline-skimming reader to insert any number of possible reasons for her apology, other stories inserted various objects of her regret, many of which changed with the reporting. In some articles, she was quoted to regret the "incident."[24] In other headlines, Winfrey was reported to feel sorry about the "media storm,"[25] the "Switzerland racism broohaha,"[26] and that the "handbag clash was 'blown up'";[27] the implication of these headlines was that Winfrey lamented that media, which should focus their attention on more important issues, devoted so much time to her ultimate pettiness about an expensive purse. Other headlines stated that Winfrey regretted "Swiss frenzy"[28] and "Switzerland's flap";[29] here the papers named the Swiss as the object of Winfrey's regret, but even these two headlines demonstrated divergent takes on the story. The first headline illustrated Winfrey allegedly lamenting Swiss anxiety over bad publicity. The second set up the idea that Winfrey condemned the whole country because one Swiss employee (supposedly) treated her poorly. This wave of "reluctant apology" themed headlines quickly devolved to a second set that named race, and revealed the press's barely-coded racism.

Another set of headlines stated that Winfrey was sorry for not just the "incident"/"storm"/"frenzy"/"hooha," but more specifically, "the storm stirred by racism story."[30] In these headlines, Winfrey bemoaned "racism flap"[31] and "racism uproar."[32] Here Winfrey was at fault for having "cried racism" as a number of outlets put it.[33] The implication behind use of the "crying racism" trope was not necessarily that Winfrey herself articulated past experiences of discrimination, but rather that Winfrey was just like all other Black Americans who stubbornly identified race-neutral encounters as racist. Crying racism was a trope that smacked of postracial ethos, what political scientist Claire Jean Kim describes as the sentiment that "the American race problem no longer consists of White racism, which is steadily declining, but rather of . . . the misguided tendency of minorities (especially Blacks) to cry racism and/or emphasize their racial identity as a strategy for getting ahead."[34] In this frame, Winfrey erroneously read an event through the prism of race when race was simply not a factor. As the papers framed Winfrey, she committed the crime of not agreeing to the lies of postracial discourse, of not agreeing to the fact that racism wasn't over, and, importantly, not being sufficiently strategic or ambiguous.

The "crying racism" frame was aided by the use of scare quotes. In one of the "crying racism" themed headlines, Winfrey didn't regret *racism*, she regretted "racism," which was emphatically placed in scare quotes.[35] In other words, the reporter's insertion of scare quotes played further on the "crying racism" trope, and erased any consideration of race as a factor. In a similar vein, one paper reported that "Oprah 'racism' just lost in translation,"[36] as language differences became the culprit for what was framed as an innocent misunderstanding. Other stories produced a similar effect by using racism as a descriptor for a made-up or exaggerated incident, as in: "She's sorry for racism flap."[37] Barely coded in these stories was the message that Winfrey should feel remorseful that her Black American hypersensitivity, her audacity in reading race into a race-less situation, victimized the blameless (and implied to be colorblind) Swiss.

In the crying racism frame, Figure 2.3 illustrates a postracial headline: the naming of "racism" only to prove that it didn't exist. The headline on gossip website TMZ labeled Winfrey as "passive aggressive" and her "apology" as "BS."[38] The article's title rhetorically cemented the frame and is paired with a photograph that furthers its work: open- and angry-mouthed, and finger-wagging, Winfrey looked anything but "apologetic." Her outsized sunglasses distanced her further, as she did not visually connect with the reader; her large drop diamond earrings showcased her tremendous wealth, further removing her from most readers of the image. There was no caption underneath the picture, so it could have been taken anywhere and at any time. But, because the website placed the picture directly under the "Passive Aggressive Oprah" headline, the reader was led to believe that the picture was taken at the time of her "BS Apology."

Figure 2.3. Crying Racism Frame. Screenshot from "Passive Aggressive Oprah—Gives BS Apology for Switzerland Racist Flap." TMZ. August 13, 2013. Viewed April 17, 2014. www.tmz.com/.

Few outlets took the opportunity to say that the Swiss store worker did not recognize her as megastar Oprah Winfrey and assumed that she was some unknown African American woman. The media could not see Winfrey as herself, Black American woman Oprah Winfrey. This misrecognition not only happened because of her mega stardom (as a star, by definition, is beyond race), but also through her own liberal use of strategic ambiguity: Winfrey has, at times, literally defined herself as being beyond race. But Blackness, as visual culture scholar Nicole Fleetwood writes, is "a troubling presence" particularly "in a visual field."[39] Because of the way popular media largely condense representations of Black people to debasing, narrow stereotypes, representations of Blackness, again in the words of Fleetwood, "require audiences to consider the very definition of blackness as problem, as perplexing, as troubling to the dominant visual field."[40] Long histories of racism dictate that Blackness can never be seen neutrally: it is always a problem. Because of the scripting of Blackness as problem, even superstar Winfrey troubled the field.

A couple of outlier sources did point out that Winfrey's treatment in Switzerland might actually offer a glimpse into the experiences of racism and xenophobia suffered by immigrants of color (the press labeled them "asylum-seekers"): in that same year of 2013, authorities banned immigrants from schools and public swimming pools in one Swiss town, and the xenophobic Swiss People's Party campaigned to ban the construction of minarets and the hijab by Muslims.[41] However, this information rarely made its way into the coverage of Winfrey's incident. Overall, from these news sources that framed the story through the "crying racism" trope, audiences could glean the idea that not only was discrimination in elite spaces implausible, but so, too, perhaps, was the existence of racialized and gendered discrimination at all. For some viewers, this might translate to the notion that *those people* were always crying racism wolf. In the words of sociologist Eduardo Bonilla-Silva, this idea demonstrates not only postrace (we have overcome race and live in a meritocracy) but also "colorblind racism": race would cease to be an issue "if blacks and other minorities would just stop thinking about the past, work hard, and complain less (particularly about racial discrimination)."[42] The logic of colorblind racism, just like its younger cousin postracial racism, is that, if race-based discrimination existed at all, it remained the fault of hypersensitive people of color. Ironically, the denial of racism's existence actually perpetuated racism.

Frame Two: Winfrey Is Uppity

While a good number of the "Oprah admits fault" headlines laced their articles with coded derision, another set of articles unsparingly and explicitly mocked "the incident" and Winfrey herself, skewering her for her supposed racial sensitivities and shifting focus to her wealth. Figure 2.4 illustrates such a sentiment. Winfrey was Photoshopped into the costume of a campy cartoon villain, "Rita Repulsa" of the Mighty Morphin Power Rangers.[43] Winfrey's cheeks were sucked in dramatically, making her appear haughtily cartoonish. The blog labeled the media (of which this blog is ostensibly not a part) as "race baiter," another postracial ploy whereby race functioned solely as a rhetorical device to unfairly blame Whites for Black people's inability to actually take responsibility. Media headlines foregrounded what they posited as the ridiculousness of the situation: one of the world's wealthiest women being treated as any (Black American woman) tourist and not as a (raceless/genderless, read: White male) billionaire. Thus, the headlines cast issues of race and gender aside as irrelevant. As one headline put it, "Oprah's just a picky shopper."[44]

By introducing the looming specter of Winfrey's well-known conspicuous consumption (an annual Christmas episode on her talk show and now a regular segment in her magazine is "Oprah's favorite things"), the logic was that, just as the luxury handbag was frivolous, so too was the idea of the incident being racialized.[45] The incident was framed as a "storm in a handbag" and "a bagful of racism,"[46] as "Oprah loses out in handbags at dawn."[47] A number of papers called this a petty fight: Winfrey was responsible for a "'racism' row,"[48] a "posh shop race row"[49] or a "bag shop race row."[50] One paper punned "shop says nope-rah to Oprah 'racist' purse di$$,"[51] and another headline proclaimed "cheesed-off Oprah bags the 'racist' Swiss."[52] As in the frame one examples, both notably put "racist" in quotes, thus efficiently mocking Winfrey's so-called racial sensitivity. Interestingly, some of the papers scorned the Swiss apology, as in the TMZ example (Figure 2.3), making Winfrey the villain who was strong-arming the Swiss into apologizing for her own racial sensitivities. One wrote: "Swiss apologize for encounter Oprah *calls* racist"[53] [my emphasis]. Another headline used quotes around "racist" once again, reporting that "Oprah gets Swiss apologies after 'racist' encounter."[54] Other papers did not code their mocking. As one headline stated: "Apology to Oprah over bags of money."[55]

Figure 2.4. Ridiculous Oprah. Screenshot from "Oprah Repulsa and Pursehead, her new $38,000 Handbag." *Chattering Teeth*, August 13, 2013. Viewed April 17, 2014. www.chatteringteeth.blogspot.com/.

The headlines undercut the validity of Winfrey's story by relying upon descriptions of her wealth, the ultimate invalidation to any intimation of race/gender discrimination. Many of the stories began with a description of Winfrey's estimated income of $77 million.[56] Most included the details that the handbag cost $38,000 and that uber-consumer Winfrey was in Zurich for the wedding of another Black American icon, Tina Turner. Such details primed the reader for the shock and disbelief that Winfrey would be denied anything, much less high-end merchandise. The details also primed the reader to believe that exceptional figures such as Turner and Winfrey were immune to a type of racism specific to Black women. By denying racism at upper socioeconomic ranks, the media eroded and invalidated the idea that racism was a structure infiltrating all arenas. Unlike the carefully controlled space of the *Entertainment Tonight* interview, where strategic ambiguity helped Winfrey articulate her critique of intersectional, historical, and interpersonal racism, when the story exploded across the popular press, postracial coding went out the window, and unbridled, uncoded, and explicit racism flew in.

The shift in frame to Winfrey's wealth also activated notions of Winfrey as not just an affluent but uppity Black woman. Winfrey faced a rhetorical double bind: because she was wealthy, she couldn't be Black; because she was Black, she couldn't be wealthy. Sociologists Maryann Erigha and Camille Z. Charles write that the "racially tinged term" *uppity* is "synonymous with the term 'presumptuous' . . . In the contemporary era, the term alludes to Whites' resentment towards Blacks who hold high-status positions of power and thus do not know their place in a society dominated by Whites."[57] Historically, journalist Brent Staples explains that it "was applied to affluent black people, who sometimes paid a horrific price for owning nice homes, cars or more successful businesses than whites." Staples adds that "forms of eloquence and assertiveness that were viewed as laudable among whites were seen as positively mutinous when practiced by people of color. As such, black men and women who looked white people squarely in the eye—and argued with them about things that mattered—were declared a threat to the racial order and persecuted whenever possible."[58]

While not using the word "uppity," Beretta Smith-Shomade describes Winfrey's "racialized chutzpah of money and blackness" as something that "propelled media propaganda about her. Winfrey's propensity to draw large sums of money both fascinated and appalled."[59] "Uppity" takes on a postracial twist with Winfrey in this particular incident. The trope of uppityness surfaced not when she refused to remain in her often performed postracial place, but when she reminded audiences that the world was not postracial and neither was she. She was Black and female, and discrimination still existed.[60] The angry response in frame two seemed to say: "can't you just be happy for your success and ignore our racism?"

Frame Three: Oprah as Angry Black Woman

A third frame in the newspapers' coverage of this incident centered on Winfrey's ostensible lies and anger. Some headlines framed Winfrey's verbal aggression through her alleged complaints: "Oprah accuses Swiss shop of racism"[61] and "Winfrey claims racism in Swiss handbag shop."[62] Other headlines ramped up the rhetoric from the language of accusation to the articulation of rage: not only did "Swiss racism upsets Oprah"[63] but the "Shop's assistant big mistake earns ire of Oprah."[64] (If Winfrey's Twitter feed provided any insight into her mental state, she tweeted about meditation during this time far more than the incident itself.) These racialized and gendered descriptions were coded not for a billionaire or a media mogul's frustration, but for a Black woman's anger. And not just any Black woman, but the well-worn stereotype of the Angry Black Woman (ABW).

The ABW was portrayed beautifully in Figure 2.5, which accompanied an online celebrity and gossip magazine's story on the incident. While hundreds of images of Winfrey exist on line, this photo with Michelle Obama was the visual the magazine chose to accompany the story. Both of the women's eyes were closed. The image was blurry and old: from Obama's hairstyle one can date the picture to the 2008 presidential election campaign, most likely before Obama's makeover and coming out as glamour goddess in the Spring of 2008 on *The View*. Perhaps most bizarrely, despite Winfrey's being featured with Michelle Obama, the text of the article provided no mention of the First Lady. Obama's pairing with Winfrey activated early 2008-election campaign memories of the First Lady labeled in the media as "angry," an incident I examined in the previous chapter. The two women's expressions were not polished, posed, or camera-ready. Since both had closed eyes, pursed (Obama) or agape (Winfrey) mouths, and no smiles in sight, and since the photograph played against the text of the article's title—"Oprah accuses Zurich shop of racist behaviour"[65]—the headline and image called up the stereotype of the Angry Black Woman.

The controlling image of the ABW is defined by hip hop scholars Marcyliena Morgan and Dionne Bennett as the emasculating, irrational shrew who serves as convenient foil to the stereotype of the "No-Good Black Man" (she's angry because he's no good; he's no good because she's angry).[66] The Angry Black Woman is a stock television character who remains a popular fixture on reality TV, the "mouthy harpy."[67] Stereotypes, which portray a narrow, flattened, dehumanizing focus on singular, repeated images, are dialectics activated by the portrayal of what they are not. In the Winfrey case, the ABW stereotype holds weight

Figure 2.5. Michelle and Oprah, Worst Pictures Ever. From "Oprah
Accused a Swiss Person of Racism," August 9, 2013. Viewed April 7,
2014. www.vice.com/.

against the foil of another ostensibly opposite group, not "the No-Good
Black Man," but the virtuous, innocent, and victimized White woman.
Black womanhood has historically been portrayed as sullied in contra-
distinction to pure White womanhood. Historian Deborah Gray White
notes the "interdependence" of Black and White womanhood:

> The white woman's sense of herself as a woman—her self-esteem and per-
> ceived superiority—depended on the racism that debased black women.
> White women were mistresses *because* black women were slaves. White
> women had real power over enslaved women because black women were
> really powerless. Black and white women had so little in common because
> the sexism they both experienced kept them apart.[68]

While, by essence of centering her White women audiences, Winfrey
wooed White women's notions of superiority, in this incident she refused

to fall victim to the historical formulation articulated by Gray White: she refused to image herself as inferior. In this particular image, the foil to Winfrey's ABW—the innocent White woman—became the assumed Oprah audience member. Her courting was not powerful enough to counter the ABW framing of the incident.

While Winfrey's careful negotiation on *ET* remained un-recounted in the mainstream media, the papers provided the Swiss shop owner's denial in detail. In order for the ABW to signify as villain, the White, Swiss salesperson became the subject and victim. As the story progressed over the course of a couple of days, the papers spun the tale into the media's righting Winfrey's wrong by giving the salesperson-framed-as-victim a voice. The Swiss woman's claims quickly ruled the headlines; her statements served to invalidate Winfrey's supposed version of the events as race-based. In this reframe, two headlines shouted: "Oprah Winfrey racism claims disputed"[69] and "Oprah handbag claim not true"[70]—guilty perpetrator billionaire Winfrey attacked innocent victim Swiss employee. Other headlines resuscitated the assistant's version as the real "truth" of the incident: "Oprah's bag-seller hits back."[71] Yet, it's important to note that Oprah refrained from responding even when, for example, the papers offered supposedly direct quotes from the assistant: "'Oprah's lying . . . I never said anything racist'"[72] and "'Why is Oprah lying? I'm just a shop girl.'"[73] As a result of the accusation, one headline states: "Oprah backtracks on racism allegations."[74]

Mainstream media framed the case in accordance with not just race but racialized gender. While Winfrey simply described the worker as "the woman working in the store," the press accounts described her as a "shopgirl." Winfrey was a woman; the store employee who refuses to show her the bag was a girl. As woman, Winfrey wielded greater power. The store employee was not just a "girl" but a "shopgirl"; this classed and aged term framed her as put-upon, powerless, innocent, young, and the real victim, as opposed to rich, untouchable, older Winfrey. The gendered, classed, and aged language bolstered the racialized connotations. The papers did not question who held the power when a White, Swiss employee in a designer store refused service to an unknown Black, American woman, but rather who held the power when a rich American megastar disliked the treatment she received from a poor shopgirl. The papers framed Winfrey as maintaining a power impenetrable to racism

Figure 2.6. The framing of innocence: smiling Swiss shop owner displaying the goods denied to Winfrey. "EXCLUSIVE: Swiss store owner at center of Oprah's 'racist' handbag storm demands to speak to star after she says 'sorry for the fuss'." Digital image. *The Daily Mail.* August 13, 2013. Accessed April 7, 2014. www.dailymail.co.uk/.

and sexism. The shop assistant and owner's denial of racism allowed for media consumers to take on a similar positionality. Historically, of course, an African American woman such as Winfrey would be perpetually described as a "girl" and not a "woman," despite her age, and the flip in language here ignores such history with a postracial "reverse racism" flair.

Crying Postrace: The Limits to Strategic Ambiguity

As media culture spun the incident, all three frames scripted Winfrey in similar ways. The papers mocked Winfrey and used loaded and racialized words like "racism" and "victim" that Winfrey never uttered. The newspapers and blogs gave readers no understanding of context, structure, or power, much less intersectionality; these were the very issues that Winfrey skillfully addressed in her *Entertainment Tonight* interview.

Instead the papers' and blogs' focus remained on the bizarreness of this individual incident (a superstar of Winfrey's stature being denied anything) as opposed to a critique that illustrated that, despite her celebrity, Winfrey's experience was neither an aberration nor an isolated incident. The story could still be summed up briefly and with tabloid outrage if they had a different frame: *even rich people can experience racism*, or *Blackness trumps wealth*. But the trope that won was that, because Oprah Winfrey—the ultimate postracial subject—transcended her race, the media were free to ignore how such an episode was part and parcel of a larger structural, social, and historical experience that still racialized African Americans and other people of color as criminal.

What might have happened had the papers used the opportunity of Winfrey's incident to examine how racism infiltrated elite or so-called unracialized spaces? In other words, instead of framing Winfrey as a spoiled, ungrateful liar, what might have happened if the papers had instead validated her experience, and linked it to other cases? What if Winfrey's story had been connected to legal theorist Patricia J. Williams's similar one? In her classic 1991 book of essays, *The Alchemy of Race and Rights*, Williams wrote of an analogous incident happening to her in 1986 at a Benetton store in New York City. Williams narrated that, when shopping in Soho at one pm on a Saturday two weeks before Christmas, a White teenager refused her entry to the store despite the visible presence of White people still shopping. After Williams "pressed my round brown face to the window and my finger to the buzzer," the teenager simply mouthed, "we're closed" before blowing a bubble in her direction.[75] In this pre-social media moment, Williams responded the next day by physically posting her written account of precisely what happened on the window of the store, and later by analyzing the incident in her writings as an example of "how the rhetoric of increased privatization, in response to racial issues, functions as the rationalizing agent of public unaccountability and, ultimately, irresponsibility."[76] Williams noted that such incidents were "outrageously demeaning [because] none of this can be called racism, even if it happens only to, or to large numbers of black people; as long as it's done with a smile, a handshake and a shrug; as long as the phantom-word 'race' is never used."[77] Winfrey was clearly not alone in her experiences of interpersonal racism in exclusive spaces, and yet the media framing alluded to precisely this claim.

And yet, to be quite clear, the framing of this story was complicated by Winfrey's own liberal use of postracial resistance and strategic ambiguity throughout her profession. Early in her career, Winfrey proclaimed "I transcend race," a statement which prompted Janice Peck to argue that Winfrey achieved tremendous success by becoming a "cultural icon of mainstream (White) America."[78] This was the problem with relying upon postracial resistance as an anti-racist strategy. Strategic ambiguity sometimes transcended, and sometimes signified, and the slippage between the two—the slipperiness of ambiguity—dictated that racism could not easily be called out with strategic ambiguity.

Nevertheless, the importance of the reporting was not that Winfrey received "fair" or "unfair" treatment, but instead how their framing played upon the new millennium tropes of postrace, which, in turn, deny very old-school forms of racism and sexism. This was the danger Winfrey risked when postracial resistance through strategic ambiguity was her go-to for managing her racialized identity. While some commentators dismissed celebrities' racialized incidents as "one percenter problems,"[79] media coverage of such events illuminated the mediated spin of the oversensitivity of Black Americans, the disease of "crying racism," and the foregone conclusion that racialized inequality must be mere fabrication. This incident demonstrated how strategic ambiguity is not always the right tool for Black women celebrities like Winfrey to fight twenty-first century, postracial, coded racism: Oprah Winfrey was caught crying postracial wolf.

This incident illustrated the limits of Winfrey's so-called racial transcendence, and how strategic ambiguity wasn't always a strong enough performance to trick (much less tame) racialized sexism in the public sphere. Interestingly, soon after this incident, her OWN cable channel became more unequivocally a Black channel by showcasing programs such as Ava DuVernay's prestige drama *Queen Sugar* (2016–present), Tyler Perry's nighttime soap opera *The Haves and the Have Nots* (2013–present), and Holly Robinson Peete's family-friendly reality television show *For Peete's Sake* (2016–present). I believe Winfrey's failure to use strategic ambiguity successfully aided the OWN network's move to become a home for African American niche programming. In the next chapter, I explore how showrunner Shonda Rhimes negotiated her own press coverage, including an interview by Ms. Winfrey herself, in another far more successful iteration of postracial resistance and strategic ambiguity.

3

"I Just Wanted a World That Looked Like the One I Know"

*The Strategically Ambiguous Respectability of a
Black Woman Showrunner*

Coming in the wake of Oprah Winfrey's tremendous success, Black women's visibility on television has undergone a sea change because of television showrunner Shonda Rhimes. Rhimes started her own tidal wave in Hollywood, flowing from the nameless, faceless writer behind the Britney Spears vehicle *Crossroads* (2002) to a cult figure whose fans and the media alike celebrated for redefining evening melodrama—some might even say television itself—with her hit shows *Grey's Anatomy* (2005–present), *Private Practice* (2007–2013), *Scandal* (2012–2018), and *How to Get Away with Murder* (2014–present). Rhimes' success belied television executives' oft-whispered reasoning that audiences want to see African American characters only on sitcoms, and it has helped usher in a new era of "diversity" on television. Offscreen, Shonda Rhimes' leading ladies preside over awards ceremonies, social media, and fashion and gossip rags. Onscreen, her Black women characters are elite, professional women whose work-lives showcase their superstar success and home-lives showcase their tempestuous and deliciously messy interpersonal relationships. They rule our TV fantasy versions of the Washington, D.C. political landscape, tony law schools and law firms, and top-tier surgery suites; they thrive in multiracial cast shows where their race is rarely, if ever, explicitly discussed; they un-self-consciously embrace interracial relationships and interracial friend groups. They are also seldom seen in community with other African American women, appearing to prefer the sisterhood of non-Black women. Race functions as but one of many personality traits in Shondaland, Rhimes' television production company and the fantasy space it represents.

The auteur of such groundbreaking and cult-like characters quite unusually garners almost as much interest in the press as her stars, or as

Oprah Winfrey herself remarked to Rhimes in Winfrey's first interview of the showrunner in O, The Oprah Magazine, "there are other hit shows, but it's rare to see so much focus on the writer." In response, Rhimes demurred: "I didn't expect this. When the press began asking me for interviews, I freaked out. My instinct is to hide."[1] But her shows' successes are partially contingent upon her own openness, or appearance thereof, in the press. In this chapter, I trace Rhimes' performance of postracial resistance through strategic ambiguity in the press during two particular moments, one in the pre-Obama era and at the beginning of her first show—Grey's Anatomy—when she stuck to a script of colorblindness and garnered entry into an elite Hollywood club, and a second in the #BlackLivesMatter moment and after a string of hits, when she called out racialized sexism and redefined Black female respectability.[2]

Rhimes' presentation of self in the media provides a precious archive of one element of strategic ambiguity that I touched upon in this book's introduction: contemporary Black female respectability politics. Historian Evelyn Brooks Higginbotham coined the phrase "the politics of respectability" to describe a late nineteenth-/early twentieth-century performance by Black church women that rigidly regulated everything from speech, to dress, to religiosity, to truly all means of presenting oneself.[3] Black female respectability, as historian Gerald Horne writes, was akin to "'putting on massa,' 'wearing a mask,' or adopting a personality."[4] A century ago, the women who enacted respectability politics "lifted as they climbed," to cite the motto of the National Association of Colored Women (NACW).[5] Respectability politics, Horne notes, "was seen as necessary to avoid being brutalized or murdered in a society suffused with white supremacy [and] was a trait developed over the centuries by Africans in North America."[6] Today Rhimes showcases herself as, in Lisa B. Thompson's words, a quintessential "Black lady,"[7] whose presentation of self features elements of such respectability.

In the decades that have passed since Higginbotham coined the term in the early 1990s, contemporary notions of African American respectability have changed, largely because of the rise of postracial ideologies that blame the victims of racism instead of racism itself. For example, figures like Bill Cosby communicated respectability in his famous 2004 "Pound Cake" rant at the NAACP's celebration of the fiftieth anniversary of Brown vs. the Board of Education of Topeka, Kansas.[8]

Cosby conjured the idea that not only are Black youth today running amuck committing petty crimes, but that when one of those youth gets "shot in the back of the head over [stealing] a piece of pound cake," we shouldn't be "outraged." In other words, disrespectable Black people provoke police violence, and Black respectability, or "pulling your pants up" as Cosby also admonished young African American men, ensures safety and success.

Cosby's version of respectability—just as sociologist Oscar Lewis put it decades earlier and Assistant Secretary of Labor Daniel Patrick Moynihan codified in his 1965 report *The Negro Family: The Case for National Action* (known popularly as the Moynihan Report)—was that Black people's problem was not disenfranchisement through racist institutions and histories; it was the "culture of poverty," the disrespectable cultural standards that Black people, and particularly pathological Black matriarchs, it maintained.[9] Black respectability politics became seen a way for elite African Americans to police and blame poor (or perceived-to-be poor) Blacks, instead of focusing the lens on either interpersonal or institutional racism. In this version, Herman Gray notes the individual focus of respectability politics where "since the social goal of racial uplift initially drove the cultural politics of respectability, the bid on black uplift and social recognition turned on black Americans collectively putting forward an imagined *black* best self"[10] [emphasis in the original]. While Rhimes did not, like Cosby, chide other African Americans for disreputable culture, she does "disavow," in the words of Higginbotham, "the folk" by featuring elite and professional Black women characters on her cult TV shows who are not in community with other Black women, and largely ignoring institutional and historical racism. In other words, Rhimes and her Black women characters garner success while remaining distanced from communities of Black women; they don't exactly "lift as they climb."

Nonetheless, this does not mean that subjects like Rhimes performing Black respectability politics remain silent regarding twenty-first century racism, and especially the racism of microaggressions. Rhimes spoke back through strategic ambiguity, a coded performance that gauges the microaggressions in the air and, if the space feels hostile to explicit resistance, performs colorblindness as a means to an end. In this chapter, I discuss how Rhimes provides another example to the modes of postracial resistance through strategic ambiguity that Michelle Obama successfully (chapter 1) and Oprah Winfrey unsuccessfully (chapter 2) enacted. Like Obama and Winfrey, Rhimes' version of postracial resistance demonstrates that a performance of strategic ambiguity is *strategic* in that is a mindful choice; it is *ambiguous* in that it deploys a primary facet of postrace, *not naming* racism. It is also *ambiguous* in that its explicit goal is to simply claim a seat at the table; it is *strategic* in that inclusion provides an opportunity to repudiate racism. Unlike the direct action of call-outs, walkouts, pickets, or sit-ins, strategic ambiguity is a safe way to respond to racism that comes in a postracial guise because it does not appear to upend the space. Strategic ambiguity is not silence or evasion; it's a choice to take on a certain amount of risk, to play with fire, to appropriate something that is used *against* you and make it work *for* you. Strategic ambiguity is one particular "Black Lady" form of refusal.

However, Rhimes' performance differs in other key ways from Higginbotham's description of respectability politics, and not simply because it is a century later. Rhimes is a Hollywood power broker; she garners a power perhaps unimagined by the Black churchwomen of Higginbotham's study. Our recently past historical moment—the Michelle Obama era—illustrated a discursive meeting of postracial ideologies and #BlackLivesMatter, a time when popular discourse toggled between proclaiming that race and racism were irrelevant in the lives of both people of color and Whites, and acknowledging the daily brutalities disproportionately suffered by Black Americans. Rhimes' performance of strategic ambiguity channeled a quiet, coded, polite form of Black female resistance that did not shout #BlackLivesMatter slogans or uncomfortably point out discrimination of an interpersonal, structural, or institutional manner.[11]

As an expression of twenty-first century Black respectability politics, strategic ambiguity functions as a sometimes conflicted, sometimes confounding, and always postracial Black feminist resistance. Strategic ambiguity knits together the contradictions of resistance in the postracial-meets-#BlackLivesMatter moment by featuring two sometimes contradictory elements—colorblindness and race-womanhood (or "wokeness")—with an exceptionally feminine grace. Reading such resistance is far from a straightforward process. Strategic ambiguity is the tool of Black respectability politics that minoritized subjects use to resist intersectional oppression when, in a postracial moment, those around them script spaces as White-only, ignore oppression, explain it away, or acknowledge it only in a single register (i.e., just racism instead of racialized sexism). Such resistance plays with and reinvents what media sociologist Herman Gray famously named as the three Black televisual discourses: assimilation and invisibility; pluralism and separate-but-equal; and multiculturalism/diversity.[12] Postracial resistance incorporates all three discourses into strategic ambiguity by sometimes performing and sometimes refuting them.

Just as all minoritized subjects seeking access to dominant forms of success often play the bait-and-switch game of strategic ambiguity, prominent Black women caught between hypervisibility and invisibility can be spotted rolling out this strategy.[13] Where Black men such as Shonda Rhimes' television star Jesse Williams are given the discursive space to speak truth to power, similarly prominent Black women do not or cannot step into such a space in a similarly forthright manner.[14] For example, when presented with a 2016 BET Humanitarian Award for producing work such as the documentary *Stay Woke: The Black Lives Matter Movement*, Williams gave a rousing speech wherein he memorialized recent Black victims of police brutality, including twelve-year-old Tamir Rice, and unflinchingly told the White audience to "sit down" if they only had "a critique for our resistance." To the Black audience he proclaimed that "what's going to happen is we are going to have equal rights and justice in our own country or we will restructure their function and ours." His comments went viral after this speech, inciting both the adulation of scores of fans across Black Twitter, among other places, and the ire of others who demanded as one online petition did that ABC "fire Jesse Williams from *Grey's Anatomy* for racist rant."[15] Rhimes, alongside celebrities such as Michelle Obama, Oprah Winfrey, and Rhimes' leading lady Kerry Washington, deploys a different form of resistance through strategic ambiguity. Indeed, when Rhimes took to Twitter to defend Williams, she quoted the last line of his speech: "Just because we're magic doesn't mean we're not real." Rhimes winked to Black Twitter audiences who knew the well-worn trope of the Magic Negro, but she did not directly name or address race or racism.

Like these other Black women celebrities, Rhimes' self-presentation in the press demonstrates a performance of postracial, carefully-controlled, twenty-first century Black respectability that allows for, in the words of literary scholars Michael Bennett and Vanessa D. Dickerson, a recovery of the Black female body through self-representation.[16] Her strategic ambiguity allows a forthright language about race and gender to wax and wane with the space that public discourse allows. Moreover, the press does not describe Rhimes in what production studies scholar John Thornton Caldwell calls the "recognizable iconic themes" of showrunners including "nocturnal and vampire-ish; a bad-boy locked in a bunker surrounded by male teenage memorabilia, rock-and-roll pretense, and an impressively odd intellectual pedigree formed by combinations of high culture, low culture, prestige, and kitsch."[17] Being neither White nor male, Rhimes is allowed none of these quirks, just as she isn't allowed to, again, in the words of Caldwell, be in this category: "the higher up a male producer is on the food chain, the more slack a company will give him to act out bad-boy and vanguard pretensions as part of the company's business habit."[18]

In this chapter, I trace two Rhimes moments. In the first moment, when Grey's Anatomy just got its legs and when the press celebrated her and her new show as a success, Rhimes performed a clenched-teeth approach to all aspects of self-disclosure and, in particular, to talking about race and gender. Then, in the second moment, and after a racialized and gendered attack, Rhimes spoke back with an unambiguous critique. She inhabited the space for racialized and gendered self-expression that the ubiquity of #BlackLivesMatter and her Gladiators—her social media fans—opened up. Rhimes' public statements reveal the magic of postracial resistance and strategic ambiguity, which facilitate her metamorphosis from colorblind to fierce Black feminist subject, all while remaining a pinnacle of feminine, Black respectability. Strategic ambiguity enabled the shift from the pre-Obama era to the #BlackLivesMatter era, where Rhimes' careful negotiation of the press demonstrated that, in the former moment, to be a respectable African American lady was to not speak frankly about race, while in the latter, respectable Black woman could and must engage in racialized self-expression, and thus redefine the bounds of respectability.

Strategically Ambiguous Rhimes: Colorblindness and the Twenty-First Century Race Woman

In the mid-2000s, colorblindness was an ideology pervading education, the law, and, of course, the media. Despite data demonstrating increasing racialized inequality, affirmative action had been dismantled in states such as California (through Proposition 209 in 1996) and Washington (through Initiative 200 in 1998), and popular discourse in newspaper editorials, educational administration, and courtrooms across the country circulated the fallacy that the twenty-first century United States was now a place of meritocracy.[19] The country was settling in to the steady erasure of racial remedies and racial talk, while simultaneously ignoring the steady climb of race-based disparities linked to such erasure. At the same time, the economy boomed, bolstered by predatory home loan practices, which were also racialized.[20] Barack Obama was a junior senator from Illinois who wowed the 2004 DNC, but wasn't yet a postracial icon. Meanwhile, television shows engaged in their own forms of representational racial disproportionality: early 2000s-era scripted network television sparingly featured supporting actors of color in popular shows such as *Lost* (2004–2010), *Heroes* (2006–2010), *Desperate Housewives* (2004–2012), and the *CSI* franchise (2000–present), while continuing to almost exclusively cast White actors in leading roles.

Rhimes' new show was greenlit in this moment. *Grey's Anatomy* is an evening hospital melodrama set in Seattle, Washington, whose White protagonist, Dr. Meredith Grey, maintains close personal and professional relationships with her many Black and White colleagues, and enjoys, in early seasons, a best-friendship with "her person," an Asian American woman doctor, and another close friendship with a Latina doctor (Figure 3.1). *Grey's* was an instant ratings success across demographic groups, or, as one publication put it rather crassly, it was "doing good business with the young, the old, the whites, the blacks."[21] When *Grey's* premiered, the press delightedly and constantly cited Rhimes as the first Black woman showrunner of an hour-long show that lasted past the first season.[22] Many articles also scripted Rhimes into her fictional stories, assuming, as media scholar Elana Levine articulated it: "We might account for *Grey's Anatomy*'s vision by considering the perspective of the

Figure 3.1. Diversity anchored by Whiteness. "Season 1 (*Grey's Anatomy*)." *Fandom.* 2005. Viewed October 7, 2017. http://greysanatomy.wikia.com/.

program's creator and showrunner, Shonda Rhimes . . . While the idea of a program's leader is only one of many factors that shape it, we have so few examples in television of an African American woman's leadership that it is difficult to know what impact Rhimes's particular perspective may have."[23] Her "particular perspective" bore tremendous weight as critics, fans, and foes alike scrutinized her shows for how they measured up to the litmus test of Black respectability.

Rhimes enacted her first performances of Black respectability both in the casting and writing of her television show; she showcased strategic ambiguity in the statements she meted out in her own press coverage. Three of the earliest articles on Rhimes came out in 2005 and 2006 in *Ebony* magazine, in *Written By: The Magazine of the Writers Guild of America, West,* and in *O: The Oprah Magazine.*[24] In *Ebony,* Rhimes said (with my emphasis): "With casting, *I don't care* what color they are. If a Black man comes in and he's great for a part and a White woman comes in and she's great for the part of his wife, well then, *suddenly* it's an interracial couple. And *I don't care.* It's about who's the *most talented* getting the parts." In *Written By,* Rhimes stated: "'I basically walked in saying I didn't write anybody's race into the [*Grey's Anatomy*] script . . . Let's make *Grey's look like the world*" [my emphasis]. Finally, in *O: Oprah Magazine,* Rhimes noted: "We read every color actor for every single part. My goal was simply to cast the *best* actors." Further, to Winfrey's inquiry—"Did you set out to elevate the country's consciousness in terms of racial diversity?"—Rhimes replied: "I just wanted a *world that looked like the one I know*"[25] [my emphasis]. Rhimes' responses both predicted and warded off journalistic assumptions that a Black woman showrunner was going to be myopically driven by race and race alone. In Rhimes' narration of her scripting and casting processes, she performed impartiality and an attitude un-swayed by race. Race was ancillary to her read of the world: she "didn't care." Providing stories about people of color or opportunities for actors of color was not a carefully scripted decision; it "suddenly" happened, never by design, but rather by happenstance. Rhimes' world was "the world" (not just "my world"), or everyone's world, a multiracial one in her scripting. She was simply holding up a mirror to her audience, not cramming diversity down their throats. By featuring "my" and "the" world on her television show, she was following sage, universal advice to all writers: write what

you know. Rhimes granted only a handful of interviews in the first season of *Grey's Anatomy* and in all of them she stayed on her main talking
point: colorblindness.

Through her interviews, Rhimes provided a blueprint of how to garner
success as a Black woman in an all-White industry: embrace the language
of colorblindness. Rhimes' careful language was strategically ambiguous
in its failure to name race or Blackness; her commitment to her colorblind brand was not just in the text of her shows, but in her own performance to the press. Her language was ambiguous in that it let readers of
all races identify themselves both in her narration of herself as a writer
and in her shows, and it was strategic in its ability to attract all audiences. Indeed, Rhimes' statements assured readers that not only is talent not racialized, but neither is access. In other words, slip in diverse
actors without fanfare or spotlight, without racially specific storylines,
and without specific mention of racialized difference. Never illuminate issues of racism in the ostensibly colorblind televisual landscape,
or the allegedly colorblind space of journalism; indeed, never mention
racialized difference at all. Journalists gleefully picked up on this trope.
For example, in *Written By*, the author did not introduce race until the
fourth page of a six-page article, and then wrote of race as just a personality trait, quipping: "Ah yes, the race thing. Rhimes, as you might have
noticed from the photographs, is African American." Rhimes' own colorblind discourse encouraged each journalist to discuss race in a cava-
lier manner because her interviews modeled a strategically ambiguous,
postracial ideology.

Early articles on Rhimes also discussed her casting process, known
as "nontraditional casting," "cross-racial casting," "colorblind casting,"
and "blindcasting." These terms essentially mean the same thing: not all-
White actors. The three 2005–2006 press quotes showed how, although
her audience changed for each publication, her colorblind message did
not. While *Ebony* is by content and design a Black women's magazine,
Rhimes did not target her message to Black women, or spin a story of
Black sisterhood. There was no "us" in her narration. The trade magazine *Written By* received a comparable message from Rhimes. She did
not name herself as different from her majority White peers, members of
Writers Guild of America (WGA) West, the key audience for this magazine. Rhimes performed similarly in *O: Oprah Magazine* (Figure 3.2).

Figure 3.2. Photographed by Kwaku Alson. "Oprah Talks to Shonda Rhimes." *O: The Oprah Magazine*. December 2006. Accessed October 7, 2017. www.oprah.com.

Rhimes did not identify through a racialized frame with Winfrey, who herself provided an earlier blueprint for strategic ambiguity, as I note in chapter 2. Winfrey primed her multiracial following of women of a certain age to hear Rhimes' message echoed in Winfrey's racially transcendent space.[26]

While the press coverage of Rhimes posited that cross-racial casting should be seen as racial progress, theater scholar Brandi Catanese argues just the opposite, writing that "cross-racial casting relies upon the assumption that structural inequality is a thing of the past: enduring cultural and racial differences are reduced to surface distractions that a discourse of colorblindness (often connected with notions of transcendence) can remedy."[27] Such "nontraditional casting practices" can be used an excuse that lets White folks off the hook for their own role in perpetuating racism. Catanese explains that cross-racial casting "risk[s] acquiescing to a hierarchy of valuation, suggesting that their only function is to improve people of color."[28] In other words, White people have nothing to do with racism or racial remediation, and their fates aren't tied to the people of color viewed on our screens. But Whiteness, indeed, is at the heart of such casting practices, as communication scholar Kristen J. Warner notes that color-blind casting, as opposed to consciously casting people of color for racially specific roles, comes from "the fear that white audiences would not tune in," which "created additional pressure for the showrunners."[29] Furthermore, critic Amy Long asserts, Rhimes certainly must feel such additional pressure, as "Rhimes had to actively point out and work against industrial assumptions that a racially unmarked character calls for a white actor."[30] The industry itself constrained forthright and explicit race conversations.

In these three interviews, Rhimes articulated an ideology of meritocracy: everyone worked equally hard for their roles, and subsequently everyone received equal payoffs. She did not tell the press that she sought to create fantasy spaces, imagining the world she hoped to see. No, she showcased the world she believed she saw and this world "didn't care" about race. Such a sentiment articulated strategic ambiguity, a 2005-era version of postracial respectability politics for a Black woman public figure. To become successful, Rhimes did not—and perhaps *could not*—spotlight Black women in a White-dominant space. This was because Rhimes, like *Grey's*, as media scholar Timothy Havens notes, "stage[d] the encounter with difference through white main characters." While Rhimes' White leading lady can (and, indeed, must) be surrounded by people of color (including, in the eleventh season of the show, a mixed-race African American half-sister), "African American characters . . . never serve as the main character identification."[31]

By being a Black Lady who articulated colorblindness, Rhimes not only avoided saying that "we live in a racist, sexist world," but she also did not make the (presumed White) audience uncomfortable (and not tune in). In addition to colorblindness, Rhimes' early press illustrated another aspect of strategic ambiguity: Rhimes scripted herself as both pleasant and an asset to her race. The author in the *Ebony* article, when describing Rhimes as someone who practiced colorblind casting, also noted that she was "a polite, low-key professional who loves the collaborative process." She was not rocking the boat. Coded in this statement is that she was a "good girl," who "got along with others." Strategic ambiguity in the pre-Obama era by a woman of color meant that she must perform gratitude for simply being included.

However, the press also framed Rhimes as performing another aspect of twenty-first century respectable race woman, one who was—in the words of historian Gerald Horne describing early twentieth-century

race women—"imbued with the ideology of racial uplift and determined to make a contribution to her people."[32] While early press coverage showed that Rhimes was conversant in the art and performance of
colorblindness, it also narrated Rhimes as a race-conscious, old-school
race woman who upheld her people with positive imagery; *Ebony* described Rhimes as having "a steely determination to avoid stereotypes
and deliver positive messages." Rhimes told the magazine that her "mandate" is: "There will never be any Black drug addicts on our show. There
will never be any Black hookers on our show. There will never be Black
pimps on our show." Rhimes explained further: "A lot of shows feel the
need and enjoy stereotyping and we're going the other way. [Perpetuat-
ing stereotypes] isn't something I'm interested in promoting."[33]

While Rhimes might not have explicitly addressed race in her show,
her move to feature images of professional and successful African

Figure 3.3. Aldore Collier, "Shonda Rhimes: The
Force Behind *Grey's Anatomy.*" *Ebony.* October 2005.

Americans, and her refusal to represent disreputable characters, spoke to a particular performance of respectability. This aspect of strategic ambiguity, flipping the script instead of addressing the power at play in damaging stereotypes, provided an entry for individual people of color who, by virtue of their "only" status, remained non-threatening, but because of colorblind storylines, had limited power to address issues of racialized inequality head-on.[34] Because Rhimes did not explicitly illustrate structural, interpersonal, or historical racism in her press on the show *Grey's Anatomy*, the unintended effect was that some audiences saw race as a choice, and that, in Rhimes' examples, getting addicted to drugs or involved in sex work instead of becoming a doctor came solely from bad choices, not racist or even racialized structures. Rhimes' interviews with the press from this 2005–6 moment circulated the same colorblind ideologies as her first show, *Grey's Anatomy*, and argued that powerful Black women must perform in a colorblind, race-woman, and strategically ambiguous manner in order to become successful in a mainstream space.

Strategic Ambiguity Turns Fierce: Rhimes' Non-Coded Response to Racialized Sexism

Shonda Rhimes' second show, *Private Practice*, premiered just two years into *Grey's Anatomy*'s run in the fall of 2007, as then-presidential candidate Barack Obama was emerging as a viable contender for the Democratic nomination. *Private Practice* was a spin-off program from *Grey's* and, like it, featured a White woman surrounded by a multiracial cast, including a Black best friend and Black and Latino love interests. But, for her third show, the cult favorite *Scandal*, which premiered in the spring of 2012 at the end of President Barack Obama's first term and well into his re-election campaign, Rhimes diverged from her White-woman-as-leading-lady formula. Internet communities and, in particular, newly formed Black Twitter were giving voice to the movement that would become #BlackLivesMatter, which shone a light on seventeen-year-old Trayvon Martin's February 26, 2012 murder, and shamed the popular media into covering the tragedy.[35] Thus, *Scandal* premiered in a media landscape very different from that of Rhimes' first two shows. While discourses of colorblindness still remained present in 2012 discourse, #BlackLivesMatter chipped away at its façade of racial equality.

As *Scandal* fictionalizes the life of Judy Smith, a real-life African American woman crisis manager or "fixer," Rhimes cast a Black woman lead, Kerry Washington. Her character Olivia Pope, like Rhimes' *Grey's* and *Private Practice* protagonists, leads a group of multiracial characters or, rather, in the case of *Scandal*, a racially mixed group of men, and a number of White women: no other women of color, outside of storylines featuring Olivia Pope's mother, share the screen with Rhimes' Black woman lead (Figure 3.4). Rhimes also counter-balanced her leading lady's Blackness with her love interests: Olivia Pope's two primary romantic partners were both White men. Shondaland's crossover approach not only worked onscreen, but also on social media. With *Scandal*, Rhimes created inventive content; she also, as media scholar Anna Everett notes, innovated "participatory and interactive show experiences and engagements, [that] arguably, have become an unparalleled game-changer in the transformed firmament of network TV production and consumption."[36] Rhimes cultivated a universe of fans on Twitter,

Figure 3.4. Olivia Pope leading her Gladiators in Season 1. *Scandal* Season 1 Cast Promotional Photo. 2012. Viewed October 7, 2017. http://images.spoilertv.com/.

a community of Pope & Associates/Shondaland "Gladiators," many of whom proudly identify as Black women and members of other minoritized groups, and, like Olivia Pope and her team, fight (or at least tweet) for good in a world of evil.

Gladiators are, of course, commonly understood as Roman Empire-era male fighters, most, although not all, of whom were of European descent. In classic Hollywood's version, White male stars such as Kirk Douglas and Lawrence Olivier embodied the personae of the gladiator in *Spartacus* (1960), while more recently White Australian actor Russell Crowe headlined the blockbuster *Gladiator* (2000). Flipping a character's presumed race and gender is a move precisely in line with what Rhimes iterated as her colorblind casting philosophy. However, Shondaland Gladiators did not simply ignore race and gender because they were happy to be included. Instead, they reveled in the racialized and gendered winks of Shondaland and transformed those winks from coded to explicit by, for example, gleefully re-tweeting quick and sly references like Olivia's "feeling a little [like] Sally Hemings," the enslaved Black woman who bore Jefferson's children.[37] On social media, self-identified Black women Gladiators proudly identified with Olivia Pope and Shonda Rhimes *because*, not despite the fact that, they were Black women.

Largely because her Gladiators catapulted *Scandal* to such fame, Rhimes rode the success of *Scandal* with the fall of 2014 premiere of *How to Get Away with Murder*, her second show with a Black woman lead. She ceded showrunner duty for the first time, but the show still bore her stamp. *How to Get Away with Murder* premiered two years into Barack Obama's second term as president and two years into the #BlackLivesMatter movement. Just as Rhimes moved from the White-female-led shows *Grey's Anatomy* and *Private Practice* to her Black-female-led shows *Scandal* and *How to Get Away With Murder*, press on her show became more focused on race, and she discussed more race questions than in early *Grey's* press, albeit still a bit reluctantly and still often in code. For example, in an *Elle* interview, Rhimes levied a critique of White privilege, stating that "the entire world is skewed from the white male perspective . . . 'Normal' is white male, and I find that to be shocking and ridiculous."[38] In this article, she also unpacked the fallacy of monolithic Blackness, stating that one of her truisms is "My Black Is

Not Your Black." Rhimes went on to explain that limited and limiting representations of African Americans are contingent upon the centering of Whiteness as "What's terrifying is that, just the same way we've all accepted that normal is white, everybody seems to buy into the idea that there's only one way to be black or one way to be Hispanic. That's as damaging as anything else."

While this critique from Rhimes markedly diverged from her previous colorblind language, in Shondaland, the showcasing of diversity of African Americans is really about the showcasing of respectable, upper-class Black folks. Strategic ambiguity, whether showcasing elements of colorblindness or race-consciousness, is on Rhimes' television shows a performance especially suited to women of color. And, to further historicize her remarks, perhaps Rhimes creates greater discursive space for Blackness with such unequivocal talk; in doing so, she enacts a positionality similar to what literary scholar Sonnet Retman describes African American novelist Sterling Brown enacting in the 1930s and 40s, a positionality that is "not . . . a representative of the black folk about whom he writes but by still identifying as black, Brown opens up a space for a more complex account of the diversity of black Southern experience, which changes with every locale and generation."[39]

Rhimes also pushed back against her earlier staid line of colorblindness in a *New York Times Magazine* article that praised her for being not only "the most powerful African-American female showrunner in television," but also "one of the most powerful show runners in the business, full stop." She responded to the intimation that all characters of color must talk about their race *ad nauseaum*, noting: "I'm a black woman every day, and I'm not confused about that. I'm not worried about that." Furthermore, equating race talk with "disempowerment," she said: "I don't need to have a discussion with you about how I feel as a black woman, because I don't feel disempowered as a black woman."[40] While Rhimes' naming Blackness might be read as refreshing to some, here Rhimes produced an equally flattening stereotype that class-privileged Black women like her only talk about race when commiserating about experiences of racism. She did not note the ways in which racialized stories, jokes, and quips are simply a part of people of color's everyday communication. Instead, Rhimes stuck with colorblindness, as she did in a *Newsweek* article where she demurred: "a good story is a good story.

It doesn't matter what the race is, and that's always been my belief." She echoed her own earlier colorblind rhetoric in this statement, but also added a race-conscious one: "That said, it was wonderful to have a story [*Scandal*] based on an African-American woman that called out for an African-American female lead. There didn't need to be a discussion about it because it was what it was."[41] What she implied—but didn't explicitly state—was that she had many of these discussions advocating for actors of color in the past. Here Rhimes' strategic ambiguity shifted with Rhimes modeling how Black respectability can also gesture towards race in a more forthright manner; she also performed as the race woman.

But in the midst of Rhimes' shift away from colorblindness in her press, she got taken down in the press *as a Black woman*. When Rhimes started commenting more on race in her shows and—perhaps more importantly—cast two Black women leads in a row, she became the target of a racist attack in the *New York Times*. Television critic Alessandra Stanley began her article "Wrought in Rhimes's Image" with the line: "When Shonda Rhimes writes her autobiography, it should be called 'How to Get Away With Being an Angry Black Woman.'"[42] In this article, ostensibly about Rhimes' new show *How to Get Away with Murder* (Rhimes executive produces but does not run this show; in fact, the showrunner is a White man), Stanley catalogued the typology of Rhimes' Black female protagonists through their "volcanic meltdowns," which she claimed they shared with their creator. Stanley wrote: "Rhimes has embraced the trite but persistent caricature of the Angry Black Woman, recast it in her own image and made it enviable." Stanley's careful language, the "recast" and the "enviable," marked this statement as postracial. By praising Rhimes, in what could be most generously described as a backhanded manner, Stanley's article wordlessly proclaimed that she couldn't possibly be racist. However, her suturing of both Rhimes and her Black female protagonists to the Angry Black Woman was not just racialized; it was racist. As chapter 2 illustrates, the Angry Black Woman stereotype operationalized against the foil of the pleasant, innocent White woman who embodied all of the grace and class the Angry Black Woman lacked. The virtuous and blameless White woman might be, in this particular case, Rhimes' White women fans, the White women actresses ostensibly losing jobs because of Rhimes, or the article's author herself.

Nevertheless, this story did not end with the triumph of a White woman reporter circulating postracial race/gender stereotypes in the nation's most venerable newspaper. Rhimes skillfully re-framed the narrative. She responded, quickly followed by her Gladiators, who unsheathed their swords in reaction to this attack and drew their shields close around her. In her response, Rhimes diverged from her then-to-date performance of controlled, respectable, strategic ambiguity. She named the article as racist and sexist, and refuted both through a number of well-stated 140 character responses. On Twitter, noteworthy as home of her Gladiators, she first blasted Stanley on the basis of inaccuracies and racialized sexism, writing (Figure 3.5): "Confused why @nytimes critic doesn't know identity of CREATOR of show she's reviewing. @petenowa did u know u were 'an angry black woman'?" Two minutes later, she again shone a light on the racist, sexist attack, posting: "Apparently we can be 'angry black women' together, because I didn't know I was one either @petenowa #LearnSomethingNewEveryday."

Her third tweet, three minutes later, also named the stereotype: "Final thing: (then I am gonna do some yoga): how come I am not 'an angry black woman' the many times [*Grey's* White protagonist] Meredith (or [*Private Practice's* White protagonist] Addison!) rants? @nytimes"[43] Here Rhimes cast off the cloak of colorblindness by stating, in no uncertain terms, that the media treated White and Black women in wildly divergent, racially stratified ways, and, by the way, racialized sexism was still very much alive. The stars of all four of Rhimes' shows and her Gladiators exploded with support across Twitter.[44] This response highlighted the racism that still exists in even vaunted spheres such as the *New York Times*, and even against celebrities such as Shonda Rhimes. Apparently mortified by the bad press, the *New York Times'* Public Editor Margaret Sullivan herself wrote: "The readers and commentators are correct to protest this story. Intended to be in praise of Ms. Rhimes, it delivered that message in a condescending way that was—at best—astonishingly tone-deaf and out of touch."[45]

While Rhimes' tweets showcased her Black feminist speaking-Twitter-truth-to-power, after this response, Rhimes didn't return to the singular colorblindness message of her early press. She moved from colorblind cover to postracial resistance; her strategic ambiguity allowed for this shift. For example, to *Entertainment Weekly*, Rhimes stated

Figure 3.5. Shonda's tweets. Screenshot from Shonda Rhimes' Twitter Account. September 19, 2014. Viewed September 20, 2014. www.twitter.com/.

that her parents were the Gladiators in her life, fighting for her "when I encountered something that felt like racism."[46] Here Rhimes named "racism" (almost rhetorically placing scare quotes around the word) but couched it in opinion, "something that felt like," instead of fact. Rhimes' critiques of the industry carefully avoided saying "White" or "racism," instead commenting in a coded manner that "we've been watching very homogenous television written by very homogenous people in very homogenous ways."[47] In another example, on NPR, Rhimes showcased her careful language, identifying the fraught-yet-necessary performance of strategic ambiguity: "Nobody wants to talk about it all the time. But if you don't talk about it, nothing changes, and that's the trap. You discuss it and spend all your time on it and let it become the only thing about you and let other people see the agenda every time they characterize you: You lose. But you don't respond, don't say what you think, don't share what you know, don't fire back when you're minimized or put down or mischaracterized: You lose."[48] In this example, Rhimes powerfully described the ways in which Black women are dismissed and demeaned . . . and yet she still doesn't name the "it." Postracial coding—the silencing of race and racism—is at the heart of strategic ambiguity. And yet, in Rhimes' press, strategic ambiguity succeeded not at silencing a powerful African American woman and her many Black women fans, but in generating new iterations of coded-and-resistant speech that politely and unobtrusively redefined African American respectability politics in a #BlackLivesMatter era.

Strategic Ambiguity: The Tool of Obfuscation and Exhilaration

Black artists carry a burden of representation. As cultural studies scholar Kobena Mercer put it over twenty years ago, "when black artists become publicly visible only one at a time, their work is burdened with a whole range of extra-artistic concerns precisely because, in their relatively isolated position as one of the few black practitioners in any given field . . . they are seen as 'representatives' who speak on behalf of, and are thus accountable to, their communities."[49] The burden of representation not only unfairly regulates prominent Black artists, but also makes all other Black people invisible: "the visibility of a few token black public figures serves to legitimate, and reproduce, the invisibility, and lack of access to public discourse, of the community as a whole."[50] Such extra weight can mean that even members of a minoritized group can read our representations as declarative statements about our identity group instead of suggestive, playful, measured performances within a particular political economy of race, gender, class, and sexuality. Rhimes' self-presentation in the press showed that the burden of representation didn't just weigh heavily in her shows: it weighed heavily on her own articulation of self.

When first becoming a showrunner, Rhimes played the game of coyly responding to the press, whether to O, Written By or Ebony, that she simply wanted to hire the best actors for the part or, as she told Winfrey: "I just wanted a world that looked like the one I know." For the early part of her career, she succeeded in rolling out some version of these lines; in other words, she was successful at appearing safe, nonthreatening, and accessible—the ultimate crossover. However, her approach changed when she began featuring Black leading ladies, then became the victim of a racist journalistic attack. What does Rhimes' shift in her messaging to the press—from colorblind subject with a coy "who me?" attitude towards diversity, to a racialized subject with a fairly forward (yet still coded) response to racialized sexism—truly signify? Between the 2005–6 interviews Rhimes granted and her 2014 Twitter responses to the Stanley article, the American political landscape changed. #BlackLivesMatter pointed the spotlight on seemingly state-sanctioned violence against Black people in the United States, and this move opened up a space for all people to cast off the cloak of colorblindness. Prominent Black women in 2014 could—and, indeed, to maintain cred with many fans and social media followers, must—call out racism and sexism. Such call-outs did not just protest physical violence, they also protested representational violence of the form Rhimes experienced in the *New York Times*. Rhimes' shift in her performance of respectability politics and strategic ambiguity meant that what constituted respectability politics changed in the #BlackLivesMatter era.

However, while Rhimes' approaches helped catapult her to the top of her game, not all critics held her strategic ambiguity in high regard. When writing about *Grey's*, Amy Long describes Rhimes' approach—both in the press and in her shows—as one of "obfuscation." Long also describes the journalists who cover Rhimes as obfuscating structural and institutional racist practices, and blames Shondaland for priming them to not see systemic racism: *Grey's Anatomy*'s "characters and storylines consistently fail to attend to the ways in which discourses and institutions structurally and systematically maintain inequalities through the reproduction of powerful gender binaries and racial hierarchies." At the same time, Long also notes that Rhimes "sometimes succeeds at challenging [racist] discourses."[51] Thus, Long reads such obfuscation into both the show and Rhimes.

Similarly, Kristen J. Warner uses the word "inconsistent" in describing Rhimes' shows and her self-presentation. On the one hand, she notes, Rhimes "neutralizes race" in order to avoid discussing issues of racial difference or racial inequality.[52] Warner lambastes Rhimes for "whitewashing" her characters of color and presenting "diversity . . . [as a] gimmick."[53] But, on the other hand, Warner also notes, her shows aren't simply hegemonic creations.[54] Warner and Long intimate that Rhimes presented her representations of difference as simply enough in and of themselves—and this was a sellout move. I contend that such obfuscation and inconsistency, which also paved a path to Rhimes' success, were key elements of a postracial resistance that ultimately subbed in new players, while not leveling the playing field. Strategic ambiguity allowed Rhimes to perform contradictory tropes of colorblindness, good girl, race woman, and even fierce Black woman critic while building her empire.

In contrast to Long and Warner's critiques of Rhimes, media scholar Anna Everett delights in Rhimes and her success, but not because of her strategic ambiguity; she unabashedly and gleefully celebrates her precisely because of her performance of "diversity." Everett gushes: "Shonda Rhimes [i]s a formidable network TV showrunner and auteur extraordinaire, and . . . a savvy media mogul who leveraged, especially, *Scandal* fans' robust Twitter activism to change the face of American network television in the age of social media, President Obama, and fragmented network TV audience-share."[55] Rhimes brought together her social media savvy with her particular brand of diversity, Everett notes, as "*Scandal*'s online gladiators have carved out a powerful racially inclusive virtual space for the type of hashtag activism organized around a jubilant multiculturalism."[56] While contemporary audience reception logic states that audiences take their cues from what's on screen, Everett makes the case that Rhimes and her vast array of cultural products take their cues from the audience, many of whom self-identify as Black women. In Everett's assessment, not only is Rhimes successful because she mobilized social media in an innovative manner, but also because she did race right in her mobilization. While I wouldn't go as far as to say that Rhimes does race right, I would say she does race strategically, and one that amounted to success in the Michelle Obama era.

But whether one believes skeptical critics like Long and Warner or celebratory ones like Everett, one thing is clear: Rhimes cracked the code through performing postracial resistance. She created a strategically ambiguous blueprint for twenty-first-century Black women's success-through-respectability, a colorblindness-meets-#BlackLivesMatter performance. In a *Wall Street Journal* article, Rhimes drew this blueprint in typically abstruse, non-racialized language: "I always say, if I'm going to go into a difficult conversation, I have to know where I'm going to draw the line before I go into the negotiation." Then, despite the results of the negotiation, "I always say I'm not surprised, I'm not disappointed, and I didn't lose—because I held my ground, and in a way, that is a victory."[57] Rhimes' rules looked like Olivia Pope, her runway strut, achingly beautiful wardrobes, and direct-gazing inquisitions announcing that she will win every negotiation.

Despite being the mistress of the President or the lawyer engaged in a serious breach of ethics (including murder), Shonda Rhimes' Black women protagonists signify as the pinnacle of Black womanhood. They speak back to the reality star vixens of *Love and Hip Hop*. They provide counternarratives to, and perhaps are even embarrassed by, the wealthy and drama-loving *Real Housewives of Atlanta*. They thrive in interracial settings. None of them has a cadre of Black women surrounding them, and therefore no Black women are dragging them down. Each flourishes in being the only, the special, the one who has transcended the imagined boundaries of Black womanhood. This is how Black women enter into and maintain respectability. In contrast, a Black-woman-led show with a Black woman protagonist on Black Entertainment Television, *Being Mary Jane*, presents an equally flawed and less-than-heroic character, but one whose community of women of color holds up a mirror to her, calls her out, and lifts her up. There is no such mirror to be had in Shonda Rhimes' creations whether in her TV characters or her creation-of-self in interviews. Nevertheless, in an interactive social media fan space her loyal Gladiators forge one for her week after week.

Both Rhimes' early success through colorblindness, and the more explicit pushing back after the racist attack are the hallmarks of strategic ambiguity. This dynamic, dialogic form of resistance allows for obfuscation, inconsistency, and jubilant multiculturalism. But its ambiguity not only slides critique past postracial racism, it lets some fans down by merely winking at audiences of color, positing that such an audience is simply pleased to see themselves, as people of color, reflected on their screens. And, for some, it might feel like a relief to experience virtual diversity without racialized strife. The surgeons at Seattle's Sloan-Grey Memorial Hospital, the doctors at Santa Monica's Seaside Wellness Center, the fixers at D.C.'s Pope and Associates, and the professor and students at Philadelphia's Middleton law school suffer through relationship crises while in interracial relationships and yet rarely bring up race. Perhaps to engage in that fantasy is empowering. But, for others, to see visual difference, to feel the weight of racialized discrimination on screen, to understand the living nature of history and yet not discuss historical legacies on racism today feels like a betrayal. Shonda Rhimes' winking commentary in her press and in her shows isn't enough to sate every viewer. Postracial resistance and strategic ambiguity might provide a blueprint for Black women's success, but it's a success only available to the lucky few, and it's a success contingent upon the performance of respectability. In the next two chapters, I look into these types of audiences: young women of color who are not satisfied with the winking, nudging, long-game approach of postracial resistance.

4

"No, But I'm Still Black"

*Women of Color Community, Hate-Watching,
and Racialized Resistance*

Thus far this book has examined postracial resistance through strategic ambiguity as a way to facilitate a successful image makeover and PR tool (Michelle Obama), an unsuccessful anti-racist tool (Oprah Winfrey), and an effective entrepreneurial mechanism (Shonda Rhimes). In the second half of the book, I take the theory of postracial resistance through strategic ambiguity from an analysis of the women we see on our screens to discussions with the real, live women in front of and behind our screens. I want to see how non-celebrity Black women and, in particular, Black women privileged by career and/or education responded to racism and sexism in the Michelle Obama era. Would their resistance look like Michelle Obama's image makeover strategy? Would it be more akin to calling on history as Oprah did? Would it be about speaking in coded language, à la Shonda Rhimes, and then, when pushed, speaking truth to power? Or perhaps something entirely different?

In these next two chapters, I investigate how a group of women completely rejected the postracial ideology of strategic ambiguity in a safe, women of color space, where the women acted as a collective and not simply as individuals. The young women saw—and critiqued—the celebrities' performances of strategic ambiguity, which signified, for them, as mere articulations of tokenism and stereotyping. This chapter examines the question of—not whether postracial resistance is a successful tool, but rather—what type of community can form when women reject strategic ambiguity as a primary response to twenty-first century postracial racism; the next chapter delineates their anti-postracial resistance and strategic ambiguity critiques. In these two chapters, I turn from the first half of the book's attention to celebrities' management of their images, to the people who make meaning of such images in multifaceted, diverse, and unexpected ways: audiences. Media sociologist Darnell Hunt notes that "how we make sense of our day-to-day experience is continuously shaped by the stories we consume. We live vicariously through the pleasures and pains of characters and their predicaments, trying these adventures on for size as we reflect on who we are, who we are not, and who we hope to be."[1] I also turn from textual analyses to audience studies. In doing so I strive to, in media studies scholar Jonathan Gray's encapsulation of classic communication studies models, "complete the communication loop from sender to receiver."[2]

Two of the receivers in this chapter are Camille and Micki,[3] students from my Black Cultural Studies undergraduate seminar, and their friends. These two women often sought me out before and after class to talk about representations of Black women on television; in the winter of 2009, they were the first people I told that I wanted to do a small audience study. They loved the idea of getting together to watch a television show, which we all agreed would have to be their then most obsessed-about program, the reality show for aspiring models, *America's Next Top Model* (*ANTM*). With my paltry promise of weekly pizza and soda, the two set off on a mission to recruit their friends and classmates to join our viewing party. These two young women were—and, indeed, still are—a force: smart, fearless, and, most importantly for this study, avid consumers of television programming featuring African American women. They quickly recruited an additional seven friends and friends-of-friends, all of whom were women of color in their late teens and early 20s, and none of whom I had met prior to our first viewing party.

After Camille, Micki, and I decided that our audience study would focus on Black women on television through the lens of *ANTM*, they eagerly jumped at the opportunity to take on all of the recruitment efforts. Before our first session met, I assumed that these two young Black women would choose other Black women to join them. However, I was surprised (but did not let on as much) when they recruited a multiracial group of women of color from their network of friends and classmates from a study abroad program to Brazil, an undergraduate Black women's student group, and the dorms. Six of the participants, Camille, Micki, Vanessa, Jen, Dezi, and McCall, identify as Black or African American, with Micki also identifying as Jamaican American and Dezi, as also Black and Filipina. Two, Lupe and Valentina, identify as Latina, and one,

Yumi, as Asian American. The diversity of the group, I believe, speaks to racialization practices on the West Coast and, more specifically, in a predominantly White city at a predominantly White university in the predominantly White Pacific Northwest, all three of which have small African American populations. The Black women in the group enjoyed women of color linkages that expanded beyond their connections with other African American women.

These next two chapters draw upon this ethnographic audience study to provide a look into how young women of color talked to each other about the types of mediated representations that I analyze in this book, and what critique looked like when it refused strategic ambiguity. This refusal took the form of the antithesis of strategic ambiguity, what I consider a reaction to the coding, double-speak, and softening in postracial resistance. Instead they preferred what I think of as not a postracial but a racialized resistance: a form of forthright pragmatism, an unambiguous, woman of color feminist critique that purposefully upheld the group over the individual, and in doing so consciously fostered community-building.

For the group of minoritized women in the study, who were very cognizant of the fact that they were still underrepresented on television, one way to arrive at such forthright pragmatism was through the act of tuning in to watch a show about which one has strong but conflicting feelings: to "hate-watch." In the popular press, the verb "hate-watch" has overtaken a related, older phrase "guilty pleasure."[4] To indulge in a guilty pleasure is to enjoy a seemingly low-quality cultural text while also flagellating oneself for doing so; one suffers remorse over consuming all-too-tasty cultural junk food. "Guilty pleasure" denotes a moment of slothful, unproductive, and passive viewing, while "hate-watching" denotes an interactive, resistant, and productive shouting-at-the-screen (and sometimes to, with, or at other viewers). Hate-watching takes on a particular force when women of color audiences watch television shows featuring women of color, whose numbers are growing in number and yet continue to feature images that, for many viewers, are frustratingly one-dimensional.

But as I set out on my journey with these young women, the idea of hate-watching and eschewing strategic ambiguity for racialized resistance was in the future. Instead I wondered how they would talk with each other about mediated images and if they would enact any form of strategic ambiguity in our setting. I wondered what they would celebrate and what they would critique as they consumed representations of Black women. What did they want of their media? Could unguarded conversations about race, gender, and representation happen with me—an adult over a decade their senior and a professor at their university—present? I had seen some of my students carefully couch their words in class when a classmate said something that struck them as racist or sexist, or just plain wrong, and then speak up more boldly if I validated their comments. I would be present at these viewing parties, but not facilitating or even participating in the discussion unless they directly invited me (and, even then, I would gently demur). But would our viewing sessions simply run like an extended version of one of my classes on race, gender, and sexuality in the media? Would they be looking to me to validate their answers? Since these next two chapters draw on a different archive and constitute a different approach than the earlier chapters, first I describe my particular form of ethnographic work and situate my project in the literature that informed this feminist, women of color, collaborative endeavor. Then I introduce the women, enter into their viewing practices, and listen to how they speak back to strategic ambiguity.

Creating a Women of Color, Feminist Audience Study

I aimed to construct the study as a community collaboration, to create a dialogic women of color feminist space. I called upon anthropologist Leith Mullings's idea that "incorporating community collaboration into research . . . allows us to uncover the cultures of resistance that stand in opposition to the dominant representations of African American women."[5] In conducting the research for and writing this chapter, I've thought a lot about how to center the audience and de-center myself. I also pondered the "truth" that emerged during our viewing sessions together. Indeed, television scholar Amanda Lotz's cautionary statement for feminist television studies ethnographers—"we must recognize the possibility that our understandings of situations are false or only partially true"[6]—felt particularly resonant for me in this study. But my goal in including the voices of audiences (or, in chapter six, television executives) in this book is not to capture some transcendental truth. My desire is to articulate how one group of young women formed community by negotiating and resisting controlling images of their racialized, gendered, and classed identities vis-à-vis televisual images and each other.

Because of this desire, I was always conscious of how my presence as both insider, as a fellow woman of color, and my status as outsider and professor gave me access to their community but also kept me apart. To combat my intrusion into their space, I tried to minimize the "me in the room" as much as possible: I was not teaching any of the women in the quarter I organized our viewing session, and I had only previously taught two of them. I tried to create a physical atmosphere where I could recede into the background. Before each session, and before any of the other women outside of Camille was present, I would set up my camera in a corner and a microphone on the coffee table. I sat with the women, but while they sat on the sofas, I grabbed a seat on the floor. In the beginning of this first session, they talked to me directly and sought out my opinion; this was the only time that I introduced prepared questions (such as "tell me about your favorite television shows" and "how much television do you watch per week?"). In subsequent sessions, I asked no questions and the women took their own conversations to a variety of locations. I also worked hard to not look at a speaker when she was speaking (something totally against my nature, culture, and upbringing); I found that I only occasionally had to gently remind them to talk to each other and not me. I also acknowledge that the measures I put in place to de-center myself as a professor could never completely erase my presence or my power in the room.[7]

Since my study was small and ethnographic, I use the terms "viewing party" and "audience study" instead of "reception analysis." I was not watching the women behind two-way glass or running the camera and leaving the room; I was always present, and my terms illustrate that presence. Furthermore, I do not claim that this group constituted a representative sample (which I'm not particularly interested in creating), but I also do not think that their opinions and interactions with each other through television were anomalous. They exemplified resistance to controlling images of Black women in media, the type of responses that happens across living rooms, dorm couches, group texts, Facebook feeds, Snapchat stories, Instagram images, and Twitter streams across the world. Like so many of these other conversations, the women's TV discussions did not linger on simply *ANTM*. They meandered through larger questions of the politics of representation; they talked about their own philosophies and lived experiences of race, gender, sexuality, and class; they questioned their university's policies and decried how unhospitable they were to women of color. To honor their conversation streams, I engaged in what communication scholar Aisha S. Durham dubs "interpretive interactionism," which "aims to illuminate the crisis of representation between the so-called real and the symbolic world. It explores lived experience and assumes that epiphanic moments—those moments of heightened awareness of the situated self—emerge from interactions that render crises of identity and/or representation."[8]

The conversation circled back a number of times to the women's need for real life role models at our university. Many of the sessions prompted them to share their experiences of racism and sexism in classes, and from there the conversation would inevitably move to their observations about the small numbers of faculty of color. Twice in the sessions, the women together listed out every tenure-track woman of color faculty member they knew of on campus. The act of naming everyone together felt ritualistic, as if saying these professors' names in and of themselves created a protective bubble around them, and helped show them a potential next stage, a successful future to imagine in the midst of their struggles. These were the moments when the women turned directly to me, and I tried to honor their desire to "talk shop," but not commandeer the conversation.

As the sessions progressed, the women registered my presence and the presence of my camera less and less, and, in fact, sometimes exclaimed, "I forgot you were here!" They spoke to each other far more boldly and more bawdily than in class, and even cursed in my presence, sometimes sheepishly glancing over at me for my reaction and only sometimes saying "sorry!," when one of their friends reminded them I was in the room. They are, to a one, young women of color who expressed clear respect for me in a way that I identified as cultural and not generational or geographic—their deferential attitude was indeed quite dissimilar to the attitudes I encountered from most White students of a similar age and from a similar geographic region. For example, while some of their White classmates nonchalantly call me by my first name without invitation, these students refused to do so in class and largely refused to do so outside of class (even with invitation); indeed, now in their late 20s, many still call me "Professor Joseph" or "Dr. Ralina."

Strategic ambiguity is a performative action, and so the performativity of the women's racialized and gendered identities in our sessions were, in a sense, the most important element of our time together. They reveled in the opportunity to perform their racialized gender in an uncompromising, unapologetic manner. In addition, although I shine a light on the performative nature of their interactions (dramatically one-upping each other to get a laugh, for example), I believe such performativity would already have characterized the young women's gatherings, perhaps even around this very show, if I were absent. In fact, some of the women said that in previous "cycles" (the show's preferred word for "seasons"), they watched *ANTM* in groups of two to five women, and I can imagine that similar conversations peppered their watching experiences. Indeed, from the very first meeting, I was relieved to discover that the tone and content of the women's commentary was far different from what I experienced in class with Micki and Camille. They were real—funny, occasionally crass, and relaxed.

While they hate-watched, this group of women gleefully flouted the preferred codes of *ANTM* and other reality shows featuring women of color. In other words, they identified against not with the host; they rooted for the characters framed as villains instead of the ones framed as heroes. As Stuart Hall's encoding/decoding model notes, audience members will not always interpret or decode the media creator's encoded or preferred meaning in either desired or unilateral ways.[9] Hall proposed that some audiences might believe the favored meanings encoded in the text, but others will believe only certain elements while rejecting other features in a negotiated manner, and still other audiences will embrace instead an entirely oppositional view. Critics such as film scholar Jacqueline Bobo employ the encoding/decoding model "for understanding how a cultural product can evoke such different viewer reactions."[10] The "different viewer reactions" these women articulate embodied what bell hooks calls the "oppositional gaze of Black female spectators."[11] For example, a couple of the women discussed whether or not a plus-sized, brown-skinned contestant from a previous cycle, Toccara Jones, had won her season's grand prize. Jones, in fact, did not win her cycle, but she did go on to have a fairly successful post-*ANTM* life on television. Camille said: "in my mind she won, so . . . !," to which Micki agreed that "she won in life [*general laughter*]." As oppositional readers, they decoded the moment of victory in the season—what the producers script as the season crescendo—as "wrong." As oppositional viewers, the young women remembered Jones as bold, spirited victor, not sad, defeated loser from an episode that aired five episodes before the finale and five booted contestants before the winner.

As I took a feminist, critical ethnographic approach to this audience study, I viewed every woman as an active participant in the process of knowledge production, and in the process of decoding. Decoding is not a straightforward process; rather, viewers who decode—and thus the scholars who write about both texts and viewers—must see texts as polysemic. Considering texts to be open is particularly necessary when assessing the constantly changing landscape of popular culture, which, as media scholar John Fiske asserts, "always is part of power relations; it always bears traces of the constant struggle between domination and subordination, between power and various forms of resistance to it or evasions of it."[12] The women in my audience study categorically resisted the forces of dominance on their screens. Like cultural studies scholar Janice Radway, who centers the voices of her audience members in her classic study, *Reading the Romance*, I draw upon theorist Stanley Fish's notion of audiences as "interpretive communities"[13] and cultural studies scholar Angela McRobbie's idea that "representations are interpretations."[14]

I give voice to, in McRobbie's words, "the patterns or regularities . . . viewers and readers bring to texts in large part because they acquire specific cultural competencies as a consequence of their particular social location."[15] As young women of color going to school, working, and living in very White contexts, they had similar "reading strategies and interpretive codes," as McRobbie puts it. In this book, moving at this point from textual analysis to audience study allows for me to make sense of the complexities of young women of color's varied strategies and codes. An audience study also presents a balanced approach to media studies, where, as Amanda Lotz states, "studying reception exposes perspectives unobtainable through textual analysis,"[16] and, as Henry Jenkins notes, scholars should "read the text from the specific perspective of particular audiences, creating our analysis in dialogue with those reception communities and in furtherance of our common interests."[17]

The "reception community," to quote Jenkins, with which I engaged was a minoritized audience who read ideologies encoded in televisual texts in a negotiated or oppositional manner. Media scholars Vicki Mayer, Miranda J. Banks, and John Thornton Caldwell note that "one place [where] academic strands weave together more complex tales about media is in the study of consumers and audiences as interpretive communities. Treating television viewers . . . as 'producers' of meaning, audience studies have mined the way that people talk about their consumer practices as formative of their identities as well as how identities shape ways of consuming and talking about consumption."[18] In their identity talk, my viewers exhibited what Jacqueline Bobo writes of as a healthy skepticism: "Black women are aware, along with others, of the oppression and harm that comes from a negative media history. But Black women are also aware that their specific experience, as Black people, as women, in a rigid class/caste system, has never been adequately dealt with in mainstream media."[19] Further, whereas, as Timothy Havens writes, "scholars have treated television as an ambivalent site for African American portrayals, at once closely linked to traditional racist stereotypes in the service of white political and economic interests," I believe resistant potential lies in the audience's interaction with the text.[20]

While textual analysis can certainly illuminate a scholar's skepticism, as exemplified by my own skeptical reads in chapters 1 through 3 of this book, centering audiences' words can provide more credence and complexity to such critique. Building on Bobo, Beretta Smith-Shomade asserts that, while "objectification of Black women exists," such objectification "can be undercut by showing moments of subjectivity achieved within television texts and within the audience's own subjectivity and identification with the character." Although my audience tended to identify against rather than with the characters on television we discussed, such moments of audience-articulated subjectivity allow for, again in Smith-Shomade's words, "moments of agency conferred upon and taken up by Black women within their circumscribed role as and within the audiences' readings of the text." Agency thus becomes "the mode of visual and content awareness of women's authority, voice, and vision."[21] I attempted to confer agency to the women by sharing drafts of chapters 4 and 5, and inviting the women to comment on and change anything that felt inaccurate, inappropriate, or simply uncomfortable to them.[22]

My desire to create agency for the young women also informed the location of the study: I conducted the viewing sessions in Camille's home. Home viewings, Amanda Lotz writes, center active audiences.[23] We watched on Camille's large television, which was positioned, like in most homes, at the center of the living space, as "television is (and always has been) more than just furniture," Ethan Thompson and Jason Mittell note. Although the women sometimes pivoted their heads and their bodies to physically address one of the other women in the room, as our gathering was predicated upon watching television, most of the women's remarks were addressed in the direction of the TV, even when the television program was paused. Thus, even when the conversation strayed far from the topic of television, the television itself structured our talk. My choice to include the voices of audiences in this book flouts the desires of what Joshua Gamson calls "the world of celebrity production" where "direct sales information (what are they buying? what are they watching?)" rules and yet "little information is sought about them."[24] Like Gamson, I seek to understand more about the texts and contexts by considering the voices of audiences.

Getting to Know the Women

Camille hosted the group at the loft apartment she shared with her fiancé Daniel in the more affordable city just north of their university. I usually arrived first at the springtime, early-evening, weeknight gathering. I unloaded the pizza, set up my equipment, and chatted with our hosts. As soon as the second woman arrived, Daniel would retreat to the bedroom to play videogames; the space became instantly and entirely female. I saw each woman heave a relaxed sigh when crossing the threshold into Camille's place, with its comfy sofas, big TV, and plenty of room for all of us to watch. We watched *ANTM* in a relaxed timeframe as we had chosen not to watch it live. Since Camille didn't have a DVR (still fairly uncommon in 2009, and certainly uncommon for college students), each week I recorded the previous week's airing of the show. We usually watched one week after the original airing dates, and the women promised each other to not watch ahead (a promise that they mostly—but not always—honored). Camille ran the remote and would generally fast-forward through commercials, although she occasionally would rewind to watch a commercial that she or one of the other women wanted to watch and discuss. At every session, I began running the camera as soon as the first two women sat on the sofas, and continued recording throughout the viewing and the postmortem of the show. Our sessions ran approximately two hours in length, although sometimes we had to double up on episodes after a missed week, or conversation kept flowing and no one was making a move to leave.

All of the women were from the West Coast, mostly from the Seattle area, but also from other places in Washington state as well as Oregon and California. They identified as lower-middle-class, "low income," situationally lower-middle-class (what one young woman called "broke college student"), and upper-middle-class. One student saw her class identity as immigrant/first generation, which, for her, meant working-class. All but one of the women identified as straight, with one identifying as queer (her word). They were social science and humanities majors, dancers and scientists, campus activists and critical observers, with many expressing hope to eventually attend graduate school. These young women were active participants in creating change in their worlds. For example, when Camille took a course on "The Other," which, in her description, was supposed to be about "origin, identity, culture, and authenticity," she balked at the absence of authors of color on the syllabus. Instead of dropping the class, like a fellow student of color did, Camille and another classmate "began to prod and poke through the professor's curriculum, required texts, and legitimacy of the course itself. We asked to edit the required reading list, to incorporate authors of color, and more women theorists."[25] When the White, male professor refused to address her concerns, Camille and her classmates created a student of color collective to address the curriculum and held a public forum with invited faculty, students, and staff from the office of minority affairs. This action resulted in that particular department's revamping their entire curriculum.

These students' connections with other young women, and particularly young women of color, constituted a lifeline of support. For example, after her father suddenly passed away, hometown student McCall transferred from the out-of-state university that she had first attended straight out of high school to our university. Her own parents, both Black alums from the university, were her link back to the school or, as she put it, "I technically wouldn't be alive without the black student rallies and blossoming trees of the quad in the late 1960's and early 1970's!" After walking on to the basketball team but not receiving much playing time, McCall worked as its manager, and she credits the three years doing so with "help[ing] my spirit and my career. After losing my biggest fan, I was able to get back to the game of basketball and made bonds with teammates and coaches that are still strong to this day."[26]

As the students bonded through shared stories like these, they co-constructed their identities in dialogue with each other. Cultural identity, as Stuart Hall famously proclaimed, is always in process and never complete.[27] In our group, the Black women's identification as such was always formed in relation to their fellow women of color, and for the purpose of community-building. However, not everyone participated equally in the processes of community-building. Even though a diversity of women of color were invited, the non-Black women did not attend the sessions as frequently as the other women and, when the non-Black women attended, they tended to speak less. A core group of five of the African American participants, McCall, Vanessa, Micki, Camille, and Jen, attended all or all-but-one of the twelve viewing sessions, over which time we watched sixteen hour-long episodes of *America's Next Top Model*, while the other four women came to the majority of the sessions, and watched the show on their own during the weeks they missed. The African American women tended to be more vocal during our sessions, and my quoting of each woman's words in this and the next chapter reflects her level of participation.

To set the scene for our viewing sessions: during the spring of 2009, this group of young women were abuzz about pop star Rihanna's brutal beating by her boyfriend and fellow musician Chris Brown, and the media's will-she-or-won't-she-go-back-to-him debate. They exclaimed, as Vanessa did, that "there is nothing that she could have done except killed his mama to deserve to get her ass beat like that," as well as puzzled over her decision, like Valentina: "But I'm saying, what are you doing going back to him?" Like the rest of the country, they scrutinized the media coverage of football player Michael Vick's dog fighting, and called out the racialized double standards of outrage at the killing of dogs but not the murders of African Americans. McCall noted that "the media completely turned on Vick," and Micki agreed, adding that "I know dog fighting's bad, like, totally, I get it—but they treated him like he had, like, serial murdered somebody." They commiserated about their hunger for and the paucity of images of women of color in media, and shared their experiences of having their excitement about Beyoncé gracing the cover of *Vogue* turn to frustration when, as Camille put it: "And so I'm like, ok, I'm, I'm literally buying this magazine just because Beyoncé's on the cover . . . [But] when I flipped through the magazine there were no other people of color, and they were just like stick figure White, blonde women."

All of the women were constantly on the hunt for images of women of color, and all of the women maintained a powerful critique of racialized patriarchy. Both of these desires found their home in discussions of their favorite television show, *America's Next Top Model*. While the show itself drew them in week after week, the show's host, supermodel Tyra Banks, roused their unmitigated disgust. They found her to be fake, a misogynist, racially biased, and unapologetically and disproportionately cruel to women of color. They did not see Banks as a woman of color role model they aspired to be like, but rather as a villainous figure against whom they identified. Most interesting to me, they didn't see her as a strategically ambiguous agent for change. They saw her as a sellout.

Throughout our sessions, the women often spoke in an easy, relaxed, and familiar manner, characteristic of what sociolinguist Maya Angela Smith describes as "a racialized narrative, in which they cut each other off, speak over each other, and repeat each other."[28] In developing their group membership, the students also exhibited another feature Smith notes, "speak[ing] in absolutes," which served to "further accentuate the us/them schism by taking isolated instances and attributing a generalization to them."[29] The "us" were young women of color and the "they"—the group against which they were performing their identities—was sometimes *ANTM*, sometimes Tyra Banks, but often, as we see in the next sections and the next chapter, young White women who functioned, interestingly, as ideological stand-ins for *ANTM* and Banks. Their sense of what it meant to be a woman of color meant not performing, among other things, postracial resistance through strategic ambiguity; instead, being a woman of color meant being unapologetic and outspoken in responses to racialized sexism.

"Yeah, That Show's Ridiculous . . . I Still Watch It, Though": Identity against Television

The women formed community through their oppositional reading of television. Throughout our sessions, they connected with each other through the prisms of their racialized and gendered identity. Their status as women of color was the connective tissue for their friendships. These connections were not happenstance but intentional, forged out of centering women of color sisterhood. They expressed their need to find each other in order to navigate their Predominantly White Institution (PWI) where a Black student walking across campus might only rarely see another familiar face. As Vanessa put it, she found Camille on Facebook after she "searched for all of the Black girls [at their university] on it freshman year." Here the media—both in connecting students and in providing alternative representations to the real life around them—was vital. This sentiment emerged often during the viewing sessions, where race and gender, alongside connections to class and sexuality, surfaced often in jokes, stories, and analysis. They bonded over discrimination as well as women of color resilience and critique. Furthermore, while they certainly lamented experiences of minoritization, they didn't do so to simply commiserate: they were working to forge a community that fought back and changed their university, city, state, country, and world.

In their community-building, these young women bonded over the constant presence in their lives: television. Indeed, in their own estimation, excessive TV consumption united all but one member of the group. Vanessa said:

> I watch so much TV just because, like, I—like, that's, like, my life. I do my homework, I hang out with my boyfriend, and then I'm online watching TV. I don't sit and, oh, show's coming on at 8, like, whatever's on online I watch it. I watch, like, 15 shows at one time. I—it's terrible [*Camille laughs knowingly*]. And it's really bad, 'cause, like, growing up I never had cable or nothing, never use to watch TV, and then when I got to college—it's horrible.

For Vanessa, just as coming to college meant having access to a community of other young women of color, so did it mean having unbridled access to an unlimited amount of television. Her experience of watching multiple shows at a time was a common one within the group. Many of the students talked about not necessarily consciously consuming programs, but having the television on constantly. Micki described television as the general background soundtrack to her life so that, in her words:

> I feel lonely if it's not on. I can't stand the silence. Like, this right now [talking before the screening without the TV on] is kind of driving me crazy. Like, I would rather have the TV on. But, like, when I was little, I used to do my homework with the TV. I used to always—and, at first, my Grandma was, like, that's bad, but then she saw that I really did get more work done with the TV on, so then she was like, well, if it works for her.

Similarly, Desiree, who, at twenty-one, was positioned as the little sister of the group, shared: "I can't say I *watch* too much TV but I like to have it on, but I don't necessarily *watch* it." McCall agreed: "I can't start my evening without watching TV," prompting Micki to one-up her, inserting: "I can't walk into my house without turning on the TV." Television was a companion to these young women: the distraction, the comfort, the constant in their lives. It also connected them as throughout their days their conversations often entailed discussions about their favorite shows and characters. Camille told me that, even now, years after graduating and geographically scattering across the country, when she and her girls get together, their conversations still center on Black women and television. Only the shows have changed: now their discussions focus on *Scandal* and *The Real Housewives of Atlanta* rather than *ANTM*.[30]

The one dissenting voice in their conversation about TV consumption came from Jen, who, at twenty-four, was the oldest member of the group; she often expressed a counter-view to many of the members. Jen balked at the idea of the TV as background noise, saying, "That's one of my pet peeves, like ambient noise of just TV in the background." Micki responded, "You don't like that?" to which Jen retorted, "I can't *stand* it [[Micki: Really?]]. Jen rejoined: "Well because you just wanna sit and chill and talk and they're like, 'Oh let me turn on the TV real quick.' Like c'mooooonnn." Jen's reaction spurred the rest of the women to murmur in general agreement: "Yeah, I do that." The TV-always-on group's sheepish reactions indicated a lighthearted performance of guilt or perhaps the acknowledgement of the background television noise as a guilty pleasure in itself. The women remained in uncharacteristic silence for a couple of seconds after Jen's comment. To break the silence, Mc-Call, the comedienne of the group, countered: "When I'm there with my roommate, I have to have the TV on, 'cause she breathes way too loud." The room erupted in laughter.

These young women were like so many Americans in that television was a constant fixture in their lives. For the women, more TV time was a result of not just freedom of parent-free dorm rooms and apartments, but also the change in technology from traditional box to multiple devices capturing television content online. Thompson and Mittell explain that "now in our era of convergence among different technologies and cultural forms, there is more TV than ever. New or emergent forms of television work alongside the residual or 'old.'"[31] "Having the TV on" did not necessarily mean running a traditional television set, but instead playing one or more TV programs in the background on various devices, a far less common practice in 2009 than at this writing in 2017. While some of the students did own traditional televisions, Vanessa, self-described as an avid consumer of television, stated, "I think TV online is more addictive [*General agreement*, "yeah"] because you could watch it whenever you're ready [*laughter*]. 'Cause, like, I don't have a TV." And yet, Vanessa would say that she "watched TV" constantly. Jen again provided an alternate viewpoint to increasing numbers of television hours: "I found that now that [I've] been kind of off [TV] in the past sixth months, I've been—I watch a lot less TV." Nonetheless, even though Jen didn't "watch TV," she knew all about the characters her friends discussed. Without actually watching television, Jen was conversant in details about past seasons of *ANTM* and other reality shows that her friends consumed.

In addition, the women's non-traditional viewing practices affirm research that television consumption has risen with its availability across multiple devices. Television studies scholar Toby Miller notes that "people who watch TV on different devices and via different services are watching more, not less, television."[32] TV watching is also racialized; Beretta Smith-Shomade documents that "Black folks watch more on the go than any other group as well—six hours per month on mobile phones and other handheld media devices."[33] Smith-Shomade's research illustrates another TV habit confirmed by my group of viewers: "Young African Americans in general . . . watch more ad-supported cable and less network affiliate programming compared to women and older demographics." Black audiences' disproportionate ad-supported cable television watching might point to a search for alternative images that, at least in 2009, were largely not available on network television, but were on channels such as BET, VH1, and the network that then aired *ANTM*, the CW.

While some of the students said that they would watch anything that happened to be on live television while watching a traditional box, they did watch thoughtfully and pragmatically: they all discussed deliberately consuming images of young Black people. And yet they experienced an ambiguous and conflicted relationship to representations of African Americans on reality television, in particular. They wanted to see women of color but despised the representations they saw. This ambiguity, at the heart of their hate-watching, stemmed from what they saw as the representations' stereotypical qualities. For example, the women constantly discussed the short-lived VH1 reality dating show, *For the Love of Ray J* (2009–2010) starring a minor child star and brother to pop singer and actress Brandy. McCall confessed, "Yeah, that show's ridiculous . . . I still watch it, though," and Micki agreed, "Me too!" Vanessa added, "It's addictive, it's like one of these, it's one of these [*puts her hands over her face like she can't watch*]." She continued, "[I watch] all bad stuff like [reality shows] *Rock of Love, I Love Money* . . . I watch like 15 hours. [*dramatic pause and intentional glance around*] A week. [*another pause and glance around*]. Way too much."

The students also discussed how the enticement of their favorite programs was almost enough to make them consider paying more for particular channels. McCall stated: "I was getting ready to invest in paying for that one channel because I thought Taneisha [a reality star from *The Bad Girls Club*] was coming back." A single character on a single show was enough of a draw for a college student to consider "investing" in a cable package with the desired channel. However, while McCall didn't end up ponying up money, the women invested *time* in watching reality TV representations of African Americans; they were gauging controlling images in the popular sphere and creating a community around critiques of the representations they watched, including critiques of strategic ambiguity.

Community, a presence and ideal divorced from the individual-focused nature of postracial resistance through strategic ambiguity, structured their watching in a variety of ways. While watching was sometimes a solitary action, it was more often than not a communal activity. Some of them watched with small groups of friends in their dorm rooms or apartments, while others attended larger gatherings for special viewing events. For example, Micki watched *The L Word* at a theater on Sundays, the same place where McCall watched the home team WNBA games when they played out of town. Interactive and community gathering around a screening was a commonplace event for these young women. If they didn't see the shows together, they talked about them. Their viewing patterns confirm what television studies scholar Toby Miller notes: television "viewing remains a collective act as well as an individual one."[34] Furthermore, the act of television viewing was intimately connected to the way in which the women negotiated their racialized and gendered identities, and provided them with endless fodder for hate-watching critique.

The women's critical views on the world, and a particular racialized and gendered critique, also linked them. Vanessa, one of the more outspoken women in the group, articulated their collective need to keep up such a critique: "we're so sexist deep down inside, women don't even realize it." This notion of internalized sexism reverberated with the group. In watching they were constantly breaking up the pleasure of the watching act with conscious critique; or, rather, they received another form of pleasure in creating critiques. Their women of color feminist oppositional gaze did not let them simply relax into the hegemonic images. They maintained a running thread throughout the discussions about double standards between men and women. In one example, Micki related a commercial that she asked Camille to rewind and replay where the men were fully dressed and the women scantily clad to a recent visit to the club:

That reminds me when we were at the uhhhhh . . . Fusion! And the bar, they have bartenders and there's the guy bartender wearing a t-shirt and jeans, and the female bartenders are wearing lingerie [[Desiree: oh yeah!]]. And I was like, am I seeing this? Like she was, they were both wearing bustiers [[Desiree: I remember that!]], like fishnets, garters, and, like, high heels, and he was wearing a freakin' Mickey Mouse t-shirt [[yeah!]] [[Lupe: was that the theme of the night?]]. No, like, it was no reason. And she looked hella tired, she was like [*pantomimes exhaustion*], she was, I was like, that makes no sense.

While the conversation in this instance emerged from Micki's critique of a commercial, the women immediately related what they saw on the screen to their real lives.

Without a doubt, the women did not see themselves in, want to see themselves in, or live vicariously through the reality television shows they eagerly watched. Nor were they unthinking dupes mindlessly consuming the images. As media studies scholar Racquel Gates writes, we must not presume " that audiences straightforwardly accept the dominant version of 'reality' that the programs carefully assemble and present to them."[35] While most of the women consumed sizable amounts of television, their consumption—often fueled by hate-watching—stoked their critiques of intersectional inequalities. Their television consumption also provided them with the new material to understand their own racialized and gendered pasts and presents, including many of the women's experiences of being "the only" growing up. As we see in the next section, their fierce critiques of power inequities in real life and in media informed the way in which they discussed—and dismissed—postracial resistance and strategic ambiguity.

"I Was the Black Senior": Tokenism and the Burden of Being "the Only"

If the participants' race and gender initially drew them to each other on their college campus, their similarly progressive and activist sensibilities bonded them further. These students were woke before the hashtag. However, even though the young women had no problem discussing their identities in their everyday lives, they hadn't necessarily spoken about their formative racialized and gendered experiences in the depth that our viewing sessions encouraged and indeed even enabled. Although some of the women had been friends for years, prior to our viewing sessions, they didn't know about one important commonality:

their similar experiences of being "the only," or, although they didn't use the word themselves, feeling like tokens.

Lamenting that her White high school classmates assumed that she shared similarities with stereotypical Black women characters on television whom she despised (and yet hate-watched), Vanessa shared her own experience of being "the only":

VANESSA: they [White high school students] have one Black kid at their school—
MCCALL: yeah!
VANESSA: —who's probably McCall or me—
MICKI: No me!—
CAMILLE: [*patting her chest*]—Or me! I was the only Black girl in my senior class—
MICKI: All of you guys are, like, the only, very little populations of Black people at your high schools?—
CAMILLE: Yeah, I was the Black senior—
JEN: By the time I got to high school there was, like, maybe like five girls. I went to junior high with no Black girls and elementary with no Black girls.

While some of the young women knew about the demographics of each other's primary and secondary schools, most of them were finding out this information for the first time. And, yet, these women were, by their description, good friends. They were so excited by this discovery that they cut each other off and spoke over one another animatedly in this discussion. Thus, through their discussions of Black representation, they discovered and connected a central component of their experience. Our viewing sessions—especially in the midst of the most spirited hate-watching critique—opened up another space of racialized and gendered connectivity and critique.

Their bonding around hating the experience of being "the only" flew in the face of postracial posturing, which can be effective by celebrating "the only" to the exclusion of her minoritized sisters. But these women identified the power inequities propagated by one aspect of postraciality: tokenization. Such connectivity and critique showed their resistance to tokenism. Social psychologists Stephen C. Wright and Donald M. Taylor define tokenism as "an intergroup context in which very few members of a disadvantaged group are accepted into positions." These positions are positioned as special, Wright and Taylor argue, because they are the ones "usually systematically denied for the vast majority of qualified disadvantaged group members."[36]

Communication scholar Subrina Robinson cites tokenism as a major concern to Black women in university settings. Because of tokenism and other forms of racial and gender bias, Robinson states that "Black women feel that they must constantly prove themselves by working harder than their White counterparts and combating negative stereotypes."[37] Robinson describes how, while tokenism might be seen as an opportunity for advancement, such advancement is contingent upon "stay[ing] within the parameters of appearing safe and unassuming to the dominant racial group even while challenging the status quo."[38] Robinson contends that, on the one hand, tokenism is a privileged position accessible to a chosen few, but, on the other hand, tokenism works to silence Black women. In other words, tokenism illuminates both the promises (being chosen) and perils (being alone) of postracial resistance and strategic ambiguity.

The women also posited that feelings of tokenism were not easy to cast off. Indeed, one is often token*ized*, and resisting this process— having the agency to speak back to the force of tokenization—can feel impossible. Our gathering, like other women of color gatherings, was a respite from feeling the oppressive force of being tokenized, of being the "chosen ones" having to hold the burden of representing their communities on their shoulders. The women roundly dismissed their experiences of being tokenized as neither exclusively harmful nor the way to gain a seat at the table. Being the only for these young women was an undesirable result of gaining access to elite spaces (although a number of them reported attending exclusive private schools prior to attending their regionally prestigious flagship state university). Furthermore, being the only meant that, to the White people around them, they became the standard-bearers of information about Black womanhood. From their own perspectives, acting as standard-bearers also meant that they were the target of stereotypes.

In this vein, the students lamented how a White woman exhibiting hypersexual behavior on a show was not going to bear the responsibility for all White women being stereotyped as hypersexual, while a Black woman felt the impetus to "lift as she climbed." Vanessa explained:

> Well, it's like when teenage white kids, like suburbia, are like, what do they talk about with their friends at, like, school and they watch [reality television star] Ray J. They don't talk about the little White girl. They're going to talk about the little Black girl. Like it totally makes Black people look terrible . . . They're comparing us to her. They know Lil' Hood [a White character from *For the Love of Ray J*] doesn't act like [White girl] Alison from next door. You know, they're going to think about how, when we're not at school, we probably act like the Black girl.

This comment resonated deeply with the other participants, as Micki agreed that their White classmates must think that "we probably do splits and do booty pop [the term that predated "twerk"]." Micki's comment animated Vanessa. She verbally positioned herself as Micki responding to an imaginary white classmate, choosing a first-person address: "I'm like, No, but I'm still Black. Booty? Like what's booty pop? Like can you define booty pop?"

Here Vanessa took on one of the strategies one can use to interrupt a microaggression: she feigned ignorance to the controlling image and asked for elaboration.[39] Psychologist Derald Wing Sue identifies one form of microaggressions as microassaults, "conscious, deliberate, and either subtle or explicit racial, gender, or sexual-orientation biased attitudes, beliefs, or behaviors that are communicated to marginalized groups through environmental cues, verbalizations, or behaviors. They are meant to attack the group identity of the person or to hurt/harm the intended victim through name-calling, avoidant behavior, or purposeful discriminatory actions."[40] Vanessa's strategy forced an individual who perpetrated a microassault—applying a racialized and gendered stereotype seen in popular media, in this case, a conjured image of a Black woman doing a stripper dance, to a real-life woman—to awkwardly define and explain use of the stereotype.

In the resistant space of their viewing session, the women validated their own experience of microassaults by cataloguing all of the stereotypical questions they had been asked. In addition to queries about dancing, Vanessa exclaimed that popular ones she got were: "Can you cook? Can you braid hair?" More of the women jumped in to reveal the ways in which they refuted the stereotypes conjured by their White classmates. Sometimes they addressed an imaginary White classmate, sometimes each other. Jen remarked, "I can't braid hair" and Micki echoed, "I can't braid my own hair . . . like what are you talking about?" Vanessa added, "Yeah, I can't help you there, pal. Can't cook fried chicken, can't do shit." Camille echoed Vanessa saying, "Everybody's like, you can't make fried chicken? I'm like nooooo." The women amped up the discussion, refuting more stereotypes. McCall said, "I don't even like the smell of watermelon!" and Vanessa added, "I don't like cornbread." The repetition of "I don't" and "I can't" added up to refusal to participate in pretending that racism—even coded, postracial racism of microaggressions—didn't exist. Such straightforward pushing back is anathema to the coded postracial resistance of strategic ambiguity.

The women had to deal with the problem of their small numbers on campus, as well as the fact that their small numbers meant that their White classmates identified them through television stereotypes. Forging connectivity fought the very notion of tokenism. Tokenism, at its core, is an experience of isolation, of loneliness. Being a good token means not allowing others in—it means fighting for scraps in a racialized and gendered economy of privilege. However, being able to name such positioning was a form of strength. By identifying each other as having similarly isolating experiences and similar critiques of media, they bonded as a community and ensured that they have somewhere to turn when being tokenized and stereotyped—what they described as a daily occurrence in their predominantly White university. The difference between their high school experiences of being "the only," without similarly positioned friends with whom to commiserate, and their experiences as college students as one of few, but with a posse of powerful women of color who also fought similar battles, was that they did not simply understand the situational nature of their "only" status, but they also understood that others were similarly positioned. They understood the ways in which White privilege functioned to minoritize and tokenize women of color across their institution, and they fostered their community of women of color precisely because of such positioning.

The women also illustrated that their experience of being "the only" shaped what they wanted from representation, but in diametrically

opposed ways. Some of the women bristled when media too closely replicated their real-life experiences. Camille told the group, "No I can't get
into this [season of the MTV reality show *The*] *Real World*. It's really
boring to me. There's no Black people on it." For Camille, being surrounded by all-White folks on campus or in her hometown was one
thing; she couldn't control the situation. She wasn't, however, going to
invite them into her home via her television. But some of the women
discussed the comfort of consuming all-White images because of their
familiarity. McCall described, in her words, the "White shows" she
liked, including the reality shows set in Orange County, *The Hills* and
Laguna Beach, and a fictionalized version of these shows, the teen drama
The OC: "That's because I, I went to a White high school, and so, the
OC kind of reminds me of what my high school kinda was." For Mc-
Call, who moved to Southern California soon after graduation, there
was something comforting about these images and perhaps the fantasy
space they represented. But that didn't mean that she was longing for
such minoritization (in fact, she expressed just the opposite). Her love
of watching White people on television did not translate to her desire
to insert herself into all-White spaces. Whether rejecting homogenous
representations because of their alienating quality or embracing them
because of their familiarity, the women were carefully thinking through
the impact of representations and constructing their community.

Racialized Resistance and the Woman of Color TV Watcher

The young women of color in my viewing session wanted a lot from
their media, and their critique of "bad" representation bonded their
community in a manner that seemed a world apart from the forms
of strategic ambiguity I elucidate in the first half of this book. They
accessed their critiques, their connections, their very understanding of
Black womanhood just as much through their co-constitutive processes
of hate-watching representations of Black women on television as their
engagement with each other. There was no careful couching of their
words, no switching of codes, no softening for others' comfort. All of the
viewers' ire emerged in the space of hate-watching. It was no accident
that their bald and bold responses occurred in a private, domestic space.
And it was no accident that the young women spoke back freely to one

of the most taboo topics in mixed company of the Michelle Obama era, racism against women of color, when surrounded by other young women of color. Hate-watching together provided the women with a tool to, quite simply, be neither strategic nor ambiguous, but racially critical and resistant.

This chapter shows one small group of progressive women of color college students at a large northwestern U.S. public university lovingly and fiercely engaging, resisting, and hate-watching mediated images of women of color while stoking their woman of color community and their critiques. The women constantly tacked between "real life" and representation, before, during, and after our viewings of *ANTM*. These young women provided a snapshot into a slice of strategic-ambiguity free life. Perhaps it was the sanctity of Camille's apartment; perhaps it was the freedom of youth. Regardless, they knew what they didn't want to be: tokenized and stereotyped. Throughout the sessions, the women combatted postrace in a particularly collective, collaborative, and gendered manner. They bonded and saw each other more fully when they engaged with representation.

In many ways, these women illustrate that their community functioned as the antidote to the individual-focused, clenched-teeth survival strategy of postracial resistance through strategic ambiguity, which flourishes alone and never in community. I further develop this idea in the next chapter as I suss out the dynamics of the women's racialized, resistant critique, and how they turned their viewing sessions into productive spaces, where they, in a sense, enacted anti-racism, anti-sexism workshops. As the young women critiqued televisual instantiations of code-switching, respectability politics, colorism, stereotyping, and the management of difference, they made sense of their own racialized and gendered lives, and turned hate-watching into a space of pleasure and productivity. In turn, the women in my viewing study inadvertently fashioned productive and pleasurable hate-watching counterscripts to strategic ambiguity.

5

"They Got Rid of the Naps, That's All They Did"

Women of Color Critiques of Respectability Politics,
Strategic Ambiguity, and Race Hazing

Throughout this book, I've assessed the gamut of stereotypes that media aim at Black women and posited that Black women celebrities performatively resist such stereotyping through the postracial resistance of strategic ambiguity. At our very first gathering before watching the first episode of the show, the women who signed up for our viewing party were already anticipating heavy use of, as Robin Means Coleman deems stereotypes, "unvarying" and "negative" portrayals. Means Coleman explains that "a stereotype is a conventional, formulaic, oversimplified conception, opinion or belief. It promotes an unvarying pattern of a group that has come to be associated with negative portrayals."[1] Valentina predicted, "I think they're gonna paint, you know, certain characters in like a certain light, that kind of thing, *based* on their ethnic background. I think a lot of it's gonna be based on . . . their ethnicity."

These young women were sophisticated consumers of media, of the type media scholar Racquel Gates describes as "ever more savvy about how reality shows are produced to convey 'reality,' . . . [and] well aware that the portrayals they see are manipulated in various ways by the process of production."[2] Such manipulation, the women in my group pointed out, was racialized and gendered, and applicable to their real lives as well as the lives they analyzed on screen. This chapter, building on the last chapter's focus on the anti-strategic ambiguity practice of community-building through hate-watching, presents the idea that a resistance to stereotyping defies strategic ambiguity through rejecting respectability politics. Although not naming it as such, they saw the behaviors I designate in this book as postracial resistance through strategic ambiguity as not just impacting the individual attempting such a posture, but negatively infecting the rest of a woman of color community; they saw strategic ambiguity, at times, as no less than a form of race hazing. Respectability politics, as a concept, sits over the whole book, and came to the fore most explicitly in chapter 3 on Shonda Rhimes' press coverage. In this chapter, I push further on what the flouting of stereotypes and respectability politics looked like when it was enacted by a group of young women of color media consumers who rejected postrace.

"It's Like Fancy Porn So You Don't Call It Porn"

The stereotypes the participants were immediately attuned to were misogynistic images of Black women. Jen, not mincing words, provided one theory: "I think some of the modeling shows are, are like porn. But it's like fancy porn so you don't call it porn . . . Yeah, like you're taking nude photos. And it's great that it's like artistic and you put like a pearl screen over them, you know, but it's still—if this other stuff is pornographic so is that." Jen posited that "this other stuff"—images labelled as pornographic—create the same dynamics as a commercial network reality television show. Jen was neither moralistically condemning nor dismissing pornography, but rather casting a wider net over what constitutes pornography. In this statement, Jen was implying that, if what we categorize as pornography is exploitative and dehumanizing, then so is the showcasing of women in reality television shows like *ANTM*.

Camille agreed that reality television functioned as another form of pornography, and she provided an example from one of their favorite shows:

> CAMILLE: "Did you see, what's-her-face on [*For the Love of*] *Ray J* when she made herself into a banana split?"
> MCCALL: Yes, that was disgusting.
> MICKI [*to me*]: Did you see that? She turned herself into a *human* banana split [*groans*].
> CAMILLE: She was in the splits, she had whipped cream on her, and she had a banana [*puts up to her face, brief thrusting motion*] like she was [*extended pause*] . . . And that was the first show! Wow!

The women identified against the positioning of Black women as mere objects of consumption, or as the symbolic embodiment of fellatio in this particular example. They balked at the misogyny to which such an image spoke, the lack of agency conferred to the woman in the show, and the way in which the woman on screen became an entirely acted-upon object and not a subject in the scene. Not only were they horrified by what they were watching on TV (perhaps more so because they were discussing it in front of me), but they were dismayed that they, and other women of color who did not make the choice to appear on a reality television show, would be identified with such representations. In assessing the sexualized positioning of Black women on television, the women were concerned about the power of stereotyping influencing other viewers' ideas about Black women or, in the words of Vanessa, what "makes Black people look so bad." The viewing women weren't able to, as theorist Jennifer Nash puts it, read "for ecstasy rather than injury," as they experienced "the preoccupation with how singular black female bodies are asked to speak for all black female bodies in the visual field, and how particular icons come to stand for black women generally."[3]

This interaction, like so many of the interactions I observed between the women, was performative and pivoted on questions of respectability politics. They spoke back to the screen, as media studies scholar Helen Wood documented in her study of women talking to their televisions, as much as they did to each other.[4] The women enjoyed the experience of naming a stereotype only to strip it of its power, of one-upping each other, and of making each other laugh. As they were refuting the stereotypes of White classmates, they were defining their own Blackness as one that pushed back against the "unvarying" and "negative" images that Means Coleman defines as at the heart of a stereotype. What such resistance meant was that there wasn't room in many interactions to reclaim and reframe a stereotype. While theorist Mirelle Miller-Young explains that "stereotypes usually have dual valences: they may also be taken up by the oppressed and refashioned to mean something quite different,"[5] the women in my group flatly condemned stereotypes. For example, in this particular interaction, none of the women could claim sex-positive notions; the only space available was one of condemnation. In their fierce refutations of stereotypes, identifying with anything remotely "stereotypical" was impossible. In another session, McCall described her own so-called inauthentic Blackness in this manner: "I guess I'll lose Black points, but my mom doesn't make sweet potato pies for holidays, like, I don't know, [she makes] pumpkin pie." Even humorously, the notion of having to preserve "Black points" or accomplish Black authenticity buttressed the respectability politics the women performed in this moment. The women equally distanced themselves from hypersexualized images or controlling notions of Blackness.

As I discussed in the previous chapter, the women frequently analyzed the racialized and gendered questions their White female classmates would ask them. Being asked about the dance that was then called "booty popping" (now, twerking) made its way into their discussions numerous times. At one such moment, after laughing about the absurdly stereotypical questions White women asked them about themselves, Jen became very serious as she launched a critique of the power dynamics inherent in White women's stereotyping of women of color:

> JEN: It's funny 'cause, like, we're kidding [about the ridiculous, stereotypical questions posed to her] but, like, I've had almost all of these questions asked to me—
> MICKI: Someone asked if you could booty pop?—
> JEN: They asked me that, and I didn't know what it was, they used a different word, but they were explaining what the women do in some of the videos, when they like lean on the car. And I was like, I don't even know what you're asking me, and it was like, "no I can't!" And then, the next question was, "well do Black guys *like* that?" And it was—after I just told you, I don't know how to do it so I wouldn't know—
> MICKI: Well, like, I'm not a Black guy—
> VANESSA: You're the expert in Black women and Black dudes—

Jen, a dance major, did not object to questions as to if she could do a specific dance, but rather the implication that as a Black woman she had greater access to her sexuality than White women.

Furthermore, the move to White women questioning Black women about Black masculinity illuminated the desire of White women to enhance their own sexual desirability by courting and catering to an imagined Black hypermasculinity. The conversation continued:

> JEN: And then, you know, another girl came up to me one time and she
>   put her arm around me and she goes, I'm really glad you're not one
>   of those ghetto Black girls, like it was a—
> MICKI: *I've* gotten that—
> JEN: —like it was a compliment. And it's kind of, you don't know—
> VANESSA: What to say—
> JEN: What to say right away, like, you don't know how to kind of—
> MICKI: [*voice thick with sarcasm*] Thanks . . . for complimenting me . . .
>   while insulting me, my race, and my people? Thank you.
> JEN: It's kind of, yeah . . . [*trails off; general agreement from the group*]
>   and it's not a leap to think that people, like, watch this stuff and start
>   thinking those things.

Here Jen, Micki, and Vanessa took on a matrix of class/race/sexuality assumptions perpetrated by White women. They exposed the racism and classism in the White women's celebration of them as non-"ghetto Black girls." The group processed this rejection of tokenization slowly and thoughtfully. Microaggression theory tells us that minoritized people spend so much time questioning whether they are correct that a comment actually qualifies as a microaggression; if they are allowed to respond to a microaggression; and if they are allowed to identify a microaggression as such. The women's community enabled them to say yes to all three modes of internal questioning. Their collective responses were incredibly validating to each other.

"People Always Think That I'm Intimidating": Negotiating White Women's Fear of Black Women's Anger

The anger the young women expressed in the viewing sessions was not simply in response to feeling read as a stereotype. They were angry that even while being insulted they had to measure and weigh their responses in order to appear nonthreatening, keep themselves safe, and avoid and handle racism, the hallmarks of strategic ambiguity. In other words, they had to serve the needs of Whiteness and negotiate through what Robin DiAngelo calls "White fragility" even while they were the victims of White racism.[6] This is one of the key predicaments to which strategic ambiguity is a solution or response. One of the stereotypes that had particular resonance with my viewing group was the stereotype of the Angry Black Woman, whose frame, as I illustrate in chapter 2, even the mighty Oprah Winfrey couldn't escape. Camille described the deployment of the Angry Black Woman stereotype on *America's Next Top Model*: "whenever there are arguments, it is always the Black girl that's the first one to kind of make the first move into the other girls' territory, or her space." In other words, the Black woman on screen is positioned as the first one who escalates disagreements and makes them physical. The women related this televisual framing to their own experiences of racialized framing. Vanessa explained the effect of the Angry Black Woman stereotype growing up: "Middle school was just, like, you better know how to fight [*Camille laughed*] 'cause you're Black. Uh, ok [*Laughter. Vanessa responds by putting her dukes up, eliciting more laughter*]." Vanessa's story resonated with Jen who turned to Camille and explained:

> Like, you know how I am. I'm not going to fight anyone. People would always say that kind of stuff to me. Like, they didn't want to make me angry because they thought I would get into a fight with them [*Vanessa nodded, agreeing*], and I was like, I'm really *calm*, like, I don't like to yell at [*laughs*] people. I'm certainly not going to get into a fight with anyone. And I would have that said to me *repeatedly* [mmm hmmm]. "I don't want to piss her off." Like, I've given you no reason to think I would just [Vanessa: Be violent], like, flex on you [*Laughs. Camille punches the air in front of her and makes a punching sound*].

Camille agreed and responded, addressing her comments initially to Micki: "People always think that I'm intimidating. It's really annoying . . . Like, in my, like, [one class] [*mmm hmm*] they would always be, like, well, you're so intimidating. It's like, is it because I'm Black? Or is it 'cause, like, I'm talking about racism and how you participate in it? Like, they'd just be like, Ooooh—and [one other student of color] was in that class, too, and, like—And presto, and they were just like, well, we just don't feel comfortable because there's like *really* intimidating people. But really, it was just *brown* people in the class [mmm hmmm]. It was just like, wow!" Here Camille argued against the codes of postracial racism, by articulating a racialized resistance.

The women expressed frustration that White people did not seem to understand the overwhelming power and the deep impact of stereotypes on women of color. Jen stated that the *invisibility* of Black women, particularly in discussions of gender and beauty, was just as harmful as the iteration of stereotypes. As in Camille's story above, the women reported that many such interactions happened in classes at their predominant White university. Jen explained:

> I sat in classes where we talked about beauty standards and people would be like, White students would be like, oh, but, that doesn't matter for like, *you*, they're talking to me as like a Black person because you're Black, so, you don't, this doesn't apply to you. Well it's like, that's even, it feels even worse 'cause you're *not* gonna get it. [Lupe: right] Like, so you can't even kind of almost, like, lie to yourself a little bit about it, be like, oh, you know, it's like, no. Like, Black is not a part of—like, what they want. So I think it affects [us]—and in a sense it makes sense that people who we think look *different* are still wanting to be on the show and care about modeling and fashion and all that stuff.

The women's frustration crested not just with the application of stereotypes to them through microassaults, but with their symbolic annihilation, the inability to be seen as women of color.[7] Communication scholar George Gerbner coined the term "symbolic annihilation" to denote representational absence;[8] many of the women's comments are about symbolic annihilation as much as stereotypes as they discussed their classmates' inability to see beautiful women of color outside of the confines of stereotypes. Lupe stated that "they make it seem like, these are such beautiful minority women as if there's not very many out there. Does that make sense? Like, the way that they talk about it or say things, it's like, oh she's really pretty, Latin women, but like, you make it sound in a way as if there's not that many out there but, you don't say, oh my gosh, she's a beautiful White woman [Micki: Exactly]. Because it's just everywhere." The beautiful women of color were singular additions, or tokens. Jen agreed: "But I felt like, uh, like, there's beauty and then people have these other kinds . . . Like, people have these quote-unquote "Black beauty" [*mmm hmmm*] and it's always, like, exceptional. So, like, they talk about the other girls being beautiful, and then the Black girls, like, they separate them out [right]. It's never, well, not that the playing field is level anyway, but I feel like shows like this . . . you see it, [girls of color] get separated out [*agreement*]." The women's objections here were that a part of stereotyping was never even being seen. In their critiques, the women questioned: was it worse to be stereotyped, or simply to be so absent from the picture that you were never considered? Or, if considered, only as an exception, registering while the rest of your people remained invisible or trapped in a stereotype?

These women struggled with representations because of how representations made their way into their daily lives. Means Coleman notes that the African American viewers of Black sitcoms whom she studied were "worried and angered" that "society would accept only the comedic depictions as an accurate portrayal of African Americans." Further, Means Coleman reports that her participants "pondered how those Whites, who know little about Blacks, learn to dislike and fear the racial group based on the shows. More than one participant observed that Black situation comedies do not create bigotry, but are an extension of a prevalent racism already in place in America."[9] My participants echoed Means Coleman's observations. Not only did the women in my group see the images on screen as flat and inadequate, but they felt the burden of having to negate such stereotyping. But, unlike those in Means Coleman's study, the women in Camille's living room were not concerned with regulating, producing, or intervening in "positive" or "negative" representations. They didn't want to counter stereotypes with strategic ambiguity. Instead, their critique amounted to a celebration of self through a multifaceted refusal of respectability politics. Their identities could not be encapsulated by the representations of their identities on screen, where, as Jonathan Gray writes, "[c]ultural identity is always in such flux, characterized by variation and difference, that any attempt to depict a group of people will at the least prove inadequate, and at the worst do great damage to an understanding of the diversity of identity."[10] Their hate-watching viewing sessions provided them with the means to exercise their anger and in doing so resist and reshape their images absent of strategic ambiguity and respectability politics.

"They Just Got Rid of the Naps, That's All They Did": Flouting Respectability Politics

The women's conversations illustrated that stereotyping, tokenization, and respectability politics went hand-in-hand. When you were "the only" and when you were keenly aware of the power of stereotypes to demean and belittle not just you, but people minoritized like you, you bore the weight of representing your entire community. What you did with that burden was one of the running questions of our sessions together. The story of Black respectability politics is one of community members questioning if representations of African Americans are noble, articulate, polished, and intelligent enough. In other words, do representations make "us" look bad in front of "them"? But such policing has had unintended consequences for groups of young women such as these television-watchers. Indeed, media historian Jane Rhodes explains that on the one hand, "the politics of respectability were a response to the racist representations of and routine attacks on black female sexuality, character, and intellect." However, Rhodes continues, these very same repressive respectability politics, "enabled black women to enact subversive strategies of resistance."[11]

Historian Kevin K. Gaines describes the urge towards respectability politics as a "self-help ideology of racial uplift." Gaines writes that "a broader vision of uplift signifying collective social aspiration, advancement, and struggle had been the legacy of the emancipation era."[12] In media, representations of the marginalized hold a special burden: instead of being singular images of individuals they bear the weight of depicting whole communities, cultures, and races. Ostensibly, representations of minoritized people are subject to respectability litmus tests from the community that aim to limit the reproduction of historic stereotypes and tropes. And yet such litmus tests are far from universally applied or accepted by community members. Respectability politics both challenges and undermines potential forms of resistance and progress in race and gender representation in popular media.[13] People play with respectability, as Beretta Smith-Shomade writes in her descriptions of the "playful piety" that often surfaces in representations of even assumed-to-be sacred spaces such as the Black church.[14]

Even though questions of respectability politics have been around for over a century, the burden of African American respectability politics loomed large in our discussions. One aspect of respectability politics the women discussed negotiating was class and its representation in deportment, clothing, and speech. Gaines argues that historically, "black elites made uplift the basis for a racialized elite identity claiming Negro improvement through class stratification as race progress."[15] These young women found themselves in a liminal class position. While they mostly (but not all) came from working-class backgrounds, as successful college students they found themselves pondering what it meant to be on their way up and out of the working class. This same question of class stratification undergirds performances of postracial resistance through strategic ambiguity. Strategic ambiguity is a performance that only those with some form of class privilege, those who are already invited to the table, can enact. Resisting postracial ideologies through performing strategic ambiguity means using the protective costumes of respectability to pass as unthreatening. This is a level of non-resistance, ambiguity, risk, and class analysis that came out in the young women's critiques.

The safe space of Camille's living room enabled the women to analyze and abandon respectability politics. Although many of the women in our viewing group enacted one form of respectability politics at times, for example, expressing dismay that "they" (White people) were going to understand "us" (women of color) along the lines of racialized stereotypes, most of them also enacted a critique and resistance. For example, some of the women critically assessed those they identified as the standard-bearers in their lives for racialized gender—their mothers— for their own respectability politics. A number of the women keenly felt the generational divide when their Black mothers celebrated Tyra Banks; they balked at such celebration. Without exception, at every session all of the women present spent time critiquing the manner in which Tyra Banks performed her classed, racialized, and gendered identity on *America's Next Top Model*. Their mothers disdained other reality show representations they consumed, like *The Flavor of Love*, but venerated Tyra Banks.

In Vanessa's words, her mother loved Banks and *America's Next Top Model* because she was simply "so happy to see some Black faces." But as her comments throughout the sessions made abundantly clear, mere representation wasn't enough for Vanessa. Micki asserted that her mother approved of Banks because she proffered a form of acceptable Black representation: "As long as you're not showing your stuff or like [unidentified woman: you know!] being hella sexual or loose or whatever, they don't care." McCall explained further: "My mom talked about Tyra today. She's like . . . yeah, I just love Tyra, she's such a wonderful young Black woman [*Jen agrees; she's heard the same remarks from her mother*]. It's like a lot of people take that for face value. Oh she's Black, she's doing something wonderful. No one looks at that she's crazy." The "crazy" that McCall referenced was the way in which Banks enacted her respectability politics: by punishing the contestants who were not able to code switch, or transgress racialized boundaries in the same way as Banks.[16]

Unlike their mothers, the women joyfully spurned respectability politics by consuming many forms of Black representation while still critiquing them. For example, they gleefully shook their heads at 1980s rapper Flavor Flav's antics on his dating reality show *The Flavor of Love*, and delighted in the ever-multiplying numbers of Black-oriented reality television programs. They were also sensitive to racialized double standards in their favorite shows. At our viewing sessions, the participants regularly dissected the complexities of respectability politics and the unfair burden placed upon Black televisual representations. The women troubled the idea that some forms of reality television featuring White people was seen as "higher-class" than similar shows featuring African Americans. Micki explained,

> See, I thought *The Bachelor* was going to be quote-unquote "classy" cause it's ABC and it's White, but then, I just lost respect for *The Bachelor* last night too [*chatter amongst the others—general agreement*—"I don't watch that"]. He picked the girl, and then like six weeks into it, after picking her and becoming engaged to her, he dropped her like a bad habit and took the other girl back [Oooooooh]. And then, on national TV like she didn't even know that he was having issues until they [mentioned it] on TV. So yeah, I think *The Bachelor* is now like on my Ray-J [in the dating reality show *For the Love of Ray J*] status.

As Micki indicated, different television networks signify different levels of prestige and respectability. Networks, like individuals, are also racialized, gendered, and classed. In 2009 when our viewing session occurred, the cable network VHI was responsible for churning out a number of reality television shows featuring African Americans, including *For the Love of Ray J* and *Flavor of Love*, but one of the big three networks, ABC, had yet (and to date, has yet) to star an African American bachelor on their landmark reality dating show and after fifteen years featured its first Black bachelorette in 2017.

And Micki wasn't alone in comparing *The Bachelor* to *The Bachelor*-inspired Black dating shows. Media scholars Rachel Dubrofsky and Antoine Hardy read *The Bachelor* and *Flavor of Love* against each other, noting "*Flavor of Love* has a Black star and predominantly Black cast but self-consciously acknowledges its appropriation of *The Bachelor*, a series with a White star and predominantly White cast."[17] Dubrofsky and Hardy also point out that *Flavor of Love* is parodic where *The Bachelor* is earnest. As a result, *Flavor of Love* as opposed to *The Bachelor*, "opens up possibilities for claiming a variety of identities at once; for foregrounding performativity and the constructedness of identities in the space of surveillance; and for complicating the requirement for authenticity in the space of White-centered RTV shows."[18] Sophisticated reality television viewers like the women in my viewing party read through the so-called respectability of *The Bachelor* to call it out as equally—if not more— misogynistic—than the predominantly Black-cast dating shows. Micki did not buy into the myth of a "classy" *Bachelor* show perhaps because of the way in which it erased Blackness so entirely that questions of racialized difference did not even enter the frame.

In addition to rejecting the notion that similar genre shows with White and Black leads were not framed as similarly respectable, the women critiqued the persistent logic that "Black shows" (i.e., Black-cast shows) should not necessarily be assessed as disrespectable to begin with and that all Black shows in a similar genre were necessarily alike. Micki went on to explain that not all Black dating shows are the same in her eyes: "[*For the Love of Ray J*] is actually better [than *Flavor of Love*] because he's a little bit more respectful . . . Like he doesn't talk to them crazy. Like, Flav, used to talk to them crazy like, [*with her Flavor Flav impression, sing-song*] "I'm Favor Flav" [*group laughter*] like he used to talk to them [Camille: [*also with her impression*] I'm Flavor Flav!]. But Ray J'll be like, "No, this isn't going to work out. Like, I'm going to need you to leave. He's a little bit more respectful, so [yeah]—it's better in that respect." Micki pushed back against the respectability politics used to flatten out all Black representation as, in this case, equally misogynistic.

"On the Acceptable End of Black": Skin Color Matters

Colorism, the privileging of light-skinned people of color in terms of beauty and overall prestige, is another form of racialized hazing that the young women critiqued. The women discussed this form of prejudice throughout our time together when they described how the media showcased light-skinned Black women to stand in for all Black women. Tyra Banks herself was most often the object of criticism both for failing to acknowledge her own privilege as a light-skinned woman, and for castigating darker-skinned contestants for their inability to sell themselves as racially flexible, which functioned as code for lighter-skinned Black women including Banks herself. A number of times the participants asked why Banks' default was stereotyping and respectability politics through the mode of colorism.

For example, the women took exception to one episode of *ANTM* in which Tyra upbraided an African American contestant for failing to apply sunscreen after turning a few shades darker. Micki commented with some irritation evident in her voice, "They were all out in the sun at the same time. Why would you say [you need to wear sunscreen] to one of the darkest people there who has the most protection from the sun?" McCall agreed, "Yeah, why would you pick her out?" Continuing, Micki responded, raising her voice slightly with more frustration, "Why would you bring that up at that point in time 'cause everyone's complimenting her on how beautiful her skin looked? [[Jen: trying to cut her down]] And then like, 'Well . . . I wouldn't be out in the sun.' It makes you sound ignorant." Jen jumped in the conversation, saying, "Well in the modeling world, yeah, dark skin doesn't fly. Unless they've got you [on a photo shoot] up in a jungle somewhere. Or in a favela where you look like you're from there [*laughter*]. Then maybe they'll give you a [photo] shoot." Even though Banks did not explicitly state, "dark skin is bad" or even, "dark skin is limiting in modeling," the women understood

Banks' denigration of the dark-skinned model to be a form of strategically ambiguous, postracial racism borne out through colorism.

The women also talked extensively about colorism when they discussed the recently aired CNN *Black in America* series.[19] Although our viewing sessions centered on *ANTM* the women often discussed other representations of people of color. The women expressed their eager anticipation for the show and their ultimate disappointment with it. Camille dubbed *Black in America* "horrible" and, Vanessa, in response, covered her face and sighed, "Oh my God, I was so disappointed." McCall interjected, "that was bad," as Vanessa continued, "It was like, bad thing after another, bad, bad, bad, bad. . . . Everything she talked about was negative, negative, negative, negative, negative, negative. Nothing positive." While McCall's designation of the show as "bad" was an unspecified blanket statement about any number of aspects of the program, Vanessa riffed off McCall's "bad" to specify its negative representations. They did not object to negative portrayals altogether: the women agreed throughout our sessions that representations of African Americans should reveal nuance and diversity. In the case of *Black in America,* as in *ANTM,* the women were not hoping for whitewashed portrayals of success playing to respectability politics. But they were also not hoping to see solely portraits of Black poverty, crime, and violence. Instead they were hoping for Black representations that showcased a variety of forms of Blackness, including all of the multifaceted ways in which they lived their Blackness as college students.

Black in America was not just disappointing to the young women because of the content—which showed what they read as excessive images of Black poverty—but because of the show's host Soledad O'Brien, a light-skinned, racially ambiguous, and mixed-race African American woman. Jen commented, "Whenever they have to talk about Black anger, [O'Brien] is like the only one they say [Yeah!] and they never talk about the fact that like, yeah, she identifies as Black but she's also like [[Micki: Everything]], really light [[Yeah] and [unidentified person from group: it's really annoying]]." Micki continued, "I had to go on the Internet and look up whether she was Black. Therefore [*slight laugh*], that doesn't really help when a person's flipping through trying to see themselves on TV and they're like– . . . I definitely googled it. I was like [*positions hands in front of her as if on a keyboard*], "Soledad O'Brien. Ethnicity, race, Black"

[*laughter*] I was like every—[[Vanessa: nationality, color]] catchword."
The women balked at O'Brien standing in for all Black women, or even
all Black people, by virtue of hosting *Black in America* because, as Camille noted, "There's a certain aesthetic that's supposed to be like "beautiful" and it's generally, more lighter-complected women." Camille felt
that the message for darker-skinned women about contingent success
was clear: "So when people come up that are darker-skinned it's kind of
just like, well . . . she *might* make it." While Camille's comments began
with a critique of televisual images, they quickly moved to a commentary
on her real-life experiences.

Indeed, our discussions frequently knitted together critiques of media
and personal reflections. The discussion of *Black in America* prompted
a discussion of the ways in which intraracial issues of colorism inter-
sect with White privilege and anti-Black racism. Jen addressed what she
believed to be White women having an unfair amount of power and
control over Black women's self-identity around their own perceptions
of skin color. Jen explained, initially addressing Vanessa, and then the
rest of the group,

> The thing you said, you know, you didn't think any of those [negative]
> things that other people thought about until you got there [[yeah]], grow-
> ing up, and I had always—I—I didn't think [my perception of my skin
> color] was a bad thing, which I'm surprised that I didn't, but I always
> thought I was very dark-skinned. [*Vanessa nods*]. And I had no idea that
> I *wasn't*. For like, until [[Camille: Until I told you?]], pretty much until
> [[Camille: light-skinned!]], pretty much until college. 'Cause everyone was
> White [Vanessa: right]. So for them it was like, if you weren't white you
> were *dark* [Vanessa: dark]. I was, I was kinda like, oh, there's, there are my
> folks, you know? [Vanessa: right, *Camille laughs*]. And like, someone had
> to be like, no [*laughter*] you're not. And, and like I had no idea, and it's
> funny like how [*beat*], like how, I'm right here, I can look in the mirror and
> see myself, but because everyone else saw me the other way, that's how I
> saw myself too. There was no separation.

In this interaction Jen revealed all of the ways in which racial identity,
particularly around skin color, is situational and relational. Because
of the way in which Whiteness worked to skew her image of herself,

especially her view of her own skin color, she could literally not see herself as other African Americans like Camille saw her. Thus, Camille had to "teach" Jen she was light-skinned compared to other African Americans. Prior to Camille's intervention, Jen could only envision herself through Whites' eyes, with no nuance about skin color. The women's conversation illustrated that the power to see ourselves comes about through comparison, including skin color comparison.

Jen's story resonated with Vanessa, who interpreted it as the power White people have to construct Black worth and identity. Commiserating and extending Jen's story to a greater critique of racialized power in beauty, Vanessa said,

> Like the weirdest thing about that too, like, White people mess your mind up, so—they always just mess your mind up, 'cause it's like we—they want Black people to be lighter and dark is bad blah blah blah, but they *tan*, and they rub that orange shit on their face . . . And I was just like, why? And, and it's like, you're trying to be like *my* people, but you want me to hate my people [yeah]. You're paying all this money to look like my ancestors, but you want me to hate that. Like that don't make *no* goddamn sense.

Vanessa related Jen's reflection about her own self-identity to the peculiarities of anti-Black racism in which White women empirically devalued Blackness and yet symbolically desired it through the process of cultural appropriation. Their appropriation of Blackness worked alongside anti-Black racism. As they spoke back to television together, the women viewers were attuned to what they read as Banks' intraracial discrimination, with the featuring of O'Brien feeding into such discrimination, and they were also alert to links between intraracial and interracial discrimination.

As the women oriented themselves (in a very *un*-strategically ambiguous manner) towards their community and not simply to themselves as individuals, they worried about messages regarding skin color affecting younger African American girls. Vanessa commented, "But like, I know people, like, the little kids at the Boys and Girls Club who just feel like we're saying light skin is better than dark skin [because] I hear someone on TV who's not like [me]—but then again, simultaneously, that's kind of how she got famous [being so light], so . . . [*trailing off*]." In saying "we" Vanessa took responsibility for the impact of colorist Black representations on young Black girls. She framed herself as someone with agency, someone who could perhaps not only bear the burden of negative imagery but also actually do something to change that imagery (or the perception of that imagery by younger girls).

Vanessa's sentiment resonated with McCall who agreed, "There's going to be some little Black girl who watches and thinks, oh, I can't go out [in the sun]. I shouldn't go out in the sun because I won't get like Tyra Banks and everyone knows Tyra Banks is the shit." Camille, responding defiantly to such notions exclaimed, "I *stay* in the sun. I do not care." Here Camille modelled how to speak back to colorism. Micki offered another response. Shaking her head, taking on the position of being a contestant on *ANTM* having to face Tyra Banks after getting darker in the sun, she said: "I was wearing sunscreen, and sunscreen is gonna protect me but it's not gonna *stop* my skin from getting darker [right]." Micki here pointed out two things: the impossibility of Banks' request as dark-skinned women will naturally tan more deeply even when wearing sunscreen, and the importance of illuminating the racism inherent in scolding darker-skinned contestants for their natural skin color.

In a later conversation, the women again discussed how featuring light-skinned women helped maintain hegemonic beauty standards. Camille noted, "Yeah, [*ANTM* is] just reproducing the same types of images. Same types of girls [*louder*]—It's not like anything is like so dramatically different in the women that they choose, and that I think, when Eva [Pigford, the first African American contestant to win a cycle of *ANTM*] was picked, it was like, Oh! Okay. But then again, Eva was very light-skinned." Jen responded, "She was on the acceptable end of Black," to which Camille added, "Is like Tyra regurgitating all these things that happened to her, placed upon these new models [Vanessa: that's so true]?" Camille raised the issue again of racialized hazing, the notion that I'm going to inflict the same harm on (vulnerable) others that was done to me.

The women noted that another mode of colorism happened when Banks, in a strategically ambiguous manner, muzzled race talk, and silenced a discussion of the role of skin color in opening or closing doors for models. The women were attendant to such silencing. For example, after breaking down all of the coded, postracial, strategically ambiguous ways that Tyra Banks engaged questions of race and colorism, Camille wanted to know if Banks had ever discussed these topics in a forthright manner. She asked, "has there ever been like Tyra talking about race or about her Blackness?" Jen responded that she remembered such a moment:

> [Banks] had like people telling her—walking into an agency office and having them be like, you might as well stop trying to model, no one's ever going to hire you [[mmm]]. Your color and stuff, and . . . like, if I made it, like, I opened doors, but she never [speaks about race directly]. So it's like she talks about being Black I feel, but she *doesn't* talk about it.

In other words, in Jen's assessment Banks defaulted to strategic ambiguity by dealing with race and gender in code. This was one of the dangers of strategic ambiguity: because of the coded ways in which she named—but, as Jen points out, doesn't name race, Banks ended up enacting racialized and gendered discrimination, in the women's eyes, despite her stated desire to break down barriers for women of color.

Race scholars Kate Russell-Cole, Midge Wilson, and Ronald E. Hall document the history and contemporary circulation of colorism, an often intraracially-discussed but both inter- and intra-racially perpetuated prejudice, which they describe as getting worse between the initial publication of their highly successful book in 1992 and a new edition in 2013. In their updated preface in the 2013 edition, Russell-Cole, Wilson, and Hall write that today, "colorism is the more legitimate form of prejudice to empirically investigate since skin tone is at least a visible and measurable attribute, whereas race is largely a social construct."[20] This is one of the many forms of racialized violence re-upped in the Obama era. In addition, critical race scholar Angela Harris names colorism an "economy of color," as a hierarchical system that is linked, but not identical to, racism. She notes that an economy of color provides important distinction to the two "most popular and scholarly discussions of racism": that of "prejudice" and that of "white supremacy." The "prejudice" approach saw racism as "interpersonal, and explores how processes of cognition, reasoning, and emotion function to make racial differences real and to make demeaning treatment of the racial 'other' seem natural, normal, and necessary," while the "white supremacy" approach "treats racism as institutional" and an effect of "political, economic, and social power."[21] The women's read of colorism drew from both the prejudice and white supremacy critiques. In hate-watching Banks spewing color-ist statements, the women girded themselves against such negativity in their own lives, just as they girded themselves against another aspect of strategic ambiguity and respectability politics: Banks' code-switching.

"Elite Moments" and "Snapping Her Neck": Rejecting Code-Switching

The participants explicitly rejected Tyra Banks' code-switching, a fun-damental performance element of strategic ambiguity and what linguist Carol Myers-Scotton describes as a tool used to signify membership in a particular group.[22] Code-switching is a central component of postra-cial resistance through strategic ambiguity; rejecting code-switching is tantamount to rejecting strategic ambiguity. The phrase "code switch," while popular not only as an academic term but a vernacular one for decades, has come into the mainstream lexicon by its use in popular culture—one example being on the National Public Radio (NPR) show and podcast "Code Switch," where journalists of color "remix race and identity" as they dive into discussions of how race "play[s] out in our lives and communities, and how all of this is shifting."[23]

Code switching is one reason the young women in my viewing group asserted that they did not identify with Tyra Banks. Vanessa put it this way, "It seems like every week she'll do her regular script, you know, blah blah blah, elite moment, and then during deliberation she has to have at least one moment where she's snapping her neck [Jen: where she reminds people she's really Black]." Turning her address to Banks herself, Vanessa asked incredulously, "What? What are you talking about? Who says that?" Vanessa noted that Banks' "regular script," or what feels like her genuine way of speaking, is "elite," which in this case means respect-able while not exactly "White" (as the women never wanted to conflate so-called "proper speech" with Whiteness), an over-enunciated parrot-ing of broadcast-friendly linguistic patterns.

Banks' "elite" or "regular script" fits media scholar Kristen J. Warner's assertion that "shows that attempt to cast African Americans as leads must ensure that their characters will not 'act' Black or perform in a manner that will offend mainstream viewers' sensibilities." At the same time, Warner goes on to explain that such performances are tricky to negotiate as, "these series continue to distance Black audiences because they 'feel' disingenuous,"[24] especially to insider audiences. Perhaps to deal with this divide, Banks clumsily (at least to these women) switches codes, "snapping her neck" to ingratiate herself to imagined Black audiences and/or appear authentically Black to White ones. However, Vanessa and Jen also noted that "elite" speech did not signify as authentically Black in a televisual space that was courting women of color audiences. In Vanessa's read, Banks made the choice to "snap her neck," or parrot a certain mode of Black female performance, in what felt like a false moment. Vanessa read Banks' code switching as an inversion of what is more regularly thought of as code switching: a lower-prestige group altering speech, dress, and mannerisms in order to gain entry to a higher prestige group. In this case the higher-powered Banks temporary abandons her "elite" or "regular" speech, to quote Vanessa, in lieu of a performance of so-called authentic Blackness. The women read such a performance as patently inauthentic.

Micki interpreted Banks' code-switching this way: "I really feel like Tyra is so like removed from the field, she has to like forge this connection [[yeah]] because she's like, 'Oh, I'm from Compton, and I'm . . .' [trailing off] but she left, what, when she was like 14? Or something like that? She's been all over the world, she has like a vastly different lifestyle than anybody else, and she'll try to be homegirl next door. It's like, let it go." Over the weeks the women expressed disdain for her inauthentic performance of Blackness that amounted, in their eyes, to a stereotype of Black womanhood. The participants pointed out that Banks' brand of code-switching was particularly dangerous because Banks narrated it as the sole path to success for women of color models. The women at the viewing sessions pointed out that such identity posturing also came from the contestants, who quickly learned how to perform a variety of racialized, classed, and gendered identities from their mentor Banks. Lupe remarked that Banks' code-switching is similar to "how [one ANTM contestant] acts like she's from the hood when she's not."

But if the women looked down on Banks' identity negotiations and rejected her attempts at performing so-called authentic Black representation as flat, they had incredible empathy for the contestants and their mandated identity play. The women paused the recording at one moment to remark about how while Banks ostensibly wanted the contestants to act respectably and not, for example, fight, she also essentially goaded a Black woman contestant into fighting by mocking her speech. Camille noted, "Tyra mimics [one of the contestants], [saying] 'yo, yo, whatsup.'" Camille explained that Banks' words caused an incident later in the show where the contestant spoke loudly "about what she'll do when disrespected." The character's anger and her quickness to fight was understandable to the women as she had just been mocked by Banks for failing to appropriately leave behind what Banks read as Black working class speech and transform to more acceptable standard English and accent. Critic Amy Adele Hasinoff describes *ANTM*'s urge to makeover unacceptable African American Vernacular English (AAVE) as part of the show's "neoliberal principles of the structural irrelevance of race, the importance of individual responsibility, the necessity for workers to become flexible to the demands of the market, and the need to continually undertake projects of individual self-improvement to attempt to succeed within the constraints of the system."[25] Such "self-improvement" on *ANTM* is often racialized and, as the women pointed out, part of the mandate to code switch, or present oneself as strategically ambiguous.

As savvy viewers, the women asserted that Banks postured in racialized ways to forge multiple identifications with the audience, a classic strategy of strategic ambiguity. While her "elite moment," in Vanessa's words, might have made her acceptable to their mothers, for example, her "snapping her neck" moment was designed for those who desired stereotypes of Black womanhood. However, neither of these performances rang true for these young women. Micki noted that the latter moment was animated by a desire of Banks to ensure that "she doesn't want people to forget . . . it's ok 'cause she's one of us too." The "it's" here is Banks' abuse of the contestants and particularly the women of color contestants. In other words, in Micki's critique, Banks' racialized and gendered hazing of the contestants was positioned by the show as understandable and forgivable because she shared race/gender identities with those who bore the brunt of her attack. The women didn't give any benefit of the doubt to the women as performing in certain ways because of the coaching of producers. In other words, they did not express any sympathy towards the structures in place which might have dictated some of Banks' behavior. The women of color viewers thus rejected a key component of strategic ambiguity and respectability politics by rejecting code-switching.

"She Is Already Different. They'll Cut Her": Managing Difference

Disingenuous racialized and gendered behavior was precisely what the women were attuned to in their discussions of the ways in which *ANTM* promoted colorism and code-switching, and managed difference writ large. The students pointed out regularly that Banks was trying to churn out models in her same mode, or, in Dez's words, "I know she gets upset when people are not like her." Dez's comments on scripting reality television personae echoed those of media scholar Laurie Ouelette who writes, "One of the things that ANTM teaches is that self-enterprise is similar to being female," which she deems "an entrepreneurial relationship to the self."[26] This entrepreneurialism of, in Oluette's words, "self-invention," amounts to hiding, showcasing, or altering often racialized aspects of themselves in tandem with other identity categories in order to progress in the competition. What Dez illustrated is that this "self-invention" was always along the lines of Banks' own persona. The young women's commentary demonstrated that they understood that the show was structured around fetishizing multiple differences, not just race.

One difference they noted was the management of physical difference, where, in one case, the contestants included a burn victim. While rooting for the contestant the group collectively burst into laughter in response to what felt like a scripted, false moment: Banks remarked that it was wonderful to have a burn survivor competing on the show. Jen noted that while this contestant was included on *ANTM* to highlight her difference, an explicitly stated desire of the show, she would not go far in the contest because of the show's urge for uniformity. In Jen's words, "she is already different. They'll cut her." In response Valentina defended the inclusion of this contestant, saying, "I think the, the whole point of picking a burn victim, though, is to like, be like something, not to be stigmatized about." Not satisfied with this answer, Jen interjected, "But that's like the whole point of *America's Next Top Model*. 'If I win,' but they're not going to win." Jen read through the stated script of the show of diversity to uncover its hidden message of homogeneity. Lupe came around to Jen's argument and expressed a common sentiment within the group: "It's *so* fake."

The women's reads on the management of physical difference in the show illustrated their careful attention to the show's emotional manipulation of the audience around difference. If we define difference as "deviation from the norm," such showcasing to create a reality show spectacle perhaps made sense.[27] And the women noted that the spectacle of difference wasn't just about physicality on the show. Jen discussed another moment she described from a previous cycle: "I saw one time, one of the girl's *mom* had been in a plane crash, her mom died on top of her, and they asked her to tell the story, you know, on that first interview things, and then they had the nerve to be like, 'Now that's the kind of thing that gives you strength to be in the modeling industry' [*laughter*]. I swear." Camille added, "That's why I think it's so harmful in some way is that you set yourself up to be critiqued in a certain way . . . I mean, we see the same type of girls being picked [yeah] to be on *Top Model* so—and in the end you know what type of girl they're looking for, yet these women still come up there and bare their all [because they hoped to get picked], and then they're hurt and wondering, well, 'why didn't they pick me?' [*slight laughter*, yeah]." Camille's response to the question she posed was one of difference. The show's message posits equivalency between, in her words summarizing Banks in judging the girls: "Well, I mean, you're a little dark, so—or your hair's not this way or your eyes are a little bit together." Difference in race, body, or even traumatic past was flattened out into simply another attribute—not a marker of power, privilege, or lack thereof—in order to temporarily showcase and then dismiss such complexities.

While many of the conversations pivoted around comparisons to Whiteness, others were Black or women of color specific, like the conversations on hair. Respectability politics often centers on women's hair, and no session would be complete without some mention of it.

Sessions often started with women's comments on hair products, hair-dressers, and all aspects of each other's hair, especially if a woman's hair was freshly done or worn in a new style. The hair discussions ex-tended from the living room to the screen as the women invoked their own experiences of hair and racialization. For example, Jen said that the judging panel the end of each episode of *America's Next Top Model*,

> reminds me of like going up through junior high and high school and whenever it is, and like, if you did, if you did different dance teams or whatever it was and, they would require your hair to be a certain way, and the only way that you could meet that requirement would be if you straightened your hair, most likely if you permed it, 'cause it's a constant thing. And it was like—and I never did drill. I couldn't stand stuff like that but it was just, it was *mandatory* [yeah] like to have your hair be a certain way.

Dance major Jen rejected the expectations of respectability and con-formity in her grade school dance groups. Jen continued, hair as a synecdoche for whole person, summed up her critique of hair-straightening: "It's just kinda like—and you look really, they look really *flat* to me now, there's nothing that *pops* anymore. And not that you can't straighten your hair *sometimes*, but the fact that's not a choice of like, a style, it's just your like base all the time." Switching from personal and real-life observations to observations of *ANTM*'s makeovers on Black women contestants, Jen continued, "And they just they don't even *do* anything to their hair, it's not like they give them these awesome hair-cuts like the other girls; they *just* put weaves and straighten it . . . They just got rid of the naps, that's all they did." Ayana D. Byrd and Lori L. Tharps note that "more than one hundred years after the terms 'good' and 'bad' hair became part of the Black American lexicon, the concepts endure."[28] Furthermore, communication scholars Regina E. Spellers and Kimberly R. Moffit explain that "if it is true that the physical body rep-resents a community of the self, then it must also be true that the degree to which the body is read as political statement creates interesting ideas about how the self is defined and (mis)understood."[29] In other words, attempted regulation of hair and body stifle far more than just those physical aspects of self.

Jen asserted that the hegemony of respectability politics was so intense that the contestants are essentially hazed, in the manner of Jen's drill team, in order to get them to perform as respectable subjects. Racialized hazing happened both on screen and off in a reciprocal manner. Again, Jen commented:

> I don't know when people are, like, Tyra Banks, blazing trails and stuff, it's like, no she's not. She's just, she's just doing [*pause*] . . . what was done to her. 'Cause she talked about that, I watched in her interviews talk about like, oh it's so hard being Black and or, or being the size that I was, I overcame this and that, but none of that is reflected in the people she chooses; in the end, whoever ends up winning really . . . [*trails off*]. I don't feel like this show, it's just like you guys said, it just reproduces, it's not changing anything.

Jen pointed out that Banks' respectability politics did not align with the ostensible mission of the show: to open up the modeling profession to more women of color and other so-called non-standard beauties. Instead, the show strictly regulated perceived difference. Through the logic of hazing, such regulation reproduced what was "done to her." The women's resistant commentary identified the cycle of hazing on screen, and hence ensured that it would not happen with them. They constructed their racialized critique in opposition to the images on screen.

The structure of *ANTM* made all differences equivalent by providing no discussion of social inequality. In their classic study on *The Cosby Show*, Sut Jhally and Justin Lewis explain a similar phenomenon, writing that "the series throws a veil of confusion over black people who are trying to comprehend the inequities of modern racism. It derails dissatisfaction with the system and converts it, almost miraculously, into acceptance of its values." Jhally and Lewis explain that the impact of such veiling is that, "in a culture where white people now refuse to acknowledge the existence of unequal opportunities, the political consequences of this acceptance are, for black people, disastrous."[30] *ANTM* also flattened structural difference to serve the myth of meritocracy, hard work, and the American dream. Instead of acknowledging that race, gender, or other identity categories held real weight as structures that enable or prevent success, as the women pointed out repeatedly, the show reframed difference. Jen put it this way: "she said you're quirky, your quirkiness, yours is your age, your height, for you it's your color."

Another physical difference that was racialized on *ANTM,* and that the women viewing the episodes often returned to, was weight and body image. In the women's estimation, managing size, or limiting the number of "plus size" models or how far they went in the competition, was another way of managing difference and creating an ultimate desire for uniformity and Whiteness, as in the women's discussions about skin color. Vanessa compared *ANTM*'s rejection of larger women to her own experiences with White women's relationship to her body and their bodies. Vanessa said that her self-image shifted because of her White female classmates. One aspect of her shifting self-image had to do with race and class: "I never, I never thought that I was, like, ghetto, or Black this, or Black that till I went to an all-White school . . . Like, I never . . . cause, like, I don't think I am! Like when I was in [a racially diverse] school from K-10, it was like, I'm the White girl, I talk White, I'm bougie, I'm this, I'm that."

Vanessa explained that, in settings with other African Americans, her own upper middle class upbringing (even as it was demeaned as "White") was visible to her classmates, but that, when she went to a predominantly White school, Blackness could only be seen as "ghetto." Similarly, when in a diverse school, she felt like, "I'm too skinny, I need to eat a backyard burger," a comment that prompted uproarious laughter from all of the women including Vanessa herself. Vanessa continued, "but then [*laughter*] when I [*laughter continues; McCall asks what's a backyard burger; Jen asks if it has to do with booty*]. Yeah, booty [*more laughter*]. But then when I go to, like, the White girls' schools, I'm the fat girl, like, I'm not. 'Oh, you're so fat,' [unidentified woman: "they say that?"] no, they don't say that. But it was, like, those girls were so daggone skinny . . . [yeah]. Like, I always thought I was small, but I don't know if they just don't feed White girls [*laughter*] where I was growing up, or, like, if it's just celery and asparagus." Camille interjected, "I think their body image is a lot different," to which Vanessa replied, "it must be, because, when I'm fat, so weird, 16 years old and you're that small."

As a college student, Vanessa could identify how her high school racialized and gendered sense of self was warped by her White female classmates' regulation of her body. Vanessa's critique of *ANTM* enabled her to name and critique the systems that affected her own self-worth. The conversation drifted back to skewed body image through representation on the show, allowing Micki to have the final word and remind everyone: "We're not talking about normal people [*Dez laughed*]. Fashion people [*beat*]. They think a size zero could be fat." Ending on a note of humor bolstered their spirits, re-centered their critiques as valid, and further built their collective, consciously racialized anti-strategically ambiguous, anti-respectability politics resistance.

Finally, the women also noted the ways in which *ANTM* managed difference by whitewashing history. The young women critiqued one episode shot with the theme of immigrants arriving voluntarily to Ellis Island. Jen commented: "having the Black people at Ellis Island like, they came of their own free will?" In one episode, the contestants completed a photoshoot in a Brazilian favela, an extremely poor neighborhood, something at which three of the students who had studied abroad in Brazil particularly recoiled. On that note, and furthering Jen's critique, Camille exclaimed: "Yeah, it was just kind of absurd to kind of just look at this huge photoshoot going on in the middle of a favela." Micki stated: "I wonder if they talk to the people, you know, we're going to be here, what's going on." In response to Micki, Camille remarked: "They're not really trying to explore Brazil, but they're in Brazil to understand that it's a fashion capital of the globe. And, like, everyone that they went and saw, all the designers, are White Brazilians. So it's kind of, like, this is a continuance of the American fashion industry, it's the same thing as everywhere else you go." Communication scholar Manoucheka Celeste notes that reality television shows that feature non-U.S. locations present "cultural and racial differences . . . primarily through signifiers ('tropical' music, fruit, and language) and the symbolic presence of those local populations (in stores, in streets, and on the beaches)."[31] In a similar vein, in his analysis of the reality television show *The Amazing Race*, Jonathan Gray writes: "This reduction of 'the Other' to backdrop, though, has been a key component of the simplistic rendering of foreign cultures for centuries."[32] Whether critiquing colorism, code-switching, size-ism, or physical appearance, the women rejected the abuses of power that characterized *ANTM*'s management of difference.

"What Was the Point of That in Relation to the Prize?": Reading Through Postrace

At one of our viewing sessions, we watched Tyra Banks recite a statistic that one-fifth of all teenagers wanted to be teen mothers, thus "you, as a model, have a responsibility." The group responded with collective groans and incredulous laughter. Micki complained: "What was the point of that in relation to the prize?" *ANTM* deployed statistics about teenage motherhood, which were particularly racialized as a coded, postracial racism. But not all audiences were enculturated, as these women demonstrate. The women's critiques of respectability politics and strategic ambiguity made it clear that, while they consumed a variety of Black representations, they were not consuming them blindly in search of role models, and they were not trying to mimic performances of respectability politics (which they took as facile), or center excessively thin White or light-skinned women or color (which they found problematic).

This chapter provided a look into what happened when women of color created a safe space for each other to abandon strategic ambiguity. What emerged was uncompromising critique. These young women provided a snapshot into a slice of strategic-ambiguity-free life. They knew what they didn't want to be: strategically ambiguous figures such as Tyra Banks. As they critiqued televisual instantiations of code-switching, respectability politics, colorism, stereotyping, and the management of difference, they made sense of their own racialized and gendered lives, and created racialized resistance, an anti-postracial, anti-strategically ambiguous response to respectability politics. In the next chapter, I will examine if the stories of television executives wield similar critiques, or if their identity negotiations look more like the celebrities I examine in part one of this book.

"Do Not Run Away from Your Blackness"

Black Women Television Workers and the Flouting of Strategic Ambiguity

Throughout this book, I have argued that women of color's access to privilege and power in mainstream or ostensibly egalitarian, meritocratic spaces, is contingent upon strategic ambiguity, the tricky dance of postracial resistance, which I define as a performance that uses the rhetorical tools of postrace in order to resist its ideological tenets. Thought of another way: strategic ambiguity is a coping strategy designed to deal with disproportionality. This book has talked about what it looks, sounds, and feels like when Black women manage to be successful despite having to constantly fight the everyday iterations of such disproportionality. Televisual representations, as the last two chapters demonstrate, can provide us with a much-needed reprieve. But what, precisely, do the microaggressions, the everyday moments of racialized sexism look, sound, and feel like for Black women television professionals who create diverse images in Hollywood, that grant us such a reprieve? And how do these women use strategic ambiguity, if at all?

Methodologically following the circuit of culture,[1] this book has arced from textual analysis to audience ethnography. In this final chapter, I move to another area of the circuit as I consider the creators of images, the ones who, in Stuart Hall's encoding/decoding model, are sending messages as, in John Caldwell's description, "prestige" (i.e., on the creative and executive end) cultural workers (by, through, and with the mitigating corporate forces of their studios).[2] Even though many media scholars utilize Hall's model, most of us don't examine how messages are encoded, even though, as Douglas Kellner explains, Hall hits all areas of the circuit by "focusing on how media institutions produce messages, how they circulate, and how audiences use or decode the messages to produce meaning."[3] In the last two chapters, I examined how certain audiences, a group of women of color sitting in front of screens, responded to racialized sexism; in this chapter, I look at the responses of the Black women who are behind the scenes in television, the writers, producers, directors, and studio executives. Would their responses look like the strategic ambiguity enacted by celebrities such as Michelle Obama, Oprah Winfrey, and Shonda Rhimes? Or would they articulate a form of resistance more like the audiences?

Between 2014 and 2016, I had a series of conversations with four prominent Black women in the Hollywood television industry, whom I call "Yvonne," "Cherise," "Yolanda," and "Valerie."[4] They are all in their 40s and 50s, and are successful writers, producers, directors, and executives, in addition to being mothers, wives, sisters, and daughters. None are Los Angeles natives; all came to LA in order to chase their dreams in the entertainment industry. Without the benefit of insider status or nepotism of any kind, they worked their ways up their ladders, proved themselves, and grabbed mentorship where they could. All expressed their gratitude at being in their current positions. These women, all of whom I met through colleagues, friends, or friends-of-friends, are well-established in Hollywood and boast scores of credits to their names. They knew I was writing a book and that it had something to do with Black women and television. All of the women wished me well, and offered generous and (often) unsolicited advice; as Yvonne said to me as a prelude to one such moment, "you're asking me for my path but I'm also giving you advice."

When interviewing them, my goal was not to capture some existential truth about Hollywood or make generalizations about all Black women Hollywood workers. Instead I hoped to hear their stories and see how they connected to my audience study as well as the celebrity performances I analyze in the first half of the book. I wanted to know how these incredibly successful women navigated elite spaces in Hollywood; I wanted to hear about their paths, their experiences, and the lessons that they had learned in the process. I did not describe postracial resistance or strategic ambiguity to them so as not to foreground my agenda in an interview situation or to bias them towards articulating what I "wanted to hear." But I listened to understand where they encountered racialized sexism, where they had to mete out their own critiques, and where they had to compromise themselves—particularly in a racialized and gendered way. This chapter provides notes towards a different form of resistance that falls somewhere between the celebrities and audiences, and somewhere between oppositional and negotiated resistance. I wanted to illustrate where the overlaps and similarities between approaches occurred. Moments of apparent redundancy are intentional to emphatically illustrate the points of overlap in these women's stories. As this chapter makes a foray into yet another area of media studies, I begin by considering scholarship in production and media industry studies.

Analyzing the "Culture of Performance": Production and Media Industry Studies of Race and Gender

Just as in the last two chapters, in this chapter, I claim larger cultural significance and not representativeness for all Black women or all women of color in Hollywood. I analyze a slice of what John Caldwell calls the "local cultures and social communities" of Hollywood workers by using media industry and production studies. This emerging area of media studies, Caldwell asserts, illuminates how "film/TV production communities" are not simply incidental to readings of the text, but are, into themselves, "cultural expressions."[5] In this chapter, I continue, in the words of Amanda Lotz, "assembling a toolkit"; adding the burgeoning field of media industry studies to my toolkit "emphasize[s] practices and processes of text creation and circulation that precede, although are constitutive of, audience creation."[6] Taking such a tack is timely at this particular moment, industry scholar David Hesmondalgh explains, because "media industries research and education are booming. Since hitting a low point of fashionability in the postmodernist and post-Marxist 1990s, media production and media industries research has bounced back."[7]

Production studies, Vicki Mayer, Miranda J. Banks, and John Thornton Caldwell note, "itself is a cultural production, mythological and branded much like the onscreen textual culture that media industries produce." This chapter, as my inroad into production studies, "draw[s its] intellectual impetus from cultural studies to look at the ways that culture both constitutes and reflects the relationships of power."[8] Including production studies ensures that the theory of postracial resistance through strategic ambiguity gets exercised across all aspects of media; as Banks writes, "production studies of media are predicated on the assumption that knowledge of the cultural and industrial modes of production will not just inform but alter one's reading not only of the media text, but of the media."[9] This chapter analyzes reflections of what Felicia D. Henderson calls the "culture of performance . . . how gender, race, and class figure into the rules, roles, and rituals that inhabit the writers' room"[10] in addition to other industry spaces. Indeed, Henderson, a media studies scholar and successful Black woman television producer in her own right, notes that "much of what happens in the creation of weekly storylines has very little to do with the actual writing of scripts. The human interactions in writers' rooms are forms of collective authorship because the sociocultural dynamics there heavily influence the narrative that finds its way to the page, and eventually to the screen."[11]

I draw from Henderson's notion of "collective authorship." Furthermore, while I do not claim that the women I interviewed represent all Black women in Hollywood, their experiences are worthy of study because they indicate larger race/gender dynamics. According to UCLA's Ralph J. Bunche Center for African American Studies's annual Hollywood Diversity Report (begun in 2014 and analyzing data from two years prior), in the 2013–14 television season, writers of color accounted for just 9.7% (a match to the previous season); this means that television writers of color were underrepresented that season by a factor of almost four to one.[12] Women were also underrepresented as TV writers but not nearly as dramatically, as they accounted for 32.5% of all writers credited for broadcast scripted shows. Race and gender are not analyzed together in these reports, so there are no factors for, for example, Black women. However, in 2012, African Americans comprised 4% of all WGA members, a small increase from 3.4% in 2007.[13] Over that same time period, women writers in WGA slightly decreased from 24.7% to 24.2%.[14] Looking at another measure, the wage gap, we can see that, over that same period of time, for every White man's dollar, women's earnings rose from $.80 to $.90, while "minority" earnings rose from $.76 to $.77.[15] Since the official reports don't disaggregate data for Black women, I asked sociologist Darnell Hunt, the lead author of the Hollywood Diversity reports, if he could share his numbers, and he generously did.

Of the 4599 total number of writers employed in 2012, there were 89 Black women writers, which amounted to 1.9 percent of all TV writers, while Black men amounted for 121 or 2.6%. To put this underrepresentation in perspective, the Black population of the U.S. is 13.2%. Furthermore, median earnings for employed Black women writers in 2012 was $98,155, as opposed to all female writers at $117,008, and all male writers at $127,537. Another measure that Hunt investigates in his reports is the 95th percentile of earners broken down by various demographic categories. 95th percentile earnings for Black women writers in 2012 was $357,191. However, the 95% earnings for White men was $704,844, which means that relative earnings for Black women writers at the 95th percentile in 2012 was 50 cents on the dollar.[16] Hunt and his team are investigating the racialized and gendered effects of what media scholars Timothy Havens and Amanda Lotz call the "political economy of media." When considering, for example, such stark disproportionality, we should also ask: "how much agency [do] we have to make our own choices?" Havens and Lotz answer that we have "a perspective of circumscribed agency, which assumes that the choices we make in our lives are not wholly our own, but neither are they simply imposed by outside forces."[17] The women I interviewed told me that they were not satisfied with circumscribed agency, and they fought for larger structural changes.

Indeed, when the successes of diverse network shows coming in the wake of Shonda Rhimes' many creations, namely *Empire* (2015–present), *Black-ish* (2014–present), *Fresh Off the Boat* (2015–present), and *Jane the Virgin* (2014–present), promised to usher in a different televisual landscape, not everyone celebrated. The backlash arrived far before the demographic data demonstrating a transformation in Hollywood. For example, one television columnist wrote of this moment: "as is the case with any sea change, the pendulum might have swung a bit too far in the opposite direction. Instead of opening the field for actors of any race to compete for any role in a color-blind manner, there has been a significant number of parts designated as ethnic this year [2015], making them off-limits for Caucasian actors, some agents signal."[18] With a dizzying array of mixed metaphors, the article continued to discuss the "flood of roles for ethnic actors" but sniped that the "talent pool of experience minority performers—especially in the younger range—is pretty limited." She went on to talk about the "quota of ethnic talent" and the subsequent shutting out of White actors. Such a column perhaps demonstrated pervasive Hollywood logic. But this columnist didn't have the last word. As I

shonda rhimes ⊘
@shondarhimes

🐦 Follow

1st Reaction:: HELL NO. Lemme take off my earrings,
somebody hold my purse!
2nd Reaction: Article is so ignorant I can't even be bothered.
9:50 PM - 24 Mar 2015

↩ ⇄ 2,494   ♥ 3,322

Figure 6.1. Rhimes' un-strategically ambiguous reaction. Image in Debbie Emery, "Shonda Rhimes Blasts Deadline Diversity Article as 'Ignorant,' Twitter Outraged." *The Wrap.* March 24, 2015. Viewed November 21, 2016. www.thewrap.com/.

demonstrated in chapter 3, Shonda Rhimes did (Figure 6.1). In reaction to this column, Rhimes wrote in an un-strategically ambiguous manner laden with Black woman code on Twitter: "1st Reaction: HELL NO. Lemme take off my earrings, somebody hold my purse! 2nd Reaction: Article is so ignorant I can't even be bothered."

At this moment, Rhimes refused to engage in coded, strategically ambiguous postracial language. Her twitter remarks gestured to the fact that disparities clearly happen behind the scenes, and in the writers' rooms. And the anti-people of color sentiment alongside the official numbers, while abysmal, only provide part of the picture. But what do Black women's stories tell us to help complete the picture? In this chapter, I focus on stories of four prominent Black women in Hollywood—three television writer/producer/directors and one studio legal counsel—to discern their thoughts on how Hollywood manages Blackness today, including the "post-Black" question and strategically ambiguous resistance through postrace. What happens when the culture the women represent butts up against television production culture? How is their membership into it both racialized and gendered, and thus considered perhaps contingent? How do they negotiate their contingent status and, in their negotiations, do they use strategic ambiguity? In the remaining parts of this chapter, I will showcase the women's stories of racialized/gendered barriers that are erected before and even once one becomes a player and, thus, how the game never ends.

"Working in the Ghetto": Segregation in Hollywood

Although all four of the women I interviewed work in television, their televisual landscapes are different, as they work in either comedy or drama, and the two genres are racialized very differently. As Cherise put it, "here's the running joke that I always say—drama is the North; it's very integrated. Comedy is the South; it's completely segregated." Valerie explained a similar sentiment, lamenting "the segregation of the Black sitcom writers and then . . . [*extended pause*] the world of drama." Cherise began working in Black comedy and moved to drama because, in her words, she didn't want to keep writing "into a stereotype that I didn't want to [uphold] . . . I didn't still want to write in it. And I didn't want to pitch, you know—I would have fights with people like, why is this woman running through the strip club with a frying pan? Aren't we trying to run away from that image? I didn't want to write in that, and [moving to drama] was a chance to write about real people to me." Whether in comedy or drama, these women fight the conventional Hollywood logic that, as Darnell Hunt articulates it, "successful programming must, first and foremost, comfort white audiences—the largest (but shrinking) racial block of viewers throughout most of commercial television's history—which is like religious doctrine whose implications for storytelling are accepted as matters of faith."[19]

Like Cherise, Yolanda made the move from comedy to drama, or what she deemed "from half hour to one hour." But Yolanda, who asserted that "I feel like one hour is friendlier to Black people in general," didn't balk at the content of half-hour Black comedies like Cherise; instead she felt the problems were structural ones. Yolanda explained that "what happened was, there used to be networks, UPN and the WB, and that's where a lot of sitcoms starring Black people were. So that's where, like, all the Black writers were. And once they went away, those two networks, you saw a lot of Black sitcom writers out of work." The shuttering of these two networks eliminated Black sitcoms, and hence jobs for Black writers. At the same time, structural problems prevented Black writers from becoming insiders because, as Yvonne said, "the staff writing position has been boxed out." With the changes in the structure of television, media scholar and showrunner Henderson explains, television writing has become an even more difficult arena in which to enter: "with the increase in short-order employment in cable and more and more examples following suit, a large number of writers—a critical mass of writers—are working on shows under the restrictive contracts."[20]

While all writers would have trouble getting jobs with this shift in industry practices, Black writers had extra difficulty finding other jobs as Hunt describes how "those with track records established on black situation comedies during UPN's heyday, were often typecast as only being able to write 'black' shows."[21] With the elimination of Black-oriented non-cable television stations, Black writers found themselves struggling to sell themselves in the segregated world of comedy. As Yolanda put it, "the thinking was, by a lot of White executive producers, 'you know, Black people can't be universal in their sense of humor. You know, White people can tell jokes for Black people *and* White people, but Black folks can only be comedic from their own perspective.'" Echoing the sentiments of all four of the women, Yolanda pointed out that racialized notions penetrate more deeply in comedy than drama. In drama, Yolanda noted, "I feel like the world is just a lot more open. It's not dependent on, you know, your sense of humor, whether that's universal or not, it's, 'I'm going to fill the room with different people who have different experiences to make my drama the best it can be,' you know?"

As opposed to comedy or half-hour, Cherise's experience in drama or one-hour was with integrated writers' rooms: "I saw a very mixed world of people just being seen as writers." Since the diversification of the writers' room was normative for Cherise throughout her career, when she got a job as an executive producer for a successful one hour drama, and "I got to hire—I replicated that. Because that's what I had come to find out . . . Come to grow up with. But a lot of people did not have that experience. Like a lot of people will say they've been on dramas where they're the only Black person." Cherise expressed optimism that, when it comes to the issue of diversity in Hollywood—"I think it's getting better"—but in the same breath she acknowledged that her optimism also comes from her experience in diverse writers' rooms which in itself makes her, in her own words, "an anomaly."

Valerie noted that "it's even hard for a Black writer to get in to get a job on a Black show, because the idea is that, 'oh you're a Black writer, you couldn't be on *Seinfeld* or on, on White sitcoms. The only voice that you could capture is that of Black sitcoms and Black characters.'" At the same time, Yvonne, whom the industry firmly identifies as a comedy writer (despite also having written a successful screenplay for a film drama), has both felt safety in Black comedy spaces, in which she describes experiencing almost all-Black writers' rooms, as well as feeling trapped into not being able to move to non-Black comedies. She started out noting: "I have to say this to the Universe, I am blessed. I have worked over twenty years in the business. I started writing the '90s when there were a lot of Black comedies on TV." But she also quickly admitted: "I have not had . . . the same financial and public success as my White counterparts, who do the same exact thing I do. I've had very few opportunities to staff on White shows. I only know of one Black co-executive producer in comedy who's gone onto a White show [This Black writer was hired onto a White show as an executive story editor and rose through the ranks]." Yvonne added: "White showrunners hire writers they've either worked with or writers who have worked with someone they know and trust, or are coming off a huge White comedy . . . which means they hire White people." Yvonne explained that such a practice of workplace discrimination and segregation in Hollywood is "called working in the ghetto." Yvonne's statements centered on two ideas: her gratitude for her success, and her understanding that her success is limited because it is contingent upon segregation and discrimination. As all four of the women asserted, this segregation and discrimination is tied to the issues of convention and genre—and the liminal position of Black women within each.

Liminality is racialized and gendered in Hollywood as in other privileged spaces across the United States. Valerie, who found herself as one of the only Black women in her workspace, explained how White executives mistook her for a secretary instead of a television executive. She explained that "you could be standing there in your [executive] outfit, with your briefcase and your navy suit and, you know, your glasses and looking like you know you could just walk right out of an ad and people would still, you know, it's just presumed . . . that you, surely, the White guy you're with who is the [secretary] must be the [executive] and you're the [secretary]." Valerie continued: "I think there's just these presumptions about particular professions that you know, that professor, doctor, lawyer, all these that just that, just not as between a White male and somebody else and that the White male gets the presumption."

Constantly navigating the misreading of one's professional identity, particularly when that identity is racialized and gendered, is exhausting.

"White Guys Run the Show": Black Women, Mentorship, and "Fitting In"

The women stressed to me numerous times that Hollywood, like so many elite industries, is not a meritocracy. What television shows they were able to work on were determined by whom they knew. They stressed how particular forms of mentorship, most often offered by White men for the career-enhancing purposes of other White men, garnered individuals entrée into elite spaces. Noting herself lucky—and unusual—to have received cross-racial mentorship, Cherise explained that she felt herself to be unique in that "there are very few people who had the opportunity to get mentored in [one long-running show she worked on], one of the fiercest camps in town." The high-profile show on which she worked and was mentored created a "springboard [that] is huge. And to have one of those, you know, king makers kind of tap you, it's— it's huge." Yolanda, who did not discuss having such mentorship, stated that, since "White guys run the shows, they want to feel comfortable, and the way they do that is surround themselves with people who look like them. And then they say and do things that aren't going to make them feel self-conscious about [being White guys]. If they happen to tell a joke that's offensive, no one is going to care, because everyone is of one race." The person of color thus functions as the fun police in this formulation, the hyper-sensitive, humorless dolt who sucks the creativity along with the enjoyment out of the room. Thus, people of color and women are rarely taken up as a mentee, a "little me" in Hollywood writers' room mentoring relationships.

Each of the women noted that beyond not registering as a "little me," women of color remain questionable in majority White male writers' rooms as those who "don't fit in." Valerie noted that the fear is "the struggle of people thinking, 'will this person fit,' 'cause that's the first thing the executive producer says when they're hiring a writer, 'how's this person gonna work in the room? Are they going to fit in?'" Furthermore, Valerie explained, while what the decision-makers might say is, "what kind of sensibility is she going to bring at the table?," really this type of coded, postracial language is "doublespeak for . . . 'is this Black woman going to fit in with the rest of the White guys or is she going to make us feel uncomfortable because she's going to bring up race issues and talk about gender and we just want to write our show?'" Valerie lamented that this issue never goes away for Black women as "the fitting in part is a constant hurdle: 'we don't know her, can she write characters who aren't Black or is she just the Black voice?'" White writers also express the presumption that diversifying the writers' room isn't really necessary: "we think we can write Black voice characters without her." In other words, before one is even allowed to interview for a job, a series of racialized and gendered assumptions limit Black women's access. In Valerie's assessment, the real challenge lay in "getting over those hurdles and that's like before anybody even looks at how well you write and all that other stuff, getting past that is what is, has been a real challenge for Black writers period."

Yvonne explained that the segregation of the genre means that Black writers simply have fewer options. She stated: "I'm sorry, I keep going back, but when you are on Black shows, you're working with Black writers . . . You know, everything is on recommendation. People hire people they know or they've worked with. So if you've only worked on Black shows, you need someone to create or get a job running a White show to hire you . . . for the most part, they're not coming off of a Black show. That White showrunner is going to need a recommendation, but he's probably not going to ask for a recommendation from someone they don't know, on a (Black) show they don't watch."

And recommendations can only take you as far as the shows that are greenlit by the studios. In Yvonne's words, "you know, when they go on, you go on. You know, you work because your reputation is set. So if they're just going onto Black shows, you're going onto Black shows." The problem is that separate is inherently unequal. Yvonne noted that the segregation of shows produces a racialized sponsorship model where "It's the White person that really has to pluck you off a Black show. Bottom line is you want to work with people who will move on to other shows, so they can hire you." She explained: "If you worked on [the White sitcom] *Frasier*, people from that show went on to run other shows and took their colleagues with them. If you were on [the Black sitcoms] *Living Single* or *Martin*, that *Frasier* showrunner won't be

looking for you." Because Black TV shows experienced a significant de-
cline in the first decade of the twenty-first century, and because writers
weren't largely in integrated writers' rooms, they didn't have the benefit
of being mentored into network television in sufficient numbers, or, in
turn, mentoring each other.

What Hollywood's racialized writers' economy means is that, again as
Valerie explained, while hiring a White writer can feel like a "sure thing,"
employing a Black writer always feels like one is "taking a chance," even
when that writer has a stellar resume. Valerie has seen how White showrunners "go to the same [White] people over and over again for the next
idea, the next show, when they think about like 'who do we wanna get
into a development deal with?'" The showrunners' first instincts will be
to say, in Valerie's words, "well, we know these ten people. They came in
and pitched us these ideas like, 'let's go with one of these ten." In Valerie's
words, "the way that the institution runs, is that showrunners pick people they know who they've worked with, who tend to look like them."
If someone tries to introduce a person of color, saying "what about this
person over here?," the response will be, "well, we don't really know that
person . . . I don't know if they can deliver." However, Valerie noted, in
the case of an inexperienced White person, "a network would be willing
to go with some relative unknown person, right, that [a White] somebody else has said is you know, credible, talented, all that, and hire a second show executive producer to back that person up because they don't
have the experience." White people are given jobs on a promise; people
of color earn jobs on the basis of over-qualifications.

In other words, Valerie has seen the situation where the network will
be so averse to diversifying the showrunners that "they're willing to take
a [White] person [with] relatively little experience . . . [and] they're willing to, like, bring in somebody else to help that person, like, get the
thing off the ground to deal with the inexperience issue." At the same
time, "like, say . . . in this other situation [we won't] take a chance per
se [with] a writer of color, who maybe comes to the table with maybe
not as much experience." But Valerie also stressed that this racist system
doesn't need to be a self-perpetuating one; laughing a bit ruefully, she
told me, "this issue [of women and people of color's exclusion] can be
overcome if there was serious push and commitment from the *top down*,
like, I don't care, I want a Black showrunner, I want, you know, I, I *insist*

that there be Black writers, women writers on the shows, and you're gonna do it or we're not hiring you." While those on the bottom can make incremental changes, true change can occur, Valerie noted, only if the most powerful members of an institution vocally and vociferously demand diversification.

"When They Go On, You Go On": Navigating Racist Culture and Racist Structures in Hollywood

In our conversations, all four of the women toggled between discussing the culture versus the structure of the industry. Both presented racialized and gendered barriers. Yvonne noted that the reproduction of White male dominance in Hollywood emerged from decisions being made, in her words, in "an ivory tower," or by an elite few White male executives within an industry that relies upon "the cult of the individual," in Durkehim's classic formulation.[22] Yvonne pointed out that "everyone wants the big star . . . and Black people, for whatever reason, have to be a really big star. Their Q [or quotient score—a rating of entertainment appeal] has to be huge so that they can get big numbers." Yvonne told me that TV executives ask: "who's the big person, who's the big get? . . . Who's hot? Who came off the hot whatever?" These questions, she said, do not set up African Americans in Hollywood for success; as she laughingly remarked, "if you are Black you don't come off the hot whatever."

Yvonne said that the heyday of Black sitcoms drew from standup— male standup where "back in the day . . . we had all these comedians that we would develop for." Standup is, of course, a very male space, as comedy scholars Mel Watkins illustrates in *On the Real Side* and Bambi Haggins notes in *Laughing Mad*.[23] A desire to write for "big stars, not big stories" means that there is no assumed universality to Black stories. Furthermore, in *Color by Fox*, Kristal Brent Zook identifies the first of the "four key elements of black-produced television" as "autobiography, meaning a tendency toward collective and individual authorship of black experience."[24] In addition, Zook notes, Black shows "have a tendency to revisit issues of deep significance to in-group audiences." She goes on to define "in-group" or "in-house" as "audience members who are not necessarily Black, but who identify with what may be described as shared 'black' positionalities, experiences, memories, or desires."[25]

Such Black shows came from a particular moment, what was produced by a particular set of programs intended to level the playing field. One of the structural ways that Hollywood has attempted to address the issues of the underrepresentation of women and people of color in writers' rooms was through various diversity initiatives, a number of which, as of this writing, are defunct. These programs were designed to, in the words of Miranda Banks, "create cultural producers with[in] a media industry [with] imagination, artistry, and inventiveness."[26] One of the first and most impactful programs, according to the women I interviewed, was the one Bill and Camille Cosby created, the currently suspended Guy Hanks and Marvin Miller Writing Program at USC. Colloquially known as the Cosby Workshop, this program for Black writers was created in 1993 for the explicit purpose of "deepen[ing] the participants [sic] appreciation for and comprehension of African American history and culture."[27] This program, which boasts alumni who "have written and produced for top ten shows on television as well as news and reality shows," chose up to fifteen participants for two evening meetings a week, one devoted to "lectures and discussions about African-American history and culture" and the second to workshopping scripts.

In a similar vein to the Cosby Workshop, ABC/Disney previously hosted a program called "the ABC Disney Diversity Program," which is also no longer active. Instead, as of this writing, ABC/Disney has a year-long "Writing Program" (no "diversity" in the title) as well as a five-week intensive program for Latino/a writers, the "National Latino Media Council (NLMC)/National Hispanic Media Coalition (NHMC) Television Writers Program."[28] Also now defunct is NBCUniversal's "Diversity Initiative for Writers."[29] As of this writing, CBS currently supports a "Writers Mentoring Program," which is listed under the network's "Diversity Institute," but, in a strikingly postracial manner, does not name race in its materials. For example, the website explains that "The CBS Writers Mentoring Program helps aspiring writers to understand the unwritten rules of breaking in and moving up. It is a combination of mentoring and networking opportunities."[30] The website does not describe race and gender in any of the actual application materials, despite the programs being organized under "diversity."

The women with whom I spoke entered the industry at an earlier moment in the 1990s, and three of the four of them reported going through previous "diversity programs." Yolanda said that her entry into Hollywood came through one of the formerly active diversity workshops. She noted that it "used to be [that] several studios had programs like this to try and get women, people of color, into the business. Because for so long, it's been a business open largely to White men." However, this workshop was not what she expected. Prior to attending the workshop, Yolanda anticipated it being a specific mentoring space for people of color, so she was surprised when on "the first day I look around, I think there was a Chinese guy, and one other Black woman, and myself. And that was it." Yolanda explained that she later found out that the studio workshop she attended became majority White after "so many White guys complained about it being unfair that [the studio] changed it . . . and it was no longer a diversity program . . . So anybody was able to get in." It appears as though the mere intimation of "reverse discrimination," absent the proof of actual demographic data, ended a series of programs intended to create a more level playing field.

In another attempt to address change structurally, the networks also created diversity initiatives designed to create incentives for showrunners to hire more people of color and women on their staff. The diversity initiatives, according to Cherise, have helped: "in terms of the mix on staff, it's getting better." However, she also noted that "there's a big problem now because of what occurred about 10 or 15 years ago, when the network started putting in diversity programs, what occurred was—and everyone feared this was going to happen—it incentivized showrunners to hire 'diverse,' but to get them free from the network." In other words, the "diverse" person, the writer of color, was not someone in which the network had made a long-term financial investment, much like hiring contingent labor (lecturers without multi-year contracts) in the university. Cherise explained that the result of this program was that, "when they were no longer free, a lot of people would fire that person and then hire another free person." As a result, "what happened was you didn't have enough people matriculating through the system. And you have a huge traffic jam at the *bottom* of the business." Echoing this sentiment, Darnell Hunt writes that "the major broadcast networks (with the exception of CBS) . . . offered programs that subsidized the placement of a 'diverse' writer on each of their current primetime shows." Hunt explains: "whether this foot in the door actually led to the long-term career opportunities for these writers is unclear. Anecdotal evidence suggests that the writers who filled the 'diverse' writer slots were sometimes marginalized in the writers' rooms, pegged as 'freebies' by other writers on staff, and frequently not asked to return after the initial season of employment."[31] This Band-Aid approach to diversity does nothing to attend to the gaping wound of underrepresentation in Hollywood.

The women also described the problem of the mere intimation of so-called reverse discrimination, what Cherise described as "a divide in the room where the White people look at the Black person or the Asian person or the Latino person as 'oh, you're the diversity person, you are already less than.'" This divide came not from facts of resumes or demographics but rather a fabricated postracial discourse of White disenfranchisement for minority enfranchisement. Cherise continued: "now you have this un- not even unspoken—this *chatter* among, you know, White people that 'the minorities are taking our jobs.' But the stats do not show that. They don't show that." Instead, what Cherise explained is that not only have people of color not taken over, but "people [of color] have not moved through [i.e., risen through the ranks to positions of power] enough. They're moving now, slowly, but enough people have not moved through. You don't have a ton of showrunners. But you have more than you had before but you don't have a ton. And you have a ton of people at the bottom who can't get to the top." Creating change from the bottom-up remained a tremendous challenge.

Like Cherise, Valerie also talked about the barriers in place that prevent diversification as she explained, from the top-down: "there's just a handful of people of color, whether it's [names two studios] you still can count the number of Black executives and know who they are throughout the company. Although you know the numbers are getting better but there's still, hmm, not where certainly I think they ought to be." Valerie described diversity in the decision-making executive roles as key to solving the "on-going challenge to get more people of color behind the camera in roles as writers, exec producers, directors, all of that." Like the other women, Valerie noted that "the industry, no matter what studio, it's sad, but it's just sort of across the board, it's just a system of nepotism and people hire the people they know and they've worked with." This nepotistic system counters the alleged spirit of diversity initiatives and as a result, "when you try to . . . just make the suggestion that, how about diverse candidates, you know, people, the showrunners feel very much put upon because they feel like you're somehow trying to lower the bar by making them hire minorities and women."

This notion of "lowering the bar" is a fallacy, Valerie illustrated, emphatically repeating herself, that hides the reality that "the people that they've *always* done business with, you know, who look like them, are the people who they feel comfortable with." This dynamic played out for Valerie when "I see that constantly on the shows that I work on, where we talk about the WGA initiatives, you know, where the company had said that we have to remind the showrunners of these initiatives; the corporate initiatives and WGA initiatives that you have to get a certain number of scripts. A fair numbers of like one or two scripts have to be given to freelance writers, and those freelance writers should be women or people of color." As a studio executive, Valerie enforced the initiatives where she must "remind them [the showrunners] constantly that they have to do it and the idea is that, well, if you gave these freelance scripts to these people of color and women, this would be an entrée and opportunity." Valerie clarified that, through the initiatives, the writers of color or female writers "wouldn't be staff writers, right, but at least they would get exposure and experience as a result of having written the script and that might open opportunities for them on other shows to get staffed."

But the response Valerie regularly received from showrunners is "like pulling teeth mentioning it on the production call [with me saying], 'hey what about the whole diversity thing, have you guys reached out?' [and them responding] 'oh yeah, we're taking [care of it], we're working on it,'" while never really making a change. The M.O. of the showrunners, Valerie explained, is that "towards the end of the season if there's 24 episodes, you know, like episode 22 and 24 are the freelance ones that finally, you know hmm, get rolled out" as diversity hires. Such tokenization means that the initiative candidate ended up "not get[ting] hired from that show at least, as a permanent person . . . [The hope is that] you get staffed as a staff writer and you move up each season, as, you know, a producer and you ultimately, you climb the ranks and hope that one day you can be a showrunner, but if you can never sorta get in the door, and follow a show for a couple of years to write so the ranks, so ultimately [never] get to a position where you could be a showrunner then." Even when programs and initiatives were rolled out to alter the structure of

Hollywood, White male culture proved itself intractable to change. The question remains of how the women dealt with such misreadings, and if they used postracial resistance through strategic ambiguity.

Not Just the First Five Names: Creating Our Own Networks

This chapter thus far has illustrated cultural and structural barriers to Black women in television that created few opportunities to even utilize postracial resistance through strategic ambiguity. But what happened when, despite all of these barriers, they made their ways into vaunted Hollywood spaces? The women I interviewed did describe performing strategic ambiguity, but it was in a manner related to, albeit markedly different, from both the celebrities whose performances I read in the first half of the book, and the young women audiences in the previous two chapters. Like the audiences and unlike the celebrity performances, what I found was their explicit *group* as opposed to *individual* orientation. In this group orientation, they described how they explicitly created their own diverse spaces. Like the celebrity women, and unlike the younger women who had yet to begin their professional careers, they had to learn how to compromise and play the long game. But the Hollywood women had their own very special inflection on strategic ambiguity.

Cherise noted that now that she had, in her word, "influence," she was able to spot how very easy it would be to hire an entirely non-diverse staff as the studio simply provides "the first five names." These first five names, Cherise clarified, are "just whoever the studio has, or the line producer gives you. Here's the first five names. It's not that they're the best, it's who that line producer knows." Instead of accepting those first five names, Cherise described her process as, "you can make more calls, you can ask." Diversifying is possible, Cherise explained, once you simply do a little more work and move beyond the preferred candidates, who are often White and male. In fact, she also noted that not just she moves beyond "the first five names": an increasingly pervasive collective orientation among her colleagues of color and female colleagues means that "an army of people . . . have reached out to me to say, 'hey, you're in the spot, here's a list of names. Here are all the inclusive names of EPs, production designers, of costumers, of writers, and that's key, you know?" Her networks are global, Cherise explained, because "now, it's like, somebody will email you from London and say, "hey, look at blah blah blah blah, I heard you're hiring, try blah blah blah blah." So, perhaps in a strategically ambiguous move, one accepts that list of the "first five names from the studio" in order to appear to accept help. However, what Cherise modeled was moving quickly to a mode of racialized resistance by refusing to follow traditional hiring scripts.

Another mode of racialized resistance comes about through fostering communities of Black television workers. Cherise noted that, now that she was in a more powerful, decision-making position, she also was able to forge a deeper connection to other African Americans in the industry. Also, notably, racial consciousness across the country has changed since 2014 with the advent of #BlackLivesMatter. As opposed to when she first moved to Hollywood, "I would say that the connection I have to my Black contemporaries is stronger now because we've woken up to" the importance of creating networks for Black folks. Cherise continued: "there's a fierceness to help and applaud and keep the momentum going for us. Whereas before, when you first get here, you're not thinking about it, you're like 'I have an audition, I want to get on the lot!' You know? You're just happy [to get any work]." Experiencing sustained rejection heightened Cherise's consciousness that true success was not just her walking through the door, but holding it open for others. This came about with her own success, but also with the change in the political tide of the country.

Creating networks for women and people of color is so vital because the rewards of working on a show long-term (and not just in a single episode or two as the "diversity hire") are tremendous, not just for community connections but for financial security. As Cherise explained about one very successful show she worked on, "when you have been on a show the duration of the show, that's your children's college money, that's a house, that's paying for your parents, that's taking a vacation to Africa or Europe, there's a lot more that can happen. And that's why the parity is so important for us." Such parity doesn't happen accidentally: "it takes work . . . You can't just say, okay, I'm going to hire [White male] Johnny" because Johnny is the one always being offered up as the expected candidate. To put it starkly: "there's been such a monopoly [of White hires in Hollywood] because there's so much money being made. And when there's money, people keep other people out." Exclusion is monetized, just as it's racialized and gendered.

"Backhanded Compliments": Resisting Postracial Racism

When the women did make it through the door to elite Hollywood spaces, as my Hollywood executives did, they experienced racism and sexism that felt hard to flush out because it was coded, postracial, and what is now more popularly deemed microaggressions. For example, Valerie described being given the, in her words, "backhanded compliment" of someone saying "I do not see race, [or see you as a] Black woman, you're just [Valerie]." To this sentiment, Valerie responded, "I don't think it's credible frankly for somebody to look at me and say [that]." She explained, "I'm okay with people seeing race," as to her seeing race was not a negative. Furthermore, she argued, "I don't think Black people are walking around and saying that they don't see race . . . [But] I think that White people think it's a source of comfort to us if they tell us that they don't see race and I think it's just quite the opposite . . . the reality is that we . . . *don't* live in a colorblind society and I don't even think that should ever be the goal, because diversity, how can you celebrate diversity if you deny that there's, there are differences?" What Valerie illuminated here is the hypocrisy of the commonly stated adage "celebrate diversity" that emerges from Hollywood studios, universities, and other institutions across the country. Her intervention—a consciously racialized one—was to point out this hypocrisy in a markedly un-postracial manner.

Cherise enacted a similar positionality when she described how the racialized sexism she received was often one of tokenization, or having to speak for her entire race. For example, "I've had experiences this way probably on every room I've been in, where someone turns to you and they say, "well, would Black people do that? What do you think? Would Black people do that?" Cherise's response was often one of humor, as she recalled remarking, "You know, I have to go to the meeting and ask them, 'cause I only know a hundred Black people. I don't know all of the Black people." But even when she responded with humor, she girded herself for the response, "oh my god, she's Black, here she goes again." In addition to humor, Cherise said one of her approaches was simply to not waste her time educating her White colleagues about their ignorance: "I'm not going to be the arbiter of Black thought for my staff."

Cherise has, however, had to respond with more than humor or ignoring ignorant responses when the racialized sexism she encountered was far from coded and polite. For example, she described how, "I've been in rooms where the n-word has been thrown out as a joke, and a lot of people have experienced this, some form of the n-word coming out, and where conversations have to be had, and where it's left rooms shocked like 'oh my gosh' and then you have to sort of deal with it." As she took her position as a role model seriously, Cherise explained that she dealt with such explicit racism head-on not only for herself but for her staff as "when you get up higher, you are higher-leveled, and other younger writers are looking up to you." In addition to workspaces like writers' rooms, she has also experienced such racist "jokes" from her colleagues in social spaces: "I've gone to the Christmas party where someone's drunk and they go, 'oh my god, here's our diversity hire!'" Cherise continued, "I've written 35 scripts for television, and I'm an executive producer, a co-executive producer, and someone says that to me. And I have to think about how, in my Christmas dress, next to my husband, to check the person and still not be Angela Davis, you know what I mean?" The stereotype of the Angry Black Woman follows her around even—or perhaps especially—when she herself is the victim of racism and, yet, unlike the celebrities dogged with this stereotype, as I examine in part one of this book, she described how she regularly responded in a forthright manner, naming and addressing the racism and sexism.

Yolanda also took a forthright tact. She described her experiences of racialized sexism as ones that functioned as singular assumptions about Blackness. For example, Yolanda explained, "I was on one show [when] someone just turned to me and said—okay this used to get me—'she doesn't sound Black.' Like, referring to an actor. We were sitting in a casting session." Yolanda immediately decoded that "what they meant was the actor sounds too educated. I always thought that was offensive because I'm like, okay, so being Black is the equivalent to sounding uneducated?" Yolanda experienced frustration with coded, postracial racism that was also classed. She wanted to tell the person: "Just say what you're trying to say. Which is: well, we want someone who is going to play an individual from a poor neighborhood." Yolanda told me that she wanted to explain to her White colleagues that "they just categorized everybody, and [they made the assumption that] suddenly if you don't sound, you know, 'ghetto,' then you're not Black." Instead, her response to such a statement, she recalled, was more strategically ambiguous. She recalled saying, "you guys, White people can have a Southern accent, or a surfer accent, all these different ways that they talk, and they're all White. You never doubt that they're White, you know? But, like, Black people, the minute they sound educated, they're sounding White. Why do you think that?" Yolanda used a classic approach of interrupting microaggressions by throwing a racist statement back in the face of the speaker and politely posing a series of questioning about the assumptions. However, Yolanda noted that this postracially resistant approach—one of strategic ambiguity that cautiously did not name ra*cism*—didn't work on her White writing colleagues: "Like some people would say, 'yeah, but you know what we mean.' You know, some people would go, 'Yeah I hear you, I hear you' . . . But they would *always* still use the words, 'he doesn't sound Black.' They would still say that. So it kind of went in one ear and out the other." While strategic ambiguity might be one type of response to racism, Yolanda's story illustrates that it did not always provide the opportunity for an anti-racist intervention. Moreover, Yolanda's postracially resistant response was too subtle for her colleagues to understand the weight of their racist comments and then take the next step: change their behavior.

"Why Does She Have to Be the Sassy Black Girl?": Interventions through Education

All of the women found their own ways of intervening in racialized sexism. One particular moment stood out for Valerie. She noted that "I have in the past given the note back about [the only Black female character on one show on which she worked], 'why does she have to be the sassy Black girl?'" Valerie balked at how this particular character often became a racialized caricature when the writers insisted that, in this diverse cast show, "she's the one that speaks the Black vernacular." Valerie always found herself saying, "why is that?" Valerie remembered one moment when the writers had the character saying, "'bed time is for suckers,' like s-u-c-k-a-s." Even though Valerie's executive job on this show was to comment on, "oh that's defamatory, can't say this, can't say that," when she saw this line in the script, she felt compelled to push back. She noted, "I just had to make a comment on this because it's just like a flood gate opened up" where she wanted to tell the writers, "you know this sounds like Aunt Esther?," the comedian LaWanda Page who co-starred in the 1970s-era sitcom *Sanford and Son*. Instead of pointing out this similarity right away, Valerie wrote a note that included a statement, "I just can't imagine one of the Obama girls saying something like this." Valerie's subtlety—her strategically ambiguous approach—did not register with the writers as "the person that got the notes wrote me back, 'not sure what the Obama reference is about on page 24? Did we mention the Obama girls in the script and I missed it . . . ?'"

When Valerie's attempt at subtlety failed, she said that while "a part of me was, like, 'don't respond any further,'" she was resigned to the fact that, "now I'm gonna have to break it down . . . really?" She sent over:

> a clip of Aunt Esther saying, you know, 'I'm gonna get . . . you sucka,' whatever . . . I'm like, this is just her getting back to an era in which Black sitcom television writing and the sassy Black girl and you know why is it that [this character doesn't] . . . speak like this but yet periodically there are things that come out of her mouth that sound like the 70's sitcom. And no, I don't imagine that President Obama's daughters ever had heard the word "'sucka" uttered in their household nor would they ever repeat it to another adult. It's not even the words of a child. It's not even like a slang term that the kids these days would say . . . It is adults who grew up in that era, who grew up watching Willis and *Different Strokes*, and . . . and you know all those 70's sitcoms and have decided *today*, that those words should come out of this child's mouth because she's Black.

This moment of educating her colleagues got them to understand their use of racist dialogue, but, more importantly, prompted them to change the script as, in Valerie's words, "they were just like [*uses a little voice*], 'okay, okay we'll change it.'" Valerie's approach was not a subtle, post-tracially resistant, strategically ambiguous one. It was an exhaustingly thorough, research-driven presentation that could leave the person making such an intervention with emotional exhaustion, or what psychologist William Smith deems "racial battle fatigue."[32]

For Valerie, this anti-racist intervention was worth all of the effort. After sharing this story, Valerie noted: "I feel like, in the position that I'm in, there are a few moments where you do have the opportunity to, to speak up and say something that will enlighten people who probably don't even . . . like, they're thinking it's funny and they're not imaging sort of how, what that term, like me sitting home at . . . five, like, with children and hearing a little Black girl on the television saying that, like . . . what, what that brings to mind." In other words, Valerie noted that the writers weren't thinking about audiences of color. While Valerie remarked that she must choose her battles, she was constantly frustrated by the fact that White "people just really don't know" about the impact of their images on perpetuating racism and sexism.

Valerie's intervention was a significant one to her, because, as she said, speaking up made her feel like "well, at least today, in this moment, I made a difference." She continued, "and that's all you can do, when there's no critical mass of Black people, or Black women, whatever the industry is. You have these moments." Such moments of education are "how you make the case of diversity other than the fact that you know it's good business and all that sort of thing, and the right thing to do and all of that but that, you know, it helps to make the programming, the content, the environment, like richer when there are more voices at the table." Notably, Valerie used the plural "voices"—advocating for more than one—as opposed to a singular "voice" at the table. Finally, speaking up "educates people who may not have thought about certain perspectives and everyone can feel more included in the process and the end-product is richer for it."

Valerie described an intervention such as this as "my little Black moment where I speak up on something." To Valerie, a "Black moment" meant refusing to remain silent in the face of racism. She noted that "if they shoot it down, I, you know I always think of what [an older Black male mentor], you know, used to say . . . : when you speak up and by so doing you may alienate people, you may end up losing at the end of the day, but you, it's a triumph, because you spoke out against an *injustice* and you tried to make a *difference*." Despite dealing with the seeming intractability of structural inequality, moments of speaking up "are the things that sort of bolster your self-esteem and allow you to, you know, sort of reconcile the conflicts sometimes of being in situations where you're like, 'am I helping or hurting the cause?'" Valerie lived by the moral code where, "when you stay silent in a moment where you know, you need to say something that even people have less respect for you for *not* saying something." She explained, "you don't necessarily want people to look around the room and say, 'hey you're Black, what do you think?,' but at the same time when something clearly comes up that's, that's . . . you could say something and you know, you're not gonna get fired for it [*laughs*] you know, why not? Why not do it?" In other words, while postracial resistance through strategic ambiguity might have been Valerie's first response, when that didn't work, she spoke up, educated people on their racism and sexism, and changed a representation before it arrived on screen.

Cherise explained her similar approach thusly: "I have made it my business to be a really straight shooter, and when I see racial shit, when I see bullshit, I call [people] on it." Cherise gave the example of illuminating racism: "I've been on shows where you hear from the network or the studio's side where it's been coded language of, 'Oh, if we're going to kill [a character] it has to be someone we care about and that normally involves blonde hair.'" Cherise called out coded postracial racism—that White lives, and particularly White female ones (as "blonde" is a shorthand here for blonde woman) are more valuable than Black ones—by name. This was the same sentiment Yvonne described as the studio logic that "you got to give White people something to look at a little bit." Another code Cherise unpacked as racist is "there's too many [people of color]—it's getting too Benetton-y. I've heard it." What this meant to Cherise was not just that the cast was getting too diverse, but rather "the coded language of a fear of too much Blackness." And Cherise responded: "when that occurs you have to fight back." Cherise provided an example of what that fighting back looked like: "when I was on a show, I wanted to do a [Hurricane] Katrina episode, and during the Katrina episode, prior to that, there had been a bunch of episodes that had minorities. I got asked, could I do the Katrina episode and make the person White. And I was like, absolutely not." In this example, Cherise noted, "I've never learned why it was happening, I was never told why it was happening, but I *knew* why it was happening." In other words, Cherise didn't need to be told that the only way that her show could make palatable what was racialized as a *Black* issue [Hurricane Katrina], was through the story of a *White* protagonist. She responded with a racially resistant "absolutely not."

This silent and default centering of Whiteness at the heart of a show has made it difficult at times for Yolanda to advocate for storylines with

Black characters. She explained: "one show I was on this [showrunner] never wanted to write stories for Black characters because, in his mind, the stories always had to do with their Blackness. As opposed to just them living their lives. And he shied away from it." The result was, Yolanda explained, "he didn't cast any Black people or they didn't have anything to do. Whereas all the White people, they're living their lives, they're having affairs, they're doing this and that, it has nothing to do with their color." In other words, White characters are allowed simple humanity in the eyes of a White showrunner, while the only personality trait Black characters are allowed is their race.

Cherise was clear that negotiating through racism and sexism was always a part of the job as "on a daily level, I've experienced so much of it." For example, she expounded, "I've experienced it with hiring someone and someone says, "well, why do you want to hire her, when there's already you?" Cherise noted that she didn't let comments such as these slide, as she remembered responding, "'oh, so she and I are both Black, we have the same kind of skin, and we have the exact same experience because we all sort of fell from the Black tree.' Like *what*?" Responding with incredulous questions was also a favorite strategy of Cherise's. Her philosophy about responding to racialized sexism was: "I don't let it fester. I snap right back." Cherise also protected herself after a racist encounter: "When I see the rest of the stuff I just sort of cut that person out of my personal existence. I don't try to figure them out because I can't, you know." This was an important point. Cherise didn't feel the need to fix an individual's racism; she felt the need to bring the racism to the light and protect herself from continuing to be hurt by the racist behavior.

At the same time, all of the women noted that responding to racism and racialized sexism could be difficult precisely because of their postracial coded nature. Yolanda explained: "You have to remember, too, a lot of times, is that the people who are writing these shows are fairly liberal and usually highly educated, like us. So even if they're thinking something, they know enough not to say it." What postracial racism can produce is a lack of ability to respond in anything but code, à la strategic ambiguity. Hollywood is known as a very White, but politically liberal space. For minoritized cultural workers and, as media studies scholar Yeidy Rivery argues, cultural critics, this presents an atmosphere that is "more challenging [as] . . . the locations in which political rule is aligned with the left but those in power have appropriated some dictatorial practices similar to those in right-wing regimes."[33] Studio systems, as described by the women, appear to have much in common with such dictatorial regimes.

Coded racism and sexism meant that one rarely if ever received confirmation that rejection was on the basis of race and gender. For Yvonne, even though she knew when studios were passing on her materials because they were too Black-woman-specific, she was not told that in a forthright manner. Instead, the studio "never give[s] you real reasons." They might say instead, "We really liked it but we have something like it." Or perhaps they might say, "we're just not sure." For Yvonne, while the language is "really vague," she was also used to the studios beaming right back to her, "but we love Yvonne. We want to be in the Yvonne business." Yvonne sees this particularly if she is trying to shop a show with "a Black female lead. If you had a Black male, for whatever [reason, it's easier]. I think White guys think they are looking at football players. I mean, look how incredibly happy are they with [former football player and current morning television host] Michael Strahan? Crazy!" What this created for Yvonne was a scenario where strategic ambiguity reigned as the most popular resistant strategy as other Black writers were "not pushing back. We need to get that job and pay our mortgage. I mean, we're just not." Yvonne's response to a studio's attempt to switch a Black lead with a White one was to say simply, "'I think you're mistaken,' and then I'm done." She chose not to fight that battle as "there's nothing" she could do to change a studio executive's mind once it was made up.

When not outright rejection, racism and sexism looked like a subtler refusal that remained coded. For example, Cherise noted, "I've seen crews turn on directors or not give a director respect and I've seen the signs of people sort of undermining somebody that could be a White woman or a person of color that is directing for the first time on a show and they do not do the same thing when there's a White male." The motivation for the crew's lack of respect was the "assumption that this person got here doing less," even though Cherise argued, "nine times out of ten, this person got here doing more." What postracial racism also looked like—stunningly similar to explicitly stated racism—was a lack of equal opportunities.

Yvonne noted that, for African American women actresses, in particular, "the opportunities are just so ridiculously small." And postracial racism in the form, ironically, of diversity rhetoric has had something to do with it. According to Yvonne, instead of wanting to cast a Black actress, "now it has become women of color." To fulfil networks' narrow check-off boxes of diversity, "if you're Latina, that's Black. If you're Indian, if you're Mindy Kaling, that's Black." As opposed to Black women, other women of color are "White-friendly with long hair and not Black. So that is your diversity, it's called women of color. It used to be that Black was the women of color. [Now] it's . . . [Latina actress] Sofia Vergara, who is the highest paid woman on television. That's your diversity highlight [*laughs*]. I mean! Really. But she's attractive to White men, Black men."

In contrast, "Black women, we do not have that standard of beauty or that standard of acceptance or whatever you want to call it. If Halle Berry can't crack that [then no Black woman can]." What this means in terms of greenlighting new shows, Yvonne noted, is that "everybody is looking for diversity as opposed to the Black show." Valerie agreed that casting Black women wasn't the networks' priority as "the number one focus of right now across the board is how do we get more of Latino-themed programing on the airways, because everybody is dialed in to the fact that, you know, Latinos are the super-majority and that everybody wants to have programming that speaks to that demographic and you see and hear about it." The multicultural universe, according to Yvonne and Valerie, has not meant greater diversity overall, or fewer White representations, just fewer Black ones. Such White supremacist logic fomented a crabs-in-a-barrel mentality, pitting groups of color against each other, and yet not significantly increasing the presence of any groups of color either in front of or behind the screens.

"Social Isolation": It's Lonely Being the Only

One of the most challenging effects of postracial racism that the women discussed was the isolation. As Cherise put it, "It's been very lonely because I think when you move out here, you believe the race stuff won't happen to you so you don't have to deal with it." What this meant was that one wasn't naming racism and sexism as they were happening, and one wasn't creating resistant communities to counter racist and sexist discourses. But eventually, Cherise explained, "time goes on and you go, 'oh my god, this is what my parents were talking about; oh my god this is what they meant by 'you have to work twice as hard', and then you go, 'oh, you actually have to work four times as hard.'" Such a realization can be devastating, Cherise noted, because, after struggling for so long, "you look up and realize you've worked yourself to death and some of your [White] contemporaries just have so much more and they did less." Having remarkable creative products or impressive collegial behavior was also no guarantee to success, as "half the stuff that you see occur, you don't necessarily see; you know that if you were Black and you did it, it would never fly."

Such struggles on the way to success were compounded by what Cherise described as "social isolation." She noted, "when I say the lonely part, I just say it because there's not enough of us to literally have camaraderie and you have to be so cautious talking about [racism] with White people because you don't want to feel like you're bringing up race all the time." Despite climbing the ladder, Cherise said, loneliness "doesn't stop, no matter how big you get." She told a story where, "I went out with [a Black Hollywood executive] recently who is very, very, very powerful, and they said to me they don't get invited to parties, they have to always re-introduce themselves when they're out, and when they were saying this, that they don't get invited to play tennis on the weekends, to drive out to Palm Springs, when they were saying this, I said, 'that's the sort of isolation, the social isolation that can happen.' I said, 'it's a battle that everyone fights.'" Cherise's response to the social isolation was to "just keep doing, just doing the work.'"

Part of what fortified all of the women in the face of loneliness was the sense that they were making a difference. All of the women paid homage to mentors and groundbreakers of the past, and the one they all mentioned with great respect and pride was Yvette Lee Bowser, creator of *Living Single* and, according to journalist and critic Kristal Brent Zook, the "first African American woman to launch a successful primetime series for network television."[34] In addition, without exception, every one of the women circled around to Shonda Rhimes at least once in their interviews. Towards the end of the interview, Cherise noted, "the last thing I'd say is that because of Shonda Rhimes, and because of how she has been able to open the door, just visually, and what she has been able to accomplish, I'd say [to aspiring TV writers] do not run away from your Blackness. Because that is your gift."

Cherise explained that, "for so long, we were not allowed to write Black leads, we were not allowed to write African American shows. If you pitched to your agent a Black drama, they would say, 'that would never sell.' And they would say that won't sell overseas." The result of being constantly rejected was that, in Cherise's words,

> a lot of Black writers unconsciously push down the Blackness thinking, in order for us to make it, we have to show that we can write [White people] really well. And we've mastered the art of writing about the Irish cop because we had to do it in order to get jobs. But [*long pause*] . . . we now exist and we're not going anywhere [*long pause*]. . . . we now exist and if you want to write about the Irish cop, go for it! Go for it—but now the studios and the networks won't laugh at you if you come in and you pitch a Black drama, a Black family drama. They won't laugh at you, so don't run from doing that because we need those stories told and we've got to—people fought so we could tell them, so don't run away from telling them . . . I see it in younger writers, and they go, "I don't know if I want to do that because it's Black," and they're so worried about getting pigeon-holed but they don't actually know the fight that occurred to finally have a diverse television landscape. So tell the stories. Just keep telling them.

For Cherise, Rhimes' success showed the value in showcasing their own Black lives on television.

On the other hand, Yolanda opined that folks shouldn't mistake Rhimes' success for major shifts in the industry. She noted, "Shonda's success is just an individual thing. And she's just like a unicorn, I mean it's just unbelievable and phenomenal. She owns ABC. It's an amazing thing." She was the only, the exception; the figure that becomes successful through strategic ambiguity. But then Yolanda countered her own position, making the clarification between behind and in front of the camera: "I think the biggest impact she's had is in front of the camera, you know? I think now people, her shows and *Empire*, have changed the way people [*trails off*] . . . they're all about money, that's all they care about, so it's not necessarily Black vs. White, it's just this show, can we sell advertising dollars? And if people buy a show with all Black people, then we don't give a shit." As she talked, Yolanda explained, "this [2015–2016 television] season, especially after *Empire*, it was like everybody was trying to put a Black person on a TV show. As if it was new information that Black people wanted to see themselves on TV." Yolanda was frustrated with this response, as it was "a product or a result of not having enough Black executives." As a result, diversification is "just a slow, slow process."

Where Yolanda calls Rhimes "a unicorn," Yvonne calls her "lighting in a bottle." She said this phrase again, repeating, "It's fantastic and . . . I can't explain it, I can't explain it. It is lightning in a bottle." Yvonne also noted a potential Shonda Rhimes trickle-down effect: "we're proud and it also makes you go . . . it does this, for me, I think. We can do more than write your momma jokes or, you know, the stories about Black people in the ghetto. We've got a lot of stories to tell. And I think, you know, I think people go, oh look at that! Maybe I will take that meeting, maybe she has something different than my momma's on crack."

Valerie noted that "Shonda Rhimes has blown up with her dramas because that's just, being able to cross over, has been a huge challenge and then once on a sitcom, getting out of the sphere of the Black shows and being perceived as a writer who had, who can capture the voice of non-Black characters, I think has been the struggle, you know for the sitcom writers." Valerie continued: "I think she's masterful. I've said this ever since *Grey's Anatomy* . . . we talk about what constitutes a Black show, is it an all-Black cast? Or is it who's behind the camera?" Valerie voted that it was, indeed, who's behind the camera, "because, you know, the imagery, that we've been so critical of from the 70's sitcoms, the way Blacks were portrayed in those shows, you know, who was behind putting those images for . . . right? So it wasn't Black, you say, you say those are Black shows because they had a Black cast but yet the stereotypes that we're reinforcing."

In contrast, Valerie asserted, with "*Grey's Anatomy*, I think Shonda Rhimes was so masterful because, she had a, you know, the protagonist was a White character but yet the cast was so multicultural." Valerie described Rhimes' approach as "it's like you're sneaking in the fact that your three leads were Black . . . And so it's the point where she gets to *Scandal* people aren't even receiving that as a Black show and you get to *How to get Away with Murder* and if you see the trailer you've got Viola Davis marries the White guy, saying you slept with that White whore . . . you know and nobody is saying oh my God it's racist . . . what is Shonda Rhimes doing?" To Valerie, Rhimes' strategically ambiguous approach was to "sneak [race] in there . . . [so] people don't even realize that you can talk about these issues." This was an impressive magic trick to Valerie, but not necessarily one she wanted to emulate.[35]

Conclusion: "You Can Never Be Sure What's Happening"

The approach I take in this chapter, one of making inroads into the emerging field of media industry studies, can, in the words of Douglas Kellner, "help individuals become aware of the connections between media and forces of domination and resistance, and can help make audiences more critical and informed consumers and producers of their culture."[36] In addition, introducing "the question of ideologies present in media texts," Timothy Havens and Amanda Lotz note, "brings us quickly to debates about the autonomy or agency of the people who work in the media industries." In other words, are "talented individuals expressing their creative visions for clear political and ideological ends, or are they merely cogs in corporate machines trying to satiate the masses by producing texts full of ideological messages that maintain the interests of those in power?" Summarizing the debates in media industry studies, Havens and Lotz note: "by the time creative workers in most industries achieve a degree of autonomy, they have already internalized the worldviews of the corporations they work for."[37] Given the opportunity I imagine that the television executives and my audience group would commiserate about the racist and sexist structures in their lives, and share strategies for flouting strategic ambiguity in order to perform postracial resistance.

I want to end here with an illustrative story from Yolanda. Echoing Oprah Winfrey in chapter 2, she noted that racialized sexism managed to bubble up just about every day—but in hard-to-pin-down ways. She explained, "the tough thing, racism—here's the thing: you can never be sure that's what's happening. That's the tough thing with racism or sexism in this business. 'Cause of course no one is going to *say* that." At the same time, Yolanda noted, "I did have an experience on one show, where I was the only woman on the show, and I was the only person to not get more than one script. I approached the EP [executive producer], and I was like, 'Why? You know all the guys got two, sometimes three scripts.' He wrote it off as, 'well, it's only because we had a truncated season, we didn't get a full season ordered; next season you'll get more.'" Yolanda patiently waited until the next season but discovered then, "the next season wasn't much better. I got two [scripts], but the second one I had to split. Whereas no one else had to do that. Even the White guys who were lower [in experience and job title] than me." It's moments like this that caused Yolanda to stop questioning herself and know that racism and sexism were to blame for her being shut out of opportunities. After going through every possibility for an alternate explanation she acknowledged, "so I was like . . . okay . . . I can't think of any other reason." This was a moment where she did not have the power to resist. And yet she squirreled this experience away and kept going. In continuing to write, to produce, to create, she met success, and moved from postracial resistance and strategic ambiguity to a racialized resistance that facilitated not just her success, but the success of large groups of other women and people of color in Hollywood.

Coda

"Have a Seat at My *Table"*

In the introduction to this book, I presented Kerry Washington's notion of taking a seat at the table as one at the heart of postracial resistance and strategic ambiguity. Washington's logic seems to go like this: in order to be invited into elite spaces, women of color must politely point out the importance of our inclusion. If we are "lucky enough" to be chosen, we join a very traditional table where we are the only or one of very few who are included. Our inclusion is contingent not only upon the majority's maintaining our numbers as small but also upon us following a series of strict rules imposed upon minoritized people by the majority. Such rules include participating politely but not taking over (possibly smiling more than talking); following gendered as well as racialized norms (perhaps keeping our feet tucked neatly behind our chairs); and veering away from contentious topics (most definitely keeping the table upright and intact). In essence, if we want to be invited, if we want to remain at the dinner party, and if we want to be asked back, we must stay resolutely and entirely in our place.

Like celebrity actress Kerry Washington, superstars Michelle Obama, Oprah Winfrey, and Shonda Rhimes have all managed to score invitations to this exclusive table. And yet, while they might have once followed these strict rules, they are now writing their own rules; the women whose images we consume today do not, by any means, appear to be cowed by any invitation they might receive. None of these women fit the description of polite ladies who stay in their place. They are groundbreakers, role models, and powerhouses, whose first experience of being invited to the table eventually turned into them being the ones doling out the invitations. But, to do so, they have also cracked a certain code of strategic ambiguity, which has meant both crossing-over and compromising. The young women in my audience study and the Black women television executives I interviewed wanted to join the table too, and, in the case of the Hollywood women, garnered their own invitations, but they saw the rules of the table differently than the celebrity icons. The women I spoke to saw the table more akin to the table that singer, songwriter, and performer Solange Knowles conjures in her 2016 album *A Seat at the Table*. Solange helps her listeners envision a new table that facilitates different modes of minoritized engagement.[1] In this third studio album, which debuted at number one on the Billboard charts, Solange pushes back on those with limited expectations of her— including music critics admonishing her to not become too radical so as not to alienate her White audiences or, as she recalls one critic put it, "bite the hand that feeds you."[2] She includes interludes from Southern rapper Master P on Black resilience, from her father Matthew Knowles on facing racialized violence when integrating his school, and from her mother Tina Lawson on Black beauty and White anger.

Critic Daphne Brooks calls Solange the bearer of "urgent, necessary, multifaceted, Black feminist sonic activism." She is, Brooks explains, "an artist who's galvanizing statements about the nature of Black freedom, Black movement, and Black imagination on the move that have quickly become the soundtrack to our current moment of ongoing resistance and resurgent struggle."[3] By creating #BlackLivesMatter era protest music, Solange urges her listeners to resist, refuse, and reject the traditional seat at the table, if taking that seat means compromising yourself. For example, in the second verse of "Weary," the second song on the album, Solange holds up a mirror to women performing strategic ambiguity, crooning: "Be leery 'bout your place in the world/You're feeling like you're chasing the world/You're leaving not a trace in the world/ But you're facing the world." Strategic ambiguity is that single-minded, individual-focused chase that doesn't connect with the strength of the collective, the strength of Black communities. The entire album is a love letter to Black people, especially Black women, and it features moments of incredible self-reflexivity and exhortations to incite change while fearlessly stepping up to "face the world."

Postracial Resistance: Black Women, Media, and the Uses of Strategic Ambiguity has traced an arc from Kerry Washington to Solange Knowles. This book has probed performances that ranged from politely slipping in critiques through a strategic ambiguity of postracial resistance, to shouting analyses through an unapologetic racialized intervention. I have argued that in the *Michelle* Obama era, a very visible group of African American women celebrities, the audiences that watch them, and the television executives who script their images sometimes used and sometimes abandoned the tools of postracial discourse—the media-propagated notion that race and race-based discrimination are over, and that race and racism no longer affect the everyday lives of both Whites and people of color—in order to resist the very tenets of postracial discourse. *Postracial Resistance* has documented Black women in three different places in media culture: Black women celebrities themselves, Black women and other women of color viewers negotiating their own ways through the limited representations available to them, and Black women writers and others working behind the scenes in television and other media to create media representations. I used a mix of methodologies—textual analysis in part one, and industry analysis and audience ethnography in part two—and a wide array of media studies strategies to paint a full picture of Black women's performance of strategic ambiguity.

While the performances of the celebrity figures in part one might have looked more coded and cautious, and the articulations of the audiences and television executives might have looked more forthright and bold, both, however, iterated their own brands of resistance. Postracial resistance of the strategic ambiguity variety coyly performed against racism and sexism of a mostly coded, implicit form. Such performance was, in some ways, complicit with the very forces it sought to unpack. Postracial resistance can proffer such a light touch that it fails to sufficiently nudge, much less wipe out, racism. This light touch is partially to blame for the regime shift from our 44th to 45th presidents. Postracial resistance didn't alert and activate those unused to reading racialized nuance enough to fear the coming of the virulent racism hiding in plain sight. Postracial resistance allowed 45 to sneak up on certain members of the complacent, Obama-loving populace. Indeed, in some ways, Americans, especially of the White liberal variety, were so enamored with the so-called postracial changes ushered in with the Obama era that the reversion to explicit forms of racism, even when Trump's dog whistle was replaced by his bullhorn, seemed impossible (until it was too late).

What the transition from the Obama to the Trump era appears to demonstrate starkly is not only that postracialism, as a tool of change, is an impossibility, but that strategic ambiguity, as an instrument of individual success, is highly fraught. Thus, a shift in frame and a shift in approach are necessary now more than ever, again, as Solange illustrates in *A Seat at the Table*. Unpacking the metaphor conjured in her album's title in an interview on NPR Solange gives her take on the seat: "We've always had a seat at the table . . . I think one of the [things about taking] seats at the table is also saying that, you know, I'm inviting *you* to have a seat at *my* table." In flipping the notion of inclusion, Solange presents the idea that *power comes from being the one who sets the terms, the one who does the inviting and not the one being invited.* Kerry Washington provides one model for women of color that she (and she alone) will join a table that is already set by someone else. That if we are patient, that if we are good girls, that if we wait our turns, then maybe someday we might get to be the one who holds the invitations in our hands. But, after we wait that long, who have we become? In a different model, Solange invites women of color to not wait. We get to be the ones in charge of the table *now*. When we invite people to join our table, we get to choose the guests, the topics of conversation, and create our own meal. We are able to center ourselves and the issues affecting our communities. We are not marginalized as the afterthought. We become unapologetically the center. And the soundtrack to the dinner party? Solange Knowles's anthem to the abandonment of strategic ambiguity, the first track on the album, "Rise": "Walk in your ways, so you won't crumble/Walk in your ways, so you can sleep at night/Walk in your ways, so you will wake up and rise."

ACKNOWLEDGMENTS

Thank you to all of the many people who sit at my scholarly, activist, and community tables, where I have had the luxury to resist and abandon strategic ambiguity. I thank all of the staff, students, and community members who make up my second home, the Center for Communication, Difference, and Equity (CCDE). In what can feel like an isolating line of work, where people lament the silos of their work-lives, I am blessed with a community of scholars with whom I can develop, share, and grow my ideas. I workshopped various portions of this book with my WIRED (Women Investigating Race, Ethnicity, and Difference) writing group members Habiba Ibrahim, LeiLani Nishime, and Sonnet Retman; my Communication Humanities writing group members Leah Ceccarelli, Christine Harold, and LeiLani Nishime; UW's Simpson Center for the Humanities Society of Scholars (with a big thanks to Kathy Woodward); and my WIRED Mediating Difference writing group members Michelle Habell-Pallán, Habiba Ibrahim, LeiLani Nishime, Sonnet Retman, Ileana Rodriguez-Silva, Stephanie Smallwood, and Sasha Su-Ling Welland. Thank you to Judy Howard for looking out for me when I couldn't be at the table, and to Jerry Baldasty for somehow knowing I was a Communication scholar before I did.

So many Comm/Race/Media warriors welcomed me to the Communication table with open arms including (but not limited to!) Mary Beltran, Robin Means Coleman, Herman Gray, Ron Jackson, Josh Kun, Lori Kido Lopez, Isabel Molina-Guzmán, Roopali Mukherjee, Beretta Smith-Shomade, Catherine Squires, Myra Washington, and Anghy Valdivia. For the past nearly twenty years, I have been, and continue to be, indebted to my mentors Jane Rhodes and Daphne Brooks, whose intellect, grace, and necessary irreverence provide me with my models for how I want (and need) to be in order to make a difference and stay sane in this career.

Thank you to the friends and colleagues who invited me to share this work at the Annenberg School at USC, the University of Illinois, Urbana-Champaign, the University of Michigan, Gonzaga University, *Black Perspectives,* and *FLOW.* Every comment and question helped shape the book. I thank Laura Helper-Ferris for our now five-year-long conversation about my writing. Thank you to all of the undergraduate and graduate students (past and present) who have worked on various portions of the book (even when you didn't know you were workshopping it! "Let me ask you guys a question . . ."), especially the Communication and Difference Research Group members (even before we had a fancy name or a fancy center).

I am grateful to all I continue to learn from my advisees Manoucheka Celeste, Elizabeth Cortez, Marcus Johnson, Monique Lacoste, Mia Lawrie, Azeb Madebo, Jennifer McClearen, Madhavi Murty, Meshell Sturgis, Riley Taitingfong, Victoria Thomas, and Anjali Vats. Thank you to the NYUP team, especially Lisha Nadkarni, Dolma Ombadykow, Aswin Punathambekar, and Eric Zinner. Thank you to all of the women in my audience group—Dezi, McCall, Vanessa, Micki, Jennifer, Yumi, Valentina, and Lupe—and most especially Camille for hosting us. Thank you to the Hollywood women who graciously endured my questioning. Thank you to Gina Aaftaab for being my Radar at the Center; your incredible ability to read my messy mind and to always generate brilliant plans has allowed the CCDE to grow and thrive while I finished this book. Thank you to the CCDE faculty, especially Carmen Gonzalez, LeiLani Nishime, and Andrea Otanez, and to all of the now 60+ WIRED women for adding so many leaves to our table that we need a new furniture set.

Thank you to my ride-or-die wing-women, my "no panel," my sisters in crime, Janine Jones, Wadiya Udell, and Joy Williamson-Lott, for enlivening my life, making me snort with laughter, and modeling three amazing and amazingly different modes of how to be the professor/mother/scholar that I strive to be. Thank you to Cherise Smith for being your brilliant, fierce self, and for introducing me to the extraordinary artist Deborah Roberts, whose incomparable piece "Untitled (Black Gloves, Big Eye, Yellow Collar)" graces the cover of this book. Thank you to my lifelong friends-from-Providence, Praveen Fernandes, Heather Reid (and Ava Hall!), and the dearly departed Jeffery Charles Mingo. Jeff, I miss your inane (and yet so on point) questions that always managed to crack open the heart of what I didn't even know I wanted to argue, while simultaneously managing to crack me up.

Thank you to my Oakland family Allison Briscoe-Smith, Mike Smith, and my godbabies Alonzo, Ava Marie, and Aria. Thank you to my Bon Secour family Jesse Meeks and Diane Sims for being the two brightest blue points in the reddest state. Thank you to my Fremont family, Diana and Ed White, for your unshakable, constant, quiet investment in me. Thank you especially to my parents, Richard and Irene Landwehr, for all of the love, support, and sacrifices that you made so that I could have the choices that you did not have the luxury of making; your sacrifices have allowed me to claim my seat at the table.

Last but always most, I dedicate this book to my James, TJ, and Naima Joseph. You are my live-in sounding boards, my first readers (and listeners), my editors, my thought-partners, and my go-to research assistants (paid only with gushing love). All is possible because of your crushing hugs, your nightly roses, thorns, and buds, and your good-natured, eye-glinting, gleeful teasing. And, yes, you're right. It's time to put the computer away. Mama owes you a vacation.

NOTES

PREFACE
1 Sue, xvi.
2 Collins, *Black Feminist Thought, 221-238.*

INTRODUCTION
1 I use the terms "Black" (capitalized) and "African American" largely interchangeably throughout this book. When, in the second half of the book, I utilize interview data I follow the wording preferences of my interview subjects.
2 "Transcended race" quoted in Peck, "Oprah Winfrey" 83. See also Peck, *The Age of Oprah, and* Pomerantz.
3 See L'Oréal Paris and Beyoncé for video links.
4 Celeste, *Race, Gender, and Citizenship* 14.
5 See National Institutes of Health.
6 See U.S. Breast Cancer Statistics.
7 See Arons and Collins, 2132–2138.
8 Guerra, 2.
9 Guerra, 2.
10 Dozier, 1833–57.
11 In 2012 the median income for Black women writers was $98,155, as opposed to all female writers at $117,008, and all male writers at $127,537. Personal correspondence with Darnell Hunt.
12 See Brinkhurst-Cuff.
13 Crenshaw, "#SayHerName".
14 Crenshaw, "#SayHerName," 1.
15 See Garza.
16 Gilroy, *Against race* 53.
17 "post-", from Latin *post* 'after, behind', quoted (?) in Oxford Dictionary website, 22 April, 2016: www.oxforddictionaries.com.
18 While numerous race critics gesture towards this phrase while writing about the paradox of race bearing social weight and yet being constructed, Richard Jenkins uses the phrase "imagined but not imaginary". See Jenkins, "Imagined but not Imaginary" 114–128.
19 Gilroy, *Against race* 12.

20 In his essay "Is the Post- in Postmodernism the Post- in Postcolonial," Kwame
   Anthony Appiah writes: "the task of chasing the word *postmodernism* through the
   pages of Jean-François Lyotard and Fredric Jameson and Jürgen Habermas, in and
   out of the *Village Voice* and the *TLS* and even the *New York Times Book Review*
   is certainly exhausting." Appiah ultimately chases philosophers and cultural
   representation to find his definitions, and I follow Appiah's lead in my search for
   postracial resistance. See Appiah, 341.

21 Featherstone, 3.

22 See McRobbie, *The Aftermath of Feminism*. I have chosen in this book to center
   my analysis and critique around "postrace" and not "postfeminism" because I
   believe postfeminism to be an unproductive analytical category for studies of
   women of color. This is a clear revision of some of my earlier work in the articles
   "Tyra Banks is Fat" and "First Lady Reframed."

23 Fleetwood, *On Racial Icons* 14.

24 Dyson, 32.

25 Dyson, 12.

26 Dyson, 20.

27 Dyson, 11.

28 Stuart Hall ("Minimal Selves") quoted in Bhabha, 45–46.

29 Crenshaw, "Foreword."

30 Gotanda, 59.

31 Nilsen and Turner, 3.

32 Pollock, 3.

33 Jackson, 78.

34 Vats, 113.

35 Smith, *Enacting Others*.

36 See Frankenberg; Morrison; Lipsitz.

37 Squires, *The post-racial mystique* 25.

38 Brooks, "All That You Can't Leave Behind 183.

39 Toby Miller notes that such tripartite methodologies of political economy, ethnography, and textual analysis derive "from Roger Chartier's tripartite historici-
   zation of books . . . This grid turns away from reflexionism, which argues that a
   text's key meaning lies in its overt or covert capacity to capture the Zeitgeist. It
   also rejects formalism's claim that close readings of sound and image can secure
   definitive meanings, because texts accrete and attenuate meanings on their travels
   as they rub up against, trope, and are troped by other fictional and social texts and
   interpreted by viewers" (147). See Kellner 1995.

40 Coleman, *African American Viewers* 12.

41 Sonnet, 258.

42 See Burke. Burke writes that while the best texts to analyze the ways in which
   an individual structures his or her rationale for a particular speech or action, in
   his words, a grammar of motives, are "theological, metaphysical, and juridical
   doctrines," other overarching themes and their connected archives are important

to consider, including the Symbolic with its analysis of "the forms and methods of art" and Rhetoric with its focus on "observations on parliamentary and diplomatic devices, editorial bias, sales methods and incidents of social sparring." At the same moment that Burke articulates his particular focus on Grammar, he also states that his goal is not "to evolve terms free of ambiguity and inconsistency" (xviii) but instead to make space for "something essentially enigmatic about the problem of motives," which means "inevitable ambiguities and inconsistencies among the terms for motives." Burke asserts that crafting an argument around the very notion of ambiguity—and a strategic one at that—brings a reader to the most crucial points of an argument. While Burke's idea has been picked up in business and the military, I haven't seen it used to a more critical end, or indeed in discussions of minoritized subjectivity and representation.

43 Conventional U.S. policy dictates that smaller powers should be prevented from utilizing strategic ambiguity, by, for example, not being allowed to refuse arms inspections, because the smaller power's weapons of mass destruction (WMDs) will continue to multiply unchecked without U.S. surveillance. However, Sandeep Baliga and Tomas Sjöström point out that strategic ambiguity, also known in military policy as "deterrence by doubt," can also decrease arms proliferation for both bigger and smaller countries even without ultimatums from the larger power (Baliga, 1023–1057).

44 See Eisenberg, 3. Eisenberg adopted Burke's phrase to denote "the human capacity to use the resources of language to communicate in ways that are both inclusive and preserve important differences" (x). Eisenberg's research is on "how people in organizations use ambiguity strategically to accomplish their goals" (5) as strategic ambiguity creates a type of "unified diversity" allowing for "multiple viewpoints in organizations . . . Strategic ambiguity is essential to organizing because it allows for multiple interpretations to exist among people who contend that they are attending to the same message . . . It is a political necessity to engage in strategic ambiguity so that different constituent groups may apply different interpretations to the symbol" (8–9). Eisenberg writes: "At the interpersonal level, strategic ambiguity can facilitate relational development. This occurs when organizational members are purposefully ambiguous and those attending to the message 'fill in' what they believe to be the appropriate context and meaning. The more ambiguous the message, the greater the room for projection. When an individual projects, he or she fills in the meaning of a message in a way which is consistent with his or her own beliefs" (11–12). Eisenberg claims that, "particularly in turbulent environments, ambiguous communication is not a kind of fudging, but rather a rational method used by communicators to orient toward multiple goals" (18).

45 Bernheim, 902–932.

46 Heller, 77–96.

47 Ceccarelli, 404. To put Ceccarelli's work on strategic ambiguity into context: In "Polysemy: Multiple Meanings in Rhetorical Criticism," Ceccarelli explicates the idea that the term polysemy, the recognition of a text's multiple meanings,

is, itself, polysemous. Ceccarelli centers not just the text but the audience in her analysis as she considers both "the agent who activates a polysemous reading (audience, rhetoric, or critic)" alongside "the social action it inspires" and "the power dynamics it puts into play" (397). Ceccarelli distinguishes the two often-confused ideas of polysemy, or varying interpretations, and polyvalence, or varying judgements, before describing three types of polysemy: resistive readings, or ones that are "audience inspired" and "undergird rebellion against a dominant authorial interpretation" (408); hermeneutic depth, where a critic "offers a new expanded way that audiences *should* read a text" (408); and strategic ambiguity. Ceccarelli's arguments are thus about method as much as theory. The critic's read isn't sufficient to make sense of a text: we also need to take reception into account (407).

48 Ceccarelli, 404.
49 Ceccarelli, 405.
50 Ceccarelli, 407.
51 Hall, "Encoding/Decoding" 128–38.
52 Gates, "Keepin' It Reality Television" 143.
53 Spivak, 214.
54 Wall, 456–458.
55 Hall, *Representation* 1.
56 See Kellner, *Media Culture*.
57 See Gaines.
58 Mitchell, 393.
59 Noble, 19.
60 Gerbner, "Living with Television" 175.
61 In "Ideology and Ideological State Apparatuses (Notes towards an Investigation)" (1972), Louis Althusser defines interpellation as the process by which people become subjects—or are hailed into being—through embracing ideology. In "The Culture Industry" (1979), Horkheimer and Adorno apply Althusser's ideas of interpellation and ideology to media, and seeing subjects as passive receptacles of media. Other scholars, including Stuart Hall in "Encoding, Decoding" (1973), resist such unidirectional interpretations of ideology while acknowledging the incredible power of media to interpellate subjects.
62 Mercer, 234.
63 Horkheimer, *Dialectic of Enlightenment*.
64 See Parker.
65 Butler, *Bodies* 219.
66 Muñoz, 31.
67 Lotz, 2.
68 Lotz, 35.
69 Hall, "The Whites of Their Eyes" 30.
70 Hall, "The Whites of Their Eyes" 31.
71 DeAngelis, 5.

72 White, 76–77.

73 Camp, 2.

74 Hine, 4.

75 Hine, 29.

76 Hine, 90.

77 Collins, 97.

78 Thompson, *Beyond the Black Lady* 3.

79 Higginbotham, "African-American women's history" 270.

80 White and Dobris, 176.

81 Hine, "Rape and the inner lives" 915.

82 See Fordham, 10. Psychologists Tracy Robinson and Janie Victoria Ward write of the difference between African American female adolescents' "resistance for survival" and "resistance for liberation." While the former "may well serve the (short-term) interest of individual survival in a hostile and oppressive environment, the latter is a "resistance in which black girls and women are encouraged to acknowledge the problems of, and to demand change in, an environment that oppresses them." (Robinson and Ward, 89.

83 Fleetwood, *On Racial Icons* 145.

84 Black women's representation in "dominant visual culture," as Fleetwood puts it, is a small but growing area of study. *Postracial Resistance* is grounded in Jacqueline Bobo's groundbreaking book *Black Women as Cultural Readers* and Beretta Smith-Shomade's incisive *Shaded Lives: African-American Women and Television.* In her 2002 book *Shaded Lives,* Smith-Shomade writes: "In the last twenty years many scholars have devoted themselves to interrogations of, by, or about African-Americans, especially Black men . . . Yet this same period offered fewer (and then typically derisive) works focused on Black women, although they have endured similar types of disrespect within American institutions" (1). This book owes much to scholarship on African American representation writ large, including Herman Gray's *Watching Race: Television and the Struggle for Blackness* and *Cultural Moves: Culture, Identity, and the Politics of Representation*, Robin Means-Coleman's *African American Viewers and the Black Situation Comedy: Situating Racial Humor*, and edited collections by Coleman (*Say it Loud!: African American Audiences, Media and Identity*) and Smith-Shomade (*Watching While Black: Centering the Television of Black Audiences*). This book joins a new renaissance of literature on Black women and representation, including Manoucheka Celeste's *Race, Gender, and Citizenship in the African Diaspora*, Kristen Warner's *The Cultural Politics of Colorblind TV Casting*, and scholarship on Black women and pornography including Mireille Miller-Young's *A Taste for Brown Sugar*, Jennifer C. Nash's *The Black Body in Ecstasy*, and Ariane Cruz's *The Color of Kink*.

85 Mask, 4.

86 Mendelberg, 109.

87 Gray, "Subject(ed) to Recognition" 771–798.

88 Smith-Shomade, *Shaded lives.*

CHAPTER 1. "OF COURSE I'M PROUD OF MY COUNTRY!"

1 Cooper, "An't I a Lady?" 41.
2 Gordon-Chipembere, 166.
3 "Presidential Ratings—The First Lady." Viewed September 21, 2016. www.gallup.com/.
4 For full disclosure, I have to admit that I am not merely an unbiased observer of our First Lady. I am a fan and so I have worked harder to substantiate my intuition about Obama's linguistic choices. However, I don't believe that my fandom makes my reading more flawed. Indeed, as Ann duCille (569) writes: "Readings are never neutral. All criticisms are local, situational. My own critical interpretations . . . are always-already colored by my race and my gender." In this chapter, I try to articulate what I imagine to be Michelle Obama's particular struggle. This is not just to help me think through the positionality of our First Lady but also to think through my own positionality. She becomes a signpost for how other women of color understand and imagine ourselves. For women of color professors ensconced in White, patriarchal departments and universities, and for scholars grounded in "biased" and "unscientific" knowledge produced through ethnic studies and feminism, when and how are we allowed to speak?
5 While this book focuses on postrace, similar cultural phenomena have occurred in the realm of gender, or in postfeminism. Scholarship in postfeminism, primarily conducted in feminist media studies, correspondingly exposes the smokescreen effect of the post (see Brunsdon, 110–116; Douglas; McRobbie, *Displacement Feminism* and "Post Feminism and Popular Culture" 255–264; Tasker; and Vavrus. In the words of communication scholar Mary D Vavrus, postfeminism, in its denials of institutionalized sexism and misogyny, "displaces critical attention from actual sources of patriarchal power and on to feminism" (223).
6 The article from which this chapter grew considered postrace and postfeminism as fairly equal and parallel intersectional identity categories; as such I discussed them in tandem through the word "post-identity," in the years that have passed since the publication of that article, I have been increasingly convinced that race is and still remains the most significant identity category, and my reliance upon racial terminology reflects that thinking. See Joseph, "'Hope is Finally Making a Comeback'" 56–77.
7 Squires, "Running through the Trenches" 213.
8 See Bonilla-Silva; Forman 175–202; Gilroy, *Against Race*; Watts, 214–222.
9 Nayak, 427.
10 St. Louis, 671.
11 See Beltran, 63–88; Springer, "Third Wave Black Feminism?" 1059–1082 and "Divas" 249–276.
12 Kellner, "Media spectacle" 707–716.
13 Rodman, 117.
14 Collins, *Black Sexual Politics* 4.
15 Kahl, 319.

16 Hall, "Cultural Identity and Diaspora" 222.

17 Obama's use of race and gender codes in lieu of speaking explicitly of race and gender discrimination illustrates her deployment of, in the words of communication scholars Lee and Morin (376–391, 387), "prior textual history" of a misogynistic, racist culture.

18 See Habell-Pallán.

19 See Smith, *Not just Race, not just Gender* xix, xv. Smith also describes how "social transformation will become possible only as we understand how these dynamics and relations [of dominance] are inscribed and produced" (xvi). We have to read "overlapping, discontinuous, and multiply interpretable discursive sites" (xviii).

20 See Crenshaw, "Mapping the Margins" 357–383.

21 Race/gender theorist Chela Sandoval gives us another way to speak back to the delimiting of women of color through her analysis of what she calls the "posttraditional era," a time she explains has also been called "'postindustrial,' 'consumer,' 'high-tech,' 'multinational,' 'transnational,' 'postcolonial,' 'postmodern,' and/or 'global.'" Although Sandoval does not use the specific term "postrace," she describes a similar rationale and function: "a new cultural dominant has overtaken the rationality of the old." In the case of postrace, the "new" cultural dominant of colorblindness presides, supposedly killing off the "old" cultural dominant of racialized sexism, and even racialized and gendered identity (9).

22 See Lyotard.

23 See Derrida.

24 Weber, 137.

25 See Trebay.

26 Crenshaw, "Mapping the Margins" 357–383.

27 See Swarns.

28 Millner, 541.

29 See Bhabha; Butler, *Gender Trouble* and *Bodies That Matter*; Chow, Ethics after Idealism; Gilroy, *The Black Atlantic*; Muñoz; and Sedgwick. Judith Roof (2003) also uses the phrase "exhaustion of identity politics" to describe why the journal *Post-Identity* was created in the late 1990s.

30 Griffin, 484.

31 See Omi.

32 See Collins, *Black Feminist Thought*.

33 James, 2.

34 See hooks, *Feminist Theory* 24.

35 Smith, *Not Just Race* 21.

36 Ceccarelli, 398.

37 Coleman, "The Gentrification of 'Black'" 88.

38 See Davis.

39 Obama's second set of remarks differed from her first because in her second she added the word "really" ("for the first time in my adult lifetime, I'm really proud of my country").

40 For a link to the speech itself see www.youtube.com/watch?v+LYY73RO_egw (viewed October 27, 2009).

41 See Habell-Pallán.

42 Davies, "Con-di-fi-cation" 76.

43 Madison, 321.

44 Kelly, 35.

45 Cloud, 458.

46 See Hovell.

47 Springer, "Third Wave Black Feminism?" 1059–1082 and "Divas" 249–276.

48 Lorde, 117.

49 See Brooks, "All that You Can't Leave Behind" 181.

50 See Piazza.

51 Spillers, 308.

52 In 2014 infant mortality rates for infants born to White women were 4.89%, and for Black women were 10.93% (T.J. Mathews, M.S., and Anne K. Driscoll, Ph.D. "Trends in Infant Mortality in the United States, 2005–2014," *NCHS Data Brief* No. 279, March 2017); the 2015–16 real median income of White households was $65,041, versus $39,490 for Black households (The U.S. Census Bureau, "Income, Poverty and Health Insurance Coverage in the United States: 2016," *Newsroom*, https://www.census.gov/newsroom/press-releases/2017/income-poverty.html. Release Number CB17–156, 2017 Race and Hispanic Origin, viewed 10 October 2017).

53 See Lugones.

54 See Steyn.

55 See Hare.

56 See Thompson.

57 See Samuels, quoting Michelle Obama.

58 Sandoval, 63.

59 Schiappa, 253–272.

60 Gordon-Chipembere, 165–80.

61 Brown, 248.

62 Williams, "The First (black) Lady" 833.

CHAPTER 2. "BECAUSE OFTEN IT'S BOTH"

1 Smith-Shomade, *Shaded Lives* 148.

2 Lofton, 6.

3 See Gabbard.

4 Ibrahim, xvii.

5 Havens, 125.

6 See Peck, *The Age of Oprah*.

7 As Alexander Weheliye writes, why are "formations of the oppressed deemed liberatory only if they resist hegemony and/or exhibit the full agency of the

oppressed? What deformations of freedom become possible in the absence of resistance and agency?" (2).

8 See Chestang.

9 Jackson, 3.

10 Sue, *Race Talk* 7.

11 Morris III, 228–244.

12 Davies, *Black Women* 21.

13 See Randhawa.

14 Winfrey references the incident on Twitter in the following manner: "Turns out that store clerk did me a favor. Just found out that bag was $38K!!! She was right I was NOT going to buy it." A couple of hours later that same day, Oprah tweets: "other than the handbag diss. I had a GREAT time in Zurich. Best spa ever @doldergrand. Would love to experience again." Viewed January 28, 2014.

15 See Rothman.

16 See Reuters.

17 This sentiment was expressed in either inferential ways in newspapers or more explicitly in blogs. For example, the Mr. Conservative blog titles its story on the topic: "Oprah Says 'Sorry' for Crying Racism After Receiving Ba-16Customer Service at Boutique" (August22, 2013), http://www.mrconservative.com/.

18 See Aesop.

19 Brüggemann, 51–58.

20 For example, see: "Oprah sorry for blown up racism row."
See also: Smith-Spark, "Oprah Winfrey: I'm sorry Switzerland racism incident got blown up").

21 See "Oprah Winfrey apologises for Swiss handbag-gate."

22 For example, see Evatt, "Oprah Winfrey expresses regret over media storm surrounding Swiss flap."

23 For example, see Hall, "Now Oprah says sorry." See also Evatt, "Oprah says sorry for Switzerland racism brouhaha."

24 See: "Oprah regrets Swiss racism incident."

25 See: "Oprah says 'sorry' for media storm linked to Swiss shopping story."

26 See Evatt, "Oprah says sorry for Switzerland racism brouhaha."

27 See Legge.

28 See: "Oprah regrets Swiss frenzy."

29 For example, see Evatt, "Oprah Winfrey expresses regret over media storm surrounding Swiss flap,"

30 See: "Winfrey regrets storm stirred by racism story."

31 See: "Oprah says sorry over Swiss racism flap."

32 See: "Oprah sorry over uproar over racism scandal."

33 See: "Oprah says 'sorry' for crying racism after receiving bad customer service at boutique."

34 Kim, 55–79.

35 See: "Winfrey sorry for 'racism' furore; Panorama around the world in 10 stories Switzerland,"

36 See: "Oprah 'racism' just lost in translation."

37 See: "She's sorry for racism flap."

38 See TMZ.

39 Fleetwood, *Troubling Vision* 3.

40 Fleetwood, *Troubling Vision* 7.

41 See Heilpern, "Oprah's Encounter with Racism Results in Apology from Swiss Tourism Office."

42 Bonilla-Silva, 1.

43 Rita Repulsa, who "was a female humanoid sorceress bent on intergalactic domination," was initially played by Japanese actress Machiko Soga and later by Asian American actress Carla Perez. Viewed October 19, 2015. http://powerrangers .wikia.com/.

44 See: "Could it be Oprah's just a picky shopper?"

45 See: "Storm in a handbag: Oprah Winfrey accuses Zurich boutique of racism."

46 See: "A bagful of racism for Oprah in Zurich."

47 See Power.

48 See: "Swiss sorry after Oprah snubbed in shop 'racism' row."

49 See Methven.

50 See: "Oprah in bag shop race row: Outrage over 'cheap' insult."

51 See Li.

52 See: "Cheesed off Oprah bags the 'racist' Swiss."

53 See Heilpern, "Swiss apologize for encounter Oprah calls racist."

54 See Dawn.

55 See: "Apology to Oprah over bags of money,"

56 See Pomerantz.

57 Erigha,441. Erigha and Charles also note that the term uppity "references historical relationships and power dynamics of subordination and domination between Blacks and Whites characterized by Jim Crow segregation and the ideology of White supremacy following the U.S. Civil War" (441). A more vernacular source, Urban Dictionary, defines uppity as "taking liberties or assuming airs beyond one's place in a social hierarchy. Assuming equality with someone higher up on the social ladder." Accessed January 7, 2014. www.urbandictionary.com.

58 See Staples.

59 Smith-Shomade, *Shaded Lives* 157.

60 Andrea O'Reilly's essay "'I come from a long line of Uppity Irate Black Women': African-American Feminist Thought on Motherhood, the Motherline and the Mother-Daughter Relationship" in *Mothers and Daughters: Connection, Empowerment, and Transformation* (143–59) takes its title from a Kate Rusin poem, "Family Tree," that begins: "I come from/a long line of/ Uppity Irate Black Women" and continues "I cultivate/Being Uppity/it's something/ my Gramon taught me" (quoted in O'Reilley, 144).

61 See: "Oprah accuses Swiss shop of racism."
62 See McKinley.
63 See: "Swiss racism upsets Oprah."
64 See: "Shop assistant's big mistake earns ire of Oprah."
65 See Battersby.
66 Morgan,485–502.
67 Springer, "Divas" 258. See also: Walley-Jean 68–86.; and Griffin, 138–157.
68 White, 6.
69 See Hall, "Oprah Winfrey racism claim disputed."
70 See: "Oprah handbag claim not true."
71 See Charter.
72 See Jefferies.
73 See Brain.
74 See Hicks.
75 See Williams, *The Alchemy of Race and Rights* 44–45.
76 Williams, *The Alchemy of Race and Rights* 47. Note that Williams writes that the line I quote here was cut out of the analysis she wrote for a law review symposium.
77 Williams, *The Alchemy of Race and Rights* 49.
78 Peck, "Oprah Winfrey" 83. See also: Peck, *The Age of Oprah.*
79 See NewsOne Staff.

CHAPTER 3. "I JUST WANTED A WORLD THAT LOOKED LIKE THE ONE I KNOW"

1 See: "Oprah Talks to Shonda Rhimes." *The Oprah Magazine*, December 2006.
2 I want to underscore the fact that I am in no way attempting to read Rhimes' intent; instead, I am reading her performance, her self-fashioning (see Staiger, 89–106).
3 Higginbotham, "African-American Women's History" 251–74, and *Righteous Discontent.*
4 See Horne.
5 See White and Dobris.
6 Horne, 4.
7 See Thompson.
8 See Cosby.
9 See Lewis.
10 Gray, "Introduction" 193.
11 One exception is a very special *Scandal* episode, "The Lawn Chair," that took on police brutality of Black men and the issues of Black protest and Black armed resistance; see Verica.
12 Gray, *Watching Race.*
13 See, for example: Brooks, "All That You Can't Leave Behind" 183, and Noble.
14 See Williams' 2016 BET Awards speech at https://www.youtube.com/watch?v=HeRIUPlxlv4.

15 See Smith, "Boycott ABC." The petition had 27,692 supporters as of October 4, 2016.

16 See Bennett.

17 Caldwell, 205.

18 Caldwell, 206.

19 See McNamee.

20 See Carey.

21 See Johnson.

22 See all of the popular press articles discussed in this piece.

23 See Levine.

24 Collier, 204–208; Johnson; "Oprah talks to Shonda Rhimes."

25 "Oprah talks to Shonda Rhimes," 321.

26 See Peck, *Age of Oprah*; and Lofton.

27 See Catanese.

28 Catanese,17.

29 Warner, "A Black Cast" 49–62.

30 Long, 1067–84.

31 Havens, *Black Television Travels*.

32 Horne, 63.

33 See Collier.

34 Another celebrated show featured a cast of color that rarely addressed racial dif-ference, *The Cosby Show*, and Sut Jhally and Justin Lewis similarly suggest that it not only did not open up racial understanding, it created greater racial animus. Here White audiences never saw Black people fighting racism, implying that it doesn't exist.

35 The #BlackLivesMatter movement was founded by three queer Black women ac-tivists who, in the words of one of them, created "a call to action for Black people after 17-year-old Trayvon Martin was post-humously [*sic*] placed on trial for his own murder and the killer, George Zimmerman, was not held accountable for the crime he committed." See Garza.

36 See Everett.

37 See Yu.

38 See Myers.

39 Retman, 98.

40 See Paskin.

41 See Samuels.

42 See Stanley.

43 See Brown, "The New York Times, Shonda Rhimes & How to Get Away With Being Racist."

44 See Goldberg.

45 See Sullivan.

46 See Maerz.

47 See Maerz, 8.

48 See Holmes.

49 Mercer, 234.

50 Mercer, 240.

51 Long, 1068.

52 Warner, "The Racial Logic of *Grey's Anatomy*" 633.

53 Warner, "The Racial Logic of *Grey's Anatomy*" 633 and 635.

54 Warner, "The Racial Logic of *Grey's Anatomy*" 638.

55 Everett, 34.

56 Everett, 37.

57 See Wolfe.

CHAPTER 4. "NO, BUT I'M STILL BLACK"

1 Hunt, "Hollywood Story" 163.

2 Gray, 66.

3 At the first session, as the women discussed and signed their human subjects forms, each participant chose her moniker for the study, and those names are what you see here.

4 Amongst communities of television fans, the buzzword "hate-watch," or to tune in to a television show simply to deride it, gained cultural cache in 2012. See Nussbaum; Franish; Davies, "'Hate watching' is mostly just being embarrassed by your own tastes."

5 Mullings, 21.

6 Lotz, "Assessing Qualitative Television" 456.

7 After I left the sessions, I typed up and expanded my scrawled comments, and developed my sparse notes into more thorough documentation of each session, as I did not want to be scribbling all during our viewing sessions. A graduate student research assistant transcribed the sessions for me within three months. While at first my RA attempted to transcribe every word spoken during the entire time the camera ran—even those spoken when the television show was on—after laboriously transcribing the first and second sessions, we agreed that she should only transcribe the moments when the TV wasn't running (before and after the show, and during the commercial breaks), and time-mark places where interesting conversation went on when the television was playing. I combed through the transcripts, watching the tapes again, making edits, and adding details with my field notes. When I incorporate the women's words in this chapter, square brackets [ ] denote something unspoken including a dropped word or phrase, as well as an interjection by another speaker. A dash or double square brackets [[ ]] denote the second speaker not just interjecting but cutting the first off, or speaking simultaneously with the first speaker. Inside of the square or double square brackets, italics denote tone, description, and nonverbal communication. Ellipses denote a pause, although—if there is a long pause—I write *pause* in italics and, if there's a pause for effect, I write *beat* in italics. I adapted this style from Maya Angela Smith's dissertation *Multilingual Practices of Senegalese Immigrants in Paris and Rome*.

8 Durham, 13.

9 Hall, "'Encoding/Decoding'" 128–36.

10 Bobo, "The Color Purple" 238.

11 hooks, "The Oppositional Gaze" 115–131.

12 Fiske, 19.

13 See Fish.

14 McRobbie, "The Politics of Feminist Research" 51.

15 As Janice Radway notes in her discussion of the romance readers in her audience study, "there are remarkable similarities to the way all the women who contributed to these studies use traditionally female form to resist their situation *as women* by enabling them to cope with the features of the situation that oppress them" (12).

16 Lotz "Assessing Qualitative Television" 449.

17 Jenkins, "'Out of the Closet and Into the Universe'" 239.

18 Mayer 3.

19 Bobo, *Black Women as Culture Readers* 102.

20 Havens, *Black Television Travels* 11.

21 Smith-Shomade, *Shaded Lives* 23.

22 Notably, none of the women sent me any requests to make changes. What did happen, however, was that I reconnected with the young women.

23 Lotz, "Assessing Qualitative Television" 449.

24 Gamson, 124.

25 Email correspondence with Camille, March 18, 2016.

26 Email correspondence with McCall, April 13, 2016.

27 Hall, "Cultural Identity and Diaspora."

28 Smith, "Multilingual Practices" 132.

29 Smith, "Multilingual Practices" 132.

30 Personal conversation with Camille, February 14, 2016.

31 Thompson and Mittell, 5.

32 Miller, 143.

33 Smith-Shomade, "Introduction: I See Black People" 4.

34 Miller, 115.

35 Gates, 143.

36 Wright, 648.

37 Robinson, 159. In this article, Robinson cites numerous studies "suggest[ing] that Black women experience gendered racism, and as a result, they face significant obstacles in the academy." Robinson coins the term "spoketokenism to denote the significance of [Black women's] voice, physical presence, and perceptions about themselves and others" (178). Robinson also notes: "'being the only one' can be an opportunity for some Black women to prove their intellect and embody an active leadership role. Conversely, if there is a lack of representation, participants felt they needed 'to bring to the table' one's race, gender, and identity politics. The

accepted status of tokenism affords some Black women the verbal leniency to strategically institute change by virtue of their insider out status" (178).

38 Robinson, 178.
39 See Kenney.
40 Sue, *Microaggressions* 28.

CHAPTER 5. "THEY GOT RID OF THE NAPS, THAT'S ALL THEY DID"

1 Coleman, *African American Viewers* 73.
2 Gates, 144.
3 Nash, 2.
4 See Wood.
5 Young, 5.
6 DiAngelo, 54–70.
7 Sue, *Microaggressions*.
8 Gerbner, "Violence in Television Drama" 44.
9 Coleman, *African American Viewers* 222.
10 Gray, "The Amazing Race: Global Othering" 96.
11 Rhodes, 202.
12 Gaines, xv.
13 Much of my thinking on Black respectability politics emerged from a panel that Khadijah White and I put together for the 2014 Seattle conference of the Society of Cinema and Media Studies, and developed through the special issue for *Souls* that Jane Rhodes and I co-edited. In addition to Dr. White and myself, other SCMS panelists included Jane Rhodes and Robin Means-Coleman.
14 Smith-Shomade, "'Don't Play with God!'" 321.
15 Gaines, 5.
16 I discuss how Banks prods her Black models to "transcend Blackness" in my chapter "Recursive Racial Transformation: Selling the Exceptional Multiracial on *America's Next Top Model*" in Joseph, *Transcending Blackness*.
17 Dubrofsky, 376.
18 Dubrofsky, 385.
19 *Black in America* premiered on CNN in July of 2008: http://www.cnn.com/, viewed October 5, 2015.
20 Russell-Cole, xv.
21 Harris, 1.
22 See Myers-Scotton.
23 See "Code Switch."
24 Warner, "A Black Cast" 60.
25 Hasinoff, 326.
26 Ouelette, 173.
27 Joseph, "What's the Difference with 'Difference'?".
28 Byrd, 182.

29 Spellers and Moffitt, 5.
30 Jhally, 129.
31 Celeste, "Entertaining Mobility" 2.
32 Gray, 98.

CHAPTER 6. "DO NOT RUN AWAY FROM YOUR BLACKNESS"

1 Jennifer Holt and Alisa Perren note that the circuit of culture that was "developed by the Center for Contemporary Cultural Studies (CCCS) at the University of Birmingham in the 1960s and 1970s prove[s] particularly useful for an emergent media industry studies" (8).
2 Caldwell, 1.
3 Kellner, "Media Industries" 100.
4 I promised the women anonymity. As a result, I have chosen first-name-only pseudonyms for them. I'm describing them by broad titles such as "television executive," and I am not naming the show(s) and network(s) for which they work.
5 Caldwell, 2.
6 Lotz, "Assembling a Toolkit" 49.
7 Hesmondalgh, 110.
8 Mayer, 2.
9 Banks, 87.
10 See Caldwell, quoting Felicia D. Henderson.
11 Caldwell, 227.
12 Hunt et al., 25–26.
13 Hunt et al., 25–26.
14 Hunt, "Turning Missed Opportunities into Realized Ones."
15 Hunt, "Turning Missed Opportunities into Realized Ones" 36.
16 Personal correspondence with Darnell Hunt, March 24, 2015.
17 Havens and Lotz, *Understanding Media Industries* 15.
18 See Andreeva.
19 Hunt, "Hollywood Story" 165.
20 Henderson, 187.
21 Hunt, "Hollywood Story" 167.
22 See Durkheim.
23 See Watkins.
24 Zook, 5.
25 Zook, 5.
26 Banks, 89.
27 See About Program.
28 See Creative Talent Development & Inclusion.
29 See NBC Universal.
30 See CBS Corporation.
31 Hunt, "Hollywood Story" 167.
32 See Smith, "Black Faculty Coping."

33 Rivero, 171.

34 Zook, 70.

35 One thing we didn't discuss was the women's positioning as executives and "creatives" and not "technical" workers. Their relative privilege in position, despite the lack of privileges conferred through their race and gender, were not a part of our conversation, nor were, in the words of Matt Stahl, the title distinctions that "do not reflect observable, noncontroversial differences in creativity, but that they actually serve to produce and/or sustain particular (im)balances of power" (65).

36 Kellner, "Media Industries" 105.

37 Havens and Lotz, *Understanding Media Industries* 13.

CODA. "HAVE A SEAT AT *MY* TABLE"

1 See Knowles.

2 See Mayard.

3 See Brooks, "Solange interview."

WORKS CITED

About Program. *The Guy A. Hanks & Marvin Screenwriting Program.* Accessed October 25, 2016. http://cinema.usc.edu/.

Aesop. *The Complete Fables.* Translated by Robert Temple and Olivia Temple. New York: Penguin Classics, 1998.

Alston, Kwaku. "Oprah Talks to Shonda Rhimes." *O, The Opera Magazine,* December 2006. www.oprah.com/omagazine/.

Althusser, Louis. "Ideology and Ideological State Apparatuses (Notes Towards an Investigation)." In *Media and Cultural Studies: Keyworks,* 79–87. Edited by Meenakshi Gigi Durham and Douglas M. Kellner, revised. Malden, MA: Blackwell Publishing, 2006.

Andreeva, Nellie. "Pilots 2015: The Year Of Ethnic Castings." *Deadline Hollywood,* March 24, 2015. http://deadline.com/.

"Apology to Oprah over bags of money." *Cape Times,* August 12, 2013. www.highbeam.com/.

Appiah, Kwame Anthony. "Is the Post- in Postmodernism the Post- in Postcolonial?" *Critical Inquiry* 17, no. 2 (1991): 336–57.

Arons, Jessica, and Madina Agénor. "Separate and Unequal: The Hyde Amendment and Women of Color." Center for American Progress, December 2010. www.americanprogress.org/.

"A bagful of racism for Oprah in Zurich." *The Independent,* August 10, 2013. Accessed February 4, 2014. www.highbeam.com.

Baliga, Sandeep, and Tomas Sjöström. "Strategic Ambiguity and Arms Proliferation." *Journal of Political Economy* 116, no. 6 (December 1, 2008): 1023–57. doi:10.1086/595016.

Banks, Miranda. "Gender Below-the-Line: Defining Feminist Production Studies." In *Production Studies: Cultural Studies of Media Industries,* 87–98. Edited by Vicky Mayer, Miranda J. Banks, and John Thornton Caldwell. New York: Routledge Press, 2009.

Battersby, Mathilda. "Oprah accuses Zurich shop of racist behavior." *Independent Press* (August 10, 2013).

Beltran, Mary. "The Racial Politics of Spectacular Post-Racial Satire: Ugly Betty and Glee." 2010. Conference presentation, *Console-ing Passions.*

Bennett, Michael, and Vanessa D. Dickerson, eds. *Recovering the Black Female Body: Self-Representation by African American Women.* New Brunswick, NJ: Rutgers University Press, 2000.

Bernheim, B. Douglas, and Michael D. Whinston. "Incomplete Contracts and Strategic Ambiguity." *American Economic Review* 88, no. 4 (1998): 902–932.

Beyoncé. "Formation (Explicit)." Quad Recording, 2016. www.youtube.com/watch?v=LrCHz1gwzTo.

Bhabha, Homi K., ed. *Identity—The Real Me: Postmodernism and the Question of Identity*. London: Institute of Contemporary Arts, 1987.

Bigelow, William. "Oprah Cries Racism Following Bad Customer Service." *Breitbart. com*, August 6, 2013. Accessed February 14, 2014. www.breitbart.com/.

Bobo, Jacqueline. *Black Women as Cultural Readers*. New York: Columbia University Press, 1995.

———. "The Color Purple: Black Women as Culture Readers." In *Cultural Theory and Popular Culture: A Reader*. New York: Pearson Education, 2006, 237–45.

Bonilla-Silva, Eduardo. *Racism without Racists: Color-blind Racism and the Persistence of Racial Inequality in the United States*. Lanham, MD: Rowman & Littlefield, 2003.

Brain, Anna. "Why is Oprah Lying? I'm just a shop girl,' bag to worse." *Sydney MX*, August 13, 2013.

Brinkhurst-Cuff, Charlie. "How #BlackGirlMagic Became a Rallying Cry for Women of Colour." *The Guardian*, April 11, 2016, sec. Life and style. www.the guardian.com/.

Brooks, Daphne. "All That You Can't Leave Behind": Black Female Soul Singing and the Politics of Surrogation in the Age of Catastrophe." *Meridians: Feminism, Race, Transnationalism* 8, no. 1 (2008): 180–204.

———. *Bodies in Dissent: Spectacular Performances of Race and Freedom, 1850–1910*. Durham, NC: Duke University Press, 2006.

———. "Solange interview at Yale University, discusses Prince's legacy." January 29, 2017. www.youtube.com/watch?v=LCB37aaP2js.

Brown, Caroline. "Marketing Michelle: Mommy Politics and Post-Feminism in the Age of Obama." *Comparative American Studies: An International Journal* 10, no. 1–2 (2013): 239–254.

Brown, Kara. "The New York Times, Shonda Rhimes & How to Get Away with Being Racist." *Jezebel*, September 19, 2014. http://jezebel.com/.

Brüggemann, Michael. "Between Frame Setting and Frame Sending: How Journalists Contribute to News Frames." *Communication Theory* 24, no.1 (2014): 61–82.

Brunsdon, Charlotte. "Feminism, Postfeminism, Martha, Martha, and Nigella." *Cinema Journal* 44 (2005): 110–116.

Burke, Kenneth. *A Grammar of Motives*. Berkeley, CA: University of California Press, 1969.

Butler, Judith. *Bodies that Matter: On the Discursive Limits of "Sex."* New York: Routledge, 1993.

———. *Gender Trouble: Feminism and the Subversion of Identity*. New York: Routledge, 1990.

Byrd, Ayana, and Lori Tharps. *Hair Story: Untangling the Roots of Black Hair in America*. New York: St. Martin's Griffin, 2001.

Caldwell, John Thornton. *Production Culture: Industrial Reflexivity and Critical Practice in Film and Television*. Durham, NC: Duke University Press, 2008.

Camp, Stephanie M. H. *Closer to Freedom: Enslaved Women and Everyday Resistance in the Plantation South*. Chapel Hill, NC: The University of North Carolina Press, 2004.

Carey, Nick. "Racial Predatory Loans Fueled U.S. Housing Crisis: Study." *Reuters*, October 4, 2010. www.reuters.com/.

Catanese, Brandi Wilkins. *The Problem of the Color[blind]: Racial Transgression and the Politics of Black Performance*. Ann Arbor, MI: University of Michigan Press, 2011.

CBS Corporation. "Writers Mentoring Program," Diversity, 2016. www.cbscorporation.com/.

Ceccarelli, Leah. "Polysemy: Multiple meanings in rhetorical criticism." *Quarterly Journal of Speech* 84, no. 1 (1998): 395–415.

Celeste, Manoucheka. "Entertaining Mobility: the racialized and gendered nation in House Hunters International." 2016. *Feminist Media Studies*, 1–16. http://dx.doi.org/10.1080/14680777.2015.1137336.

———. *Race, Gender, and Citizenship in the African Diaspora: Travelling Blackness*. New York: Routledge, 2016.

Charter, David. "Oprah's bag seller hits back at racism claims." *The Times UK*, August 13, 2013. Accessed February 4, 2014. www.thetimes.co.uk/.

"Cheesed off Oprah bags the 'racist' Swiss." *Sunday Telegraph* Australia ed., August 11, 2013.

Chestang, Raphael. "ET First: Oprah on Being a Recent Victim of Racism." *Entertainment Tonight*, August 5, 2013. Accessed on October 21, 2016. www.etonline.com/.

Chow, Rey. Ethics after Idealism: Theory—Culture—Ethnicity—Reading. Bloomington, IN: Indiana University Press, 1998.

Cloud, Dana. "Foiling the Intellectuals: Gender, Identity Framing, and the Rhetoric of the Kill in Conservative Hate Mail." *Communication, Culture & Critique* 2, no. 4 (2009): 457–479.

CNN Presents: Black in America. CNN, July 23, 2008.

"Code switch: Race and Identity Remixed." National Public Radio. Accessed on November 10, 2016. www.npr.org/sections/codeswitch/."

Coleman, Robin R. Means. *African American Viewers and the Black Situation Comedy: Situating Racial Humor*. New York: Garland Publishing, 1998.

———. "The Gentrification of "Black" in Black Popular Communication in the New Millennium." *Popular Communication* 4, no. 2 (2006): 79–94.

Collier, Aldore. "Shonda Rhimes: The Force Behind *Grey's Anatomy*." *Ebony* 60, no. 12 (August 31, 2011): 204.

Collins, James W., Richard J. David, Arden Handler, Stephen Wall, and Steven Andes. "Very Low Birthweight in African American Infants: The Role of Maternal Exposure to Interpersonal Racial Discrimination." *American Journal of Public Health* 94, no. 12 (December 2004): 2132–38.

Collins, Patricia Hill. *Black Feminist Thought: Knowledge, Consciousness, and the Politics of Empowerment*. New York: Routledge, 1991.

———. *Black Sexual Politics: African Americans, Gender, and the New Racism*. New York: Routledge, 2005. *Comparative American Studies* 10, no. 2–3 (2012): 239–54.

Cooper, Anna Julia. *The Negro as Presented in American Literature*. In *The Voice of Anna Julia Cooper*, 134–160. Edited by C. Lemert & E. Bhan. Lanham, MD: Rowman & Littlefield, 1998.

Cooper, Brittney. "A'n't I a Lady?: Race Women, Michelle Obama, and the Ever-Expanding Democratic Imagination." *MELUS: Multi-Ethnic Literature of the U.S.* 35, no. 4 (2010): 39–57.

Cosby, Bill. "Bill Cosby Famous Pound Cake Speech." Washington, DC., 2004. www .youtube.com/watch?v=_Gh3_e3mDQ8.

"Could it be Oprah's just a picky shopper?" *The Philadelphia Daily News*, August 8, 2013. Accessed April 2, 2016. http://articles.philly.com/.

Creative Talent Development & Inclusion. "Storytellers Start Here." *Disney ABC Television Group*, 2016. www.disneyabctalentdevelopment.com/.

Crenshaw, Kimberlé Williams. "Foreword: Toward a Race-Conscious Pedagogy in Legal Education." *S. Cal Rev. L. & Women's Studies* 33, no. 4 (1994).

———. "Mapping the Margins: Intersectionality, Identity Politics, and Violence against Women of Color." In *Critical Race Theory: The Key Writings that Formed the Movement*, 357–383. Edited by N. Gotanda, G. Peller & K. Thomas. New York: New Press, 1995.

Crenshaw, Kimberlé Williams, and Andrea J. Ritchie. "#SayHerName Brief." New York: African American Policy Forum; Center for Intersectionality and Social Policy Studies, 2015. www.aapf.org/.

Cruz, Ariane. *The Color of Kink: Black Women, BDSM, and Pornography*. New York: New York University Press, 2016.

Davies, Carole Boyce. *Black Women, Writing and Identity: Migrations of the Subject*. London; New York: Routledge, 1994.

———. "Con-di-fi-cation: Black women, Leadership, and Political Power." *Feminist Africa* 7 (2007).

Davies, Madeline. "'Hate watching' is mostly just being embarrassed by your own tastes." *Jezebel*, September 6, 2013. http://jezebel.com/.

Davis, Adrienne. "'Don't Let Nobody Bother Yo' Principle: The Sexual Economy of American Slavery." In *Sister Circle: Black Women and Work*, 103–127. Edited by S. Harley and the Black Women and Work Collective. New Brunswick, NJ: Rutgers University Press, 2002.

Dawn, Randee. "Oprah gets Swiss apologies after 'racist' encounter." *Today Entertainment*, August 9, 2013. Accessed February 4, 2014. www.today.com/.

DeAngelis, Michael. *Gay Fandom and Crossover Stardom: James Dean, Mel Gibson, and Keanu Reeves*. Durham, NC: Duke University Press, 2001.

Derrida, Jacques. *Writing and Difference*. Chicago: University of Chicago Press, 1978.

DiAngelo, Robin. "White Fragility." *The International Journal of Critical Pedagogy* 3, no. 3 (2011): 54–70.

Douglas, Susan, and Meredith Michaels. *The Mommy Myth*. New York: Free Press, 2004.

Dozier, Raine. "The Declining Relative Status of Black Women Workers, 1980–2002." *Social Forces* 88, no. 4 (2010): 1833–57.

Dubrofsky, Rachel E., and Antoine Hardy. "Performing Race in *Flavor of Love* and *The Bachelor*." *Critical Studies in Media Communication* 25, no. 4 (2008): 373–92. doi:10.1080/15295030802327774.

duCille, Ann. "Phallus(ies) of Interpretation: Toward Engendering the Black Critical 'I'." *Callaloo* 16, no. 3 (1993): 559–573.

Durham, Aisha S. *Home with Hip Hop Feminism: Performances in Communication and Culture*. New York: Peter Lang, 2014.

Durkheim, Émile. "Individualism and the Intellectuals." *Political Studies* 17 (1969): 14–30.

Dyson, Michael Eric. Foreword in *Who's Afraid of Post-Blackness? What It Means to Be Black Now*, by Touré. New York: Simon and Schuster, 2011.

Eisenberg, Eric M. *Strategic Ambiguities: Essays on Communication, Organization, and Identity*. Thousand Oaks, CA: SAGE Publications, Inc., 2007.

Emery, Debbie. "Shonda Rhimes Blasts Deadline Diversity Article as 'Ignorant,' Twitter Outraged." *TheWrap*, March 24, 2015. www.thewrap.com/.

Entman Robert. "Framing: Towards a Clarification of a Fractured Paradigm." *Journal of Communication* 43 (1993): 51–58.

Erigha, Maryann, and Camille Z. Charles. "Other, Uppity Obama: A Content Analysis of Race Appeals in the 2008 U.S. Presidential Election." *Du Bois Review: Social Science Research on Race* 9, no. 2 (2012): 439–56. doi:10.1017/S1742058X12000264.

Evatt, Nicole. "Oprah says sorry for Switzerland racism brouhaha." *Mail and Guardian: Africa's Best Read*, August 14, 2013. http://mg.co.za/.

———. "Oprah Winfrey expresses regret over media storm surrounding Swiss flap." *The Star*, August 13, 2013. Accessed February 14, 2014. www.thestar.com/.

Everett, Anna. "Scandalicious." *The Black Scholar* 45, no. 1 (2015): 34–43. doi:10.1080/00 064246.2014.997602.

Fandom Powered by Wikia. "Season 1 (Grey's Anatomy)." *Fandom*, 2005. http://greys anatomy.wikia.com/.

Featherstone, Mike. *Consumer Culture and Postmodernism*. 2nd edition. Los Angeles: SAGE Publications, 2007.

Fish, Stanley. *Is there a Text in This Classroom: The Authority of Interpretive Communities*. Cambridge, MA: Harvard University Press, 1982.

Fiske, John. *Understanding Popular Culture*. New York: Routledge, 1989.

Fleetwood, Nicole R. *On Racial Icons: Blackness and the Public Imagination*. New Brunswick, NJ: Rutgers University Press, 2015.

———. *Troubling Vision: Performance, Visuality, and Blackness*. Chicago: University of Chicago Press, 2011.

Fordham, Signithia. "'Those Loud Black Girls': (Black) Women, Silence, and Gender 'Passing' in the Academy." *Anthropology & Education Quarterly* 24, no. 1 (1993): 3–32.

Forman, Tyrone and Amanda Lewis. "Racial Apathy and Hurricane Katrina: The Social Anatomy of Prejudice in the Post-Civil Rights Era." *DuBois Review* 3 (2006): 175–202.

Franish, Darren. "The Rise of Hate-Watching: What TV Shows Do You Love to Despise?" *Entertainment Weekly*, August 16, 2012. http://ew.com/.

Frankenberg, Ruth. *White Women, Race Matters: The Social Construction of Whiteness*. 1st edition. Minneapolis: University of Minnesota Press, 1993.

Gabbard, Krin. *Black Magic: White Hollywood and African American Culture*. 6th edition. New Brunswick, NJ: Rutgers University Press, 2004.

Gaines, Kevin K. *Uplifting the Race: Black Leadership, Politics, and Culture in the Twentieth Century*. Chapel Hill, NC: The University of North Carolina Press, 2012.

Gamson, Joshua. *Claims to Fame: Celebrity in Contemporary America*. Berkeley: University of California Press, 2004.

Garza, Alicia. "A Herstory of the #BlackLivesMatter Movement by Alicia Garza." *The Feminist Wire*, October 7, 2014. www.thefeministwire.com/.

Gates, Racquel. "'Keepin' It Reality Television." In *Watching While Black: Centering the Television of Black Audiences*, 141–56. Edited by Beretta E. Smith-Shomade. New Brunswick, NJ: Rutgers University Press, 2012.

Gerbner, George, and Larry Gross. "Living with Television: The Violence Profile." *Journal of Communication* 26, no. 2 (June 1, 1976): 172–94. doi:10.1111/j.1460-2466.1976.tb01397.x.

———. "Violence in Television Drama: Trends and Symbolic Functions." In *Television and Social Behavior, Volume I: Media, Content and Control*. Edited by George A. Comstock and Eli A. Rubinstein. Washington, D.C.: U.S. Government Printing Office, 1972.

Gilroy, Paul. *Against Race: Imagining Political Culture Beyond the Color Line*. Cambridge, MA: Belknap Press of Harvard University Press, 2000.

———. *The Black Atlantic: Modernity and Double-Consciousness*. Reissue edition. Cambridge, MA: Harvard University Press, 1993.

Goldberg, Lesley. "30 of Shonda Rhimes' Stars Respond to *New York Times*' 'Angry Black Woman' Column." *The Hollywood*, September 22, 2014. www.hollywoodreporter.com/.

Gordon-Chipembere, Natasha. "Under Cuvier's Microscope: The Dissection of Michelle Obama in the Twenty-First Century." In *Representation and Black Womanhood*, 165–80. Edited by Natasha Gordon-Chipembere. New York: Palgrave Macmillan, 2011. doi:10.1057/9780230339262_11.

Gotanda, Neil. "A Critique of 'Our Constitution Is Color-Blind.'" *Stanford Law Review* 44, no. 1 (1991): 1–68. doi:10.2307/1228940.

Gray, Herman. "The Amazing Race: Global Othering." In *How to Watch Television*, 94–102. Edited by Ethan Thompson and Jason Mittell. New York: New York University Press, 2013.

———. *Cultural Moves: African Americans and the Politics of Representation*. American Crossroads. Berkeley: University of California Press, 2005.

———. "Introduction: Subjected to Respectability." *Souls: A Critical Journal of Black Politics, Culture, and Society* 18, no. 2–4 (October 1, 2016): 192–200. doi:10.1080/10999949.2016.1230814.

———. "Subject(ed) to Recognition." *American Quarterly* 65, no. 4 (2013): 771–98. doi:10.1353/aq.2013.0058.

———. *Watching Race: Television and the Struggle for "Blackness."* Minneapolis: University of Minnesota Press, 1995.

Gray, Jonathan. "New Audiences, New Textualities: Anti-fans and Non-fans." *International Journal of Cultural Studies* 6, no. 1 (2003): 64–81.

Griffin, Farah Jasmine. "'That the Mothers May Soar and the Daughters May Know their Names: A Retrospective of Black Feminist Literary Criticism." *Signs: A Journal of Women in Culture and Society* 32, no. 2 (2006): 483–508.

Griffin, Rachel Alicia. "I Am an Angry Black Woman: Black Feminist Autoethnography, Voice, and Resistance." *Women's Studies in Communication* 35, no. 2 (2012): 138–157.

Guerra, Maria. "Fact Sheet: The State of African American Women in the United States—Center for American Progress." Center for American Progress, November 7, 2013. www.americanprogress.org/.

Habell-Pallán, Michelle. "'An apartheid of theoretical domains': Transnational Feminism and the Disarticulation of U.S. Third World/Women of Color Feminist Theory." Paper presented at *National Women Studies Association Annual Conference* Roundtable: Decolonial Theory and Method: Examining 21st Century Challenges of Teaching at the Intersections of Women's Studies and Ethnic Studies, November, 2009. Atlanta, GA.

Haggins, Bambi. *Laughing Mad: The Black Comic Persona in Post-Soul America.* New Brunswick, NJ: Rutgers University Press, 2007.

Hall, Allan. "EXCLUSIVE: Swiss store owner at center of Oprah's 'racist' handbag storm demands to speak to star after she says 'sorry for the fuss.'" *The Daily Mail,* August 13, 2013. Accessed April 7, 2014. www.dailymail.co.uk/.

———. "Now Oprah says sorry." *Daily Mail,* August 13, 2013. Accessed February 14, 2014. www.dailymail.co.uk/.

———. "Oprah Winfrey racism claim disputed." *The Scotsman,* August 13, 2013. Accessed February 2, 2014. www.scotsman.com/.

Hall, Emily. "Oprah in bag shop race row: Outrage over 'cheap' insult." *The Daily Star,* August 10, 2013. Accessed April 27, 2014. www.dailystar.co.uk/.

Hall, Stuart. "Cultural Identity and Diaspora." In *Identity: Community, Culture, Difference.* Edited by Jonathan Rutherford. London: Lawrence of Wishart, 1990.

———. "Encoding/Decoding." In *Culture, Media, Language: Working Papers in Cultural Studies, 1972–79,* 128–136. Edited by Centre for Contemporary Cultural Studies. London: Routledge, 1993.

———, ed. *Representation, Meaning and Language.* London: Sage Publications, 2001.

———. "The Whites of their Eyes: Racist Ideologies and the Media." In *Silver Linings: Some Strategies for the Eighties,* 28–52. Edited by G. Bridges and R. Brunt. London: Lawrence & Wishart, 1981.

Hare, Breeanna. "Winslet, Michelle Obama among *People's* best-dressed." *CNN.com,* September 16, 2009. Accessed January 24, 2010. www.cnn.com/.

Harris, Angela P. "Introduction: Economies of Color." In *Shades of Difference: Why Skin Color Matters*, 1–6. Stanford, CA: Stanford University Press, 2009.

Hasinoff, Amy Adele. "Fashioning Race for the Free Market on America's Next Top Model." *Critical Studies in Media Communication* 25, no. 3 (August 1, 2008): 324–43. doi:10.1080/15295030802192012.

Havens, Timothy, and Amanda Lotz. *Black Television Travels: African American Media around the Globe*. New York: New York University Press, 2013.

———. *Understanding Media Industries*. New York: Oxford University Press, 2011.

Heilpern, John. "Oprah's Encounter with Racism Results in Apology from Swiss Tourism Office." *The Huffington Post*, August 9, 2013. Accessed November 12, 2013. www.huffingtonpost.com/.

———. "Swiss apologize for encounter Oprah calls racist." *Associated Press*, August 9, 2013. Accessed February 4, 2014. http://bigstory.ap.org/.

Heller, Monica. "Strategic Ambiguity: Codeswitching in the Management of Conflict." In *Codeswitching: Anthropological and Sociolinguistic Perspectives*, 77–96. Edited by Monica Heller. New York: Walter de Gruyter, 1988.

Henderson, Felicia D. "Options and Exclusivity: Economic Pressures on TV Writers' Compensation and the Effects on Writers' Room Culture." In *The SAGE Handbook of Television Studies*, by Manuel Alvarado, Milly Buonanno, Herman Gray, and Toby Miller, 183–92. London: SAGE Publications, 2015.

Hesmondalgh, David. "The Menace of Instrumentalism in Media Industries Research and Education." In *Media Industries: Perspectives on an Evolving Field*, 49–56. Edited by Amelia Arsenault and Alisa Perren, Media Industries Editorial Board, 2016. CreateSpace Independent Publishing Platform, 2016.

Hicks, Tony. "Hicks: Oprah backtracks on racism allegations." *San Jose Mercury News*, August 13, 2013. Accessed February 4, 2014. www.mercurynews.com/.

Higginbotham, Evelyn Brooks. "African-American Women's History and the Metalanguage of Race." *Signs* 17, no. 2 (1992): 251–74.

———. *Righteous Discontent: The Women's Movement in the Black Baptist Church, 1880–1920*. Revised, Cambridge, MA.: Harvard University Press, 1994.

Hine, Darlene Clark, and Kathleen Thompson. *A Shining Thread of Hope: The History of Black Women in America*. New York: Broadway, 1998.

Holmes, Linda. "The Only One: A Talk with Shonda Rhimes." *National Public Radio*, September 22, 2014. www.npr.org/.

Holt, Jennifer, and Alisa Perren, eds. *Media Industries: History, Theory, and Method*. Malden, MA: Wiley-Blackwell, 2009.

hooks, bell. *Feminist Theory: From Margin to Center*. Boston: South End Press, 1984.

———. "The Oppositional Gaze: Black Female Spectators." In *Black Looks: Race and Representation*, 115–131. Boston: South End Press, 1992.

Horkheimer, Max, and Theodor Adorno. "The Culture Industry: Enlightenment as Mass Deception." In *Media and Cultural Studies: Keyworks*, 41–72. Edited by Meenakshi Gigi Durham and Douglas M. Kellner. Revised, Malden, MA: Blackwell Publishing, 2006.

Horkheimer, Max, Theodor W. Adorno, and Gunzelin Schmid Noerr. *Dialectic of Enlightenment: Philosophical Fragments*. Stanford, CA: Stanford University Press, 2002.

Horne, Gerald. *Race Woman: The Lives of Shirley Graham Du Bois*. New York: New York University Press, 2002.

Hua, Julietta. "'Gucci Geishas' and Postfeminism." *Women's Studies in Communication* 32, no. 1 (2009): 63–88.

Hunt, Darnell. "Hollywood Story: Diversity, Writing and the End of Television as We Know It." In *The SAGE Handbook of Television Studies*, by Manuel Alvarado, Milly Buonanno, Herman Gray, and Toby Miller, 163–73. London: SAGE Publications, 2015.

———. "Turning Missed Opportunities into Realized Ones." *The 2014 Hollywood Writers Report*. Writers Guild of America, West, 2014.

Hunt, Darnell, Ana-Christina Ramon, and Michael Tran. "Hollywood Diversity Report: Business as Usual?" Los Angeles, CA: University of California Los Angeles, 2016.

Ibrahim, Habiba. *Troubling the Family: The Promise of Personhood and the Rise of Multiracialism*. Minneapolis, MN: University of Minnesota Press, 2012.

Jackson, John L. *Racial Paranoia: The Unintended Consequences of Political Correctness*. Reprint, New York: Basic Books, 2010.

James, Joy. "Resting in the Gardens, Battling in the Deserts: Black women's Activism." *The Black Scholar* 38, no. 4 (2009): 2–7.

Jefferies, Mark. "'Oprah's Lying . . . I never said anything racist'; Shop assistant hits back." *Daily Mirror*, August 2013.

Jenkins, Henry. "'Out of the Closet and Into the Universe': Queers and Star Trek." In *Science Fiction Audiences: Doctor Who and Star Trek*, 237–65. Edited by John Tulloch and Henry Jenkins. New York: Routledge, 1995.

Jenkins, Richard. "Imagined but Not Imaginary: Ethnicity and Nationalism in the Modern World." In *Exotic No More: Anthropology on the Front Lines*, 114–128. Edited by Jeremy MacClancy. University of Chicago Press, 2002.

Jhally, Sut, and Justin M. Lewis. *Enlightened Racism: The Cosby Show, Audiences, and the Myth of the American Dream*. Boulder, CO: Westview Press, 1992.

Johnson, Pamela K. "The Cutting Edge: Shonda Rhimes Dissects Grey's Anatomy." *Written By: The Magazine of the Writers Guild of America, West*, September 2005. www.wga.org/.

Joseph, Ralina L. "'Hope Is Finally Making a Comeback': First Lady Reframed." *Communication, Culture & Critique* 4, no. 1 (2011): 56–77. doi:10.1111/j.1753–9137.2010.01093.x.

———. *Transcending Blackness: From the New Millennium Mulatta to the Exceptional Multiracial*. Durham, NC: Duke University Press, 2013.

———. "What's the Difference with 'Difference'?" University of Washington Distinguished Public Lecture. Seattle, WA, January 14, 2016.

Kahl, Mary L. "First Lady Michelle Obama: Advocate for Strong Families." *Communication and Critical/Cultural Studies* 6, no. 3 (2009): 316–320.

Kellner, Douglas. "Cultural Studies, Multiculturalism, and Media Culture." In *Gender, Race, and Class in Media: A Critical Reader*, 5–17. Thousand Oaks, CA: Sage Publications, 1995.

———. "Media Industries, Political Economy, and Media/Cultural Studies: An Articulation." In *Media Industries: History, Theory, and Method*, 107–112. Edited by Jennifer Holt and Alisa Perren. Malden, MA: Wiley-Blackwell, 2009.

———. "Media spectacle and the 2008 presidential election." *Cultural Studies < = > Critical Methodologies* 9, no. 6 (2009): 707–716.

———. *Media Culture: Cultural Studies, Identity and Politics between the Modern and the Post-Modern*. New York: Routledge, 1995.

Kelly, Raina. "A Real Wife, in a Real Marriage." *Newsweek*, February 25, 2008. www.newsweek.com/.

Kenney, Greta. "Interrupting Microaggressions." College of the Holy Cross, Diversity Leadership & Education. www.uua.org/.

Kim, Claire Jean. "Managing the Racial Breach: Clinton, Black-White Polarization, and the Race Initiative." *Political Science Quarterly* 117.1 (2002): 55–79.

Knowles, Solange. *A Seat at the Table*. Saint Records and Columbia Records, 2016, digital.

L'Oréal Paris. "Beyonce Knowles Singer—L'Oreal Paris: Celebrity Endorsements, Celebrity Advertisements, Celebrity Endorsed Products." *Celebrity Fashionation*, 2003. www.celebrityendorsementads.com/.

Lee, Ronald, and Aysel Morin. "Using the 2008 Presidential Election to Think About 'Playing the Race Card.'" *Communication Studies* 60 no. 4 (2009): 376–391.

Legge, James. "Oprah Winfrey: I'm really sorry that Swiss racism story got 'blown up.'" *The Independent*, August 14, 2013. www.independent.co.uk/.

Levine, Elana. "Grey's Anatomy: Feminism." In *How to Watch Television*, 139–147. Edited by Ethan Thompson and Jason Mittell. New York: New York University Press, 2013.

Lewis, Oscar. *Five Families: Mexican Case Studies in the Culture of Poverty*. New York: Basic Books, 1975.

Li, David. "Shop says nope-rah to Oprah 'racist' purse di$$." *The New York Post*, August 10, 2013. www.newshour24.com/.

Lipsitz, George. *The Possessive Investment in Whiteness: How White People Profit from Identity Politics, Revised and Expanded Edition*. Philadelphia: Temple University Press, 2006.

Lofton, Kathryn. *Oprah: The Gospel of an Icon*. Berkeley: University of California Press, 2011.

Long, Amy. "Diagnosing Drama: Grey's Anatomy, Blind Casting, and the Politics of Representation." *The Journal of Popular Culture* 44, no. 5 (2011): 1067–84. doi:10.1111/j.1540-5931.2011.00888.x.

Lorde, Audre. *Sister Outsider: Essays and Speeches*. Berkeley: Crossing Press, 1984.

Lotz, Amanda D. "Assembling a Toolkit." In *Media Industries: Perspectives on an Evolving Field*, 107–112. Edited by Amelia Arsenault and Alisa Perren. CreateSpace Independent Publishing Platform, 2016.

———. "Assessing Qualitative Television Audience Research: Incorporating Feminist and Anthropological Theoretical Innovation." *Communication Theory* 10, no. 4 (2000): 447–67. doi:10.1111/j.1468-2885.2000.tb00202.x.

———. *The Television Will Be Revolutionized*. New York: New York University Press, 2007.

Lugones, Maria. "The Coloniality of Gender." *Worlds and Knowledge Otherwise*, 2008. Accessed January 24, 2010. www.jhfc.duke.edu/.

Lyotard, Jean-Francois. *The Postmodern Condition: A Report on Knowledge*. Minneapolis: University of Minnesota Press, 1993.

Madison, D. Soyini. "Crazy Patriotism and Angry (Post)Black Women." *Communication and Critical/Cultural Studies* 6, no. 3 (2009): 321–326.

Maerz, Melissa. "The Anatomy of How to Get Away with Scandalously Good TV." *Entertainment Weekly*, September 11, 2015. 22–30.

Mask, Mia. *Divas on Screen: Black Women in American Film*. Urbana and Chicago: University of Illinois Press, 2010.

Mayard, Judnick. "A Seat with Us: A Conversation Between Solange Knowles, Mrs. Tina Lawson, & Judnick Mayard." *Saint Heron*, September 20, 2016. Accessed June 14, 2017. http://saintheron.com/.

Mayer, Vicky, Miranda J. Banks, and John Thornton Caldwell. "Introduction: Production Studies: Routes and Roots." In *Production Studies: Cultural Studies of Media Industries,* 1–12. Edited by Vicky Mayer, Miranda J. Banks, and John Thornton Caldwell. New York: Routledge Press, 2009.

McKinley, Christopher. "Winfrey claims racism in Swiss handbag shop: TV host says assistant refused to get EUR 28,500 crocodile bag for her because of its cost." *Irish Times*, August 10, 2013. Accessed February 4, 2014. www.highbeam.com/.

McNamee, Stephen J., and Robert K. Miller, Jr. *The Meritocracy Myth*. 3rd edition. Lanham: Rowman & Littlefield Publishers, Inc, 2009.

McRobbie, Angela. "Post Feminism and Popular Culture." *Feminist Media Studies* 4 (2004): 255–264.

———. "The Politics of Feminist Research: Between Talk, Text and Action." *Feminist Review* no. 12 (1982): 46–57. doi:10.2307/1394881.

———. *Displacement Feminism: Gender, Culture and Social Change*. Thousand Oaks, CA: Sage, 2008.

———. *The Aftermath of Feminism: Gender, Culture and Social Change*. Los Angeles: SAGE Publications, 2009.

Means Coleman, Robin ed. *Say It Loud!: African American Audiences, Media and Identity*. New York: Routledge, 2002.

Mendelberg, Tali. "Racial Priming Revived." Perspectives on Politics 6, no. 01 (2008): 109-12. doi: 10.1017/S1537592708080092.

Mercer, Kobena. *Welcome to the Jungle: New Positions in Black Cultural Studies*. New York: Routledge, 1994.

Methven, Nicola. "TV legend Oprah in 'posh shop race row." *The Mirror*, August 10, 2013. Accessed February 4, 2014. www.highbeam.com/.

Michelle Obama. "Michelle Obama Pt 1A of 4." *The View*, ABC, June 18, 2008. Accessed January 24, 2010. www.youtube.com/watch?v=6cdQQAdUeVE.

Miller, Toby. *Television Studies: The Basics*. New York: Routledge, 2010.

Miller-Young, Mireille. *A Taste for Brown Sugar: Black Women in Pornography*. Durham, NC: Duke University Press, 2014.

Millner, Michael. "Review: Post Post-Identity." *American Quarterly* 57, no. 2 (2005): 541–554.

Mitchell, W. J. Thomas. "Seeing Disability." *Public Culture* 13, no. 3 (September 1, 2001): 391–97.

Morgan, Marcyliena, and Dionne Bennett. "Getting off of Black Women's Backs: Love Her or Leave Her Alone." *DuBois Review* 3, no. 2 (2006): 485–502.

Morris III, Charles E. "Pink Herring & the Fourth Persona: J. Edgar Hoover's Sex Crime Panic." Quarterly Journal of Speech 88, no. 2 (May 1, 2002): 228–44. doi:10.1080/00335630209384372.

Morrison, Toni. *Playing in the Dark: Whiteness and the Literary Imagination*. Reprint, New York: Vintage, 2007.

Moynihan, Daniel P. "The Negro Family: The Case for National Action." *Office of Policy Planning and Research*. Washington, D.C.: U.S. Department of Labor, 1965.

Mullings, Leith. "African-American women making themselves: Notes on the role of black feminist research." *SOULS: A Critical Journal of Black Politics, Culture, and Society* 2, no. 4 (2000): 18–29.

Muñoz, José Esteban. *Disidentifications: Queers of Color and the Performance of Politics*. Cultural Studies of the Americas. Minneapolis, MN: University of Minnesota Press, 1999.

Myers, Robbie. "Shonda Rhimes on Power, Feminism, and Police Brutality." *Elle*, September 23, 2015. www.elle.com/.

Myers-Scotton, Carol. *Duelling Languages: Grammatical Structure in Codeswitching*. Oxford: Clarendon Press, 1993.

Nash, Jennifer C. *The Black Body in Ecstasy: Reading Race, Reading Pornography*. Durham, NC: Duke University Press, 2014.

National Institutes of Health. "Women of Color Health Information Collection: Cardiovascular Disease." *U.S. Department of Health and Human Services*, 2012, 8. http://orwh.od.nih.gov/.

National Public Radio. "Code Switch: Race and Identity, Remixed." *NPR.org*, April 7, 2013. www.npr.org/.

Nayak, Anoop. "After Race: Ethnography, Race and Post-Race Theory." *Ethnic and Racial Studies* 29, no. 3 (2006): 411–430.

NBC Universal. "Diversity Initiative for Writers." *NBC Universal Careers*, 2016. www.nbcunicareers.com/.

NewsOne Staff. "Melissa Harris-Perry Mocks Oprah's 'Racist' Experience As '1-Percenter Problems.'" *Newsone.com*, August 12, 2013. Accessed February 10, 2014 http://newsone.com/.

Nilsen, Sarah, and Sarah E. Turner eds. *The Colorblind Screen: Television in Post-Racial America*. New York, NY: NYU Press, 2014.

Noble, Safiya Umoja. "Google Search: Hyper-Visibility as a Means of Rendering Black Women and Girls." *InVisible Culture: An Electronic Journal for Visual Culture* 19 (2013).

Nussbaum, Emily. "Hate-Watching Smash." *New Yorker*, April 27, 2012. www.new yorker.com/.

O'Keefe, Ed. "Cindy McCain Presses Obama Patriotism Case." ABC News Blog, June 18, 2008. http://blogs.abcnews.com/.

O'Reilly, Andrea. "I come from a long line of Uppity Irate Black Women." In *Mothers and Daughters: Connection, Empowerment, and Transformation*, 143–159. Edited by Andrea O'Reilly and Sharon Abbey. Lanham, MD: Rowman & Littlefield, 2000.

Omi, Michael, and Howard Winant. *Racial Formation in the United States*. New York: Routledge, 1996.

"Oprah accuses Swiss shop of racism." *Canberra Times*, August 11, 2013. Australia edition.

"Oprah handbag claim not true." *Daily Mail*, August 13, 2013.

"Oprah 'racism' just lost in translation." *The Sunday-Star Times*, August 11, 2013.

"Oprah regrets Swiss frenzy." *Cape Times*, August 14, 2013. South Africa. Accessed February 4, 2014. www.highbeam.com/.

"Oprah regrets Swiss racism incident." *ABC News Radio*, August 14, 2013. Accessed February 14, 2014. www.classichitsandoldies.com/.

"Oprah Repulsa and Pursehead, her new $38,000 handbag." *Chatteringteeth Blog*, August 13, 2013. Accessed April 17, 2014. chatteringteeth.blogspot.com/.

"Oprah Says 'Sorry' For Crying Racism After Receiving Bad Customer Service at Boutique." *MrConservative.com*, August 13, 2013. www.mrconservative.com/.

"Oprah says 'sorry' for media storm linked to Swiss shopping story." *CTV News*, August 14, 2013. Accessed February 14, 2014. www.ctvnews.ca/.

"Oprah says sorry over Switzerland racism flap." *Fox News*, August 13, 2013. Accessed February 4, 2014. www.foxnews.com/.

"Oprah sorry for blown up racism row." *Irish Independent*, August 14, 2013. Accessed February 14, 2014. www.independent.ie/.

"Oprah sorry over uproar over racism scandal." *The Hype: Yahoo Entertainment*, August 14, 2013. Accessed February 14, 2014. http://au.thehype.yahoo.com/.

"Oprah Talks to Shonda Rhimes." *The Oprah Magazine* no. 12 (December 1, 2016): 7,.

"Oprah Winfrey apologises for Swiss handbag-gate." *Euronews*, August 13, 2013. Accessed February 14, 2014. www.euronews.com/.

Ouelette, Laurie. "*America's Next Top Model*: Neoliberal Labor." In *How to Watch Television*, 168–76. Edited by Ethan Thompson and Jason Mittell. New York: New York University Press, 2013.

Page, Susan. "Poll: Michelle Obama Gets High Marks." *USA Today*, April 24, 2009. http://usatoday30.usatoday.com/.

Parker, Morgan. "Why I'm Moving Out of Shondaland." *For Harriet: Celebrating the Fullness of Black Womanhood.* December 15, 2014. www.forharriet.com/.

Paskin, Willa. "Network TV Is Broken. So How Does Shonda Rhimes Keep Making Hits?" *The New York Times,* May 9, 2013. www.nytimes.com/.

Peck, Janice. "Oprah Winfrey: Cultural Icon of Mainstream (White) America." In *The Colorblind Screen: Television in Post-Racial America,* 83–107. Edited by Sarah Nilsen and Sarah E. Turner. New York: New York University Press, 2014.

———. *The Age of Oprah: Cultural Icon for the Neoliberal Era.* Boulder, CO: Routledge, 2008.

Piazza, Jo. "Mad rush for $148 dress Michelle Obama wore on 'The View.'" *Daily News,* June 20, 2008. Accessed January 24, 2010. www.nydailynews.com/.

Pollock, Mica. Colormute: Race Talk Dilemmas in an American School. Princeton, NJ: Princeton University Press, 2005.

Pomerantz, Dorothy. "Oprah Winfrey Regains No. 1 Slot on Forbes 2013 List of the Most Powerful Celebrities." *Forbes,* June 26, 2013. Accessed October 31, 2013 www.forbes.com/sites/.

Power, Brenda. "Oprah loses out on handbags at dawn." *Irish Daily Mail,* August 17, 2013. Accessed February 2, 2014. http://connection.ebscohost.com/.

Radway, Janice A. *Reading the Romance: Women, Patriarchy, and Popular Literature.* Chapel Hill, NC: The University of North Carolina Press, 1984.

Randhawa, Kirin. "'That Bag Is Too Expensive for You': Oprah Winfrey Says 'Racist 'Assistant Refused to Serve Her in Zurich." *Evening Standard,* August 9, 2013. www.standard.co.uk/.

Retman, Sonnet. "'Return of the Native': Sterling Brown's A Negro Looks at the South and the Work of Signifing Ethnography." *American Literature* 88: 1. March 2014: 87–115.

Reuters. "Oprah Opens The 'Handbag' Issue At 'The Butler' Premiere." Accessed February 2, 2014. www.youtube.com/watch?v=oHhsYnlVf2k/.

Rhimes, Shonda. "Confused Why @nytimes Critic Doesn't Know Identity of CREATOR of Show She's Reviewing. @petenowa Did U Know U Were 'an Angry Black Woman'?" Microblog. @shondarhimes, September 19, 2014. https://twitter.com/.

Rhodes, Jane. "Pedagogies of Respectability: Race, Media, and Black Womanhood in the Early 20th Century." *Souls: A Critical Journal of Black Politics, Culture, and Society* 18, no. 2–4 (October 1, 2016): 201–14. doi:10.1080/10999949.2016.1230814.

Rita Repulsa. *RangerWiki.* Accessed October 19, 2015. http://powerrangers.wikia.com/.

Rivero, Yeidy. "Politically Charged Media Sites: The 'Right,' the 'Left,' and the Self in Research." In *Media Industries: Perspectives on an Evolving Field,* 171–176. Edited by Amelia Arsenault and Alisa Perren, Media Industries Editorial Board. CreateSpace Independent Publishing Platform, 2016.

Robinson, Subrina J. "Spoketokenism: Black Women Talking Back about Graduate School Experiences." *Race Ethnicity and Education* 16, no. 2 (2013): 155–81. doi:10.1080/13613324.2011.645567.

Robinson, Tracy, and Janie Victoria Ward. "A Belief in Self Far Greater Than Anyone's Disbelief': Cultivating Resistance Among African American Female Adolescents."

In *Women, Girls & Psychotherapy: Reframing Resistance*, 87–104. Edited by Carol Gilligan, Annie G. Rogers, and Deborah L. Tolman. Binghamton, NY: Harington Park Press, 1991.

Rodman, Gilbert B. "Race . . . and Other Four Letter Words: Eminem and the Cultural Politics of Authenticity." *Popular Communication* 4, no. 2, (2006): 95–121.

Roof, Judith. "Thinking Post-identity." *The Journal of the Midwest Modern Language Association* 36, no. 1 (2003): 1–5.

Rothman, Michael. "Oprah gets Swiss apology for racist diss in handbag shop." *ABC NEWS*, October 2013. http://abcnews.go.com/.

Russell-Cole, Kathy, Midge Wilson, and Ronald E. Hall. *The Color Complex: The Politics of Skin Color in a New Millennium*. New York: Random House, 1992.

Samuels, Allison. "How Scandal on ABC Got off the Ground." *Newsweek*, March 5, 2012. www.newsweek.com/.

Sandoval, Chela. *Methodology of the Oppressed: Theory out of Bounds*. Minneapolis: University of Minnesota Press, 2000.

Scandal Season 1 Cast Promotional Photo. Photograph, 2012. http://images.spoilertv .com/.

Schiappa, Edward. "The Rhetoric of Nukespeak." *Communication Monographs* 56, no. 3 (1989): 253–272.

Sedgwick, Eve Kosofsky. *Epistemology of the Closet*. Berkeley: University of California Press, 1990.

"She's sorry for racism flap." *Newsday*, August 14, 2013.

Shilling, Dave. "Oprah Accused a Swiss Person of Racism." *Vice.com*, August 9, 2013. Accessed April 7, 2014. www.vice.com/.

"Shop assistant's big mistake earns ire of Oprah." *Cape Argus*, August 10, 2013. www.iol .co.za/.

Smith, Cherise. *Enacting Others: Politics of Identity in Eleanor Antin, Nikki S. Lee, Adrian Piper, and Anna Deavere Smith*. Durham, NC: Duke University Press, 2011.

Smith, Erin. "Boycott ABC & Sign petition to fire Jesse Williams from Grey's Anatomy for racist ran." Accessed on October 4, 2016. www.change.org/.

Smith, Maya Angela. "Multilingual Practices of Senegalese Immigrants in Paris and Rome: A Comparative Study of Language Use and Identity Construction." Doctoral Dissertation, University of California, Berkeley, 2013. http://escholarship.org/uc/item /3px5k06d.

———. "Multilingual Practices of Senegalese Immigrants in Rome: Construction of Identities and Negotiation of Boundaries." *Italian Culture* 33, no. 2 (2015): 126–46. doi:10.1179/0161462215Z.00000000037.

Smith, Valerie. *Not just Race, not just Gender: Black Feminist Readings*. New York: Routledge, 1998.

Smith, William A. "Black Faculty Coping with Racial Battle Fatigue: The Campus Racial Climate in a Post-Civil Rights Era." *A Long Way to Go: Conversations about Race by African American Faculty and Graduate Students*. Edited by Darrel Cleveland. New York: Peter Lang, 2004.

Smith-Shomade, Beretta E. "'Don't Play with God!': Black Church, Play, and Possibilities." *Souls* 18, no. 2–4 (October 1, 2016): 321–37. doi:10.1080/10999949.2016.1230820.

———. *Shaded Lives: African-American Women and Television.* New Brunswick, NJ: Rutgers University Press, 2002.

———. Beretta E. *Watching While Black: Centering the Television of Black Audiences.* New Brunswick, NJ: Rutgers University Press, 2013.

Smith-Spark, Laura, and KJ Matthews. "Oprah Winfrey: I'm sorry Switzerland racism incident got blown up." *CNN,* August 13, 2013. Accessed February 14, 2014. www.cnn .com/.

Sonnet, Esther. "'Ju envisioning the audience as a *construct* st a Book,' She Said . . .': Reconfiguring Ethnography for the Female Readers of Sexual Fiction." In *The Audience Studies Reader,* 254–79. Edited by Will Brooker and Deborah Jermyn. London and New York: Psychology Press, 2003.

Spellers, Regina, and Kimberly Moffitt. Introduction in *Blackberries and Redbones: Critical Articulations of Black Hair/Body Politics in Africana Communities.* Cresskill, NJ: Hampton Press, 2010.

Spillers, Hortense. "Views of the East Wing: On Michelle Obama." *Communication & Critical/Cultural Studies* 6, no. 3 (2009): 307–310.

Spivak, Gayatri. "Subaltern Studies." In *Deconstruction: Critical Concepts in Literary and Cultural Studies,* IV:220–44. Edited by Jonathan D. Culler. New York: Routledge, 2003.

Springer, Kimberly. "Divas, Evil Black Bitches, and Bitter Black Women: African American Women in Postfeminist and Post-Civil Rights Popular Culture." In *Interrogating Postfeminism,* 249–276. Edited by Y. Tasker and D. Negra. Durham, NC: Duke University Press, 2007.

———. "Third Wave Black Feminism?" *Signs: Journal of Women in Culture and Society* 27 (2002): 1059–1082.

Squires, Catherine R. *The Post-Racial Mystique: Media and Race in the Twenty-First Century.* Critical Cultural Communication. New York: New York University Press, 2014.

———. "Running Through the Trenches: Or, an Introduction to the Undead Culture Wars and Dead Serious Identity Politics." *Journal of Communication Theory* 34, no. 3 (2010): 211–214.

St. Louis, Brett. "Post-Race/Post-Politics? Activist-Intellectualism and the Reification of Race. *Ethnic and Racial Studies* 25, no. 4 (2002): 652–675.

Stahl, Matt. "Privilege and Distinction in Production Worlds: Copyright, Collective Bargaining, and Working Conditions in Media Making." In *Production Studies: Cultural Studies of Media Industries,* 54–68. Edited by Vicky Mayer, Miranda J. Banks, and John Thornton Caldwell. New York: Routledge Press, 2009.

Staiger, Janet. "Analysing Self-Fashioning in Authoring and Reception." In *Ingmar Bergman Revisited: Performance, Cinema and the Arts,* 89–106. Edited by Maaret Koskinen and Liv Ullmann. London: Wallflower, 2008.

Stanley, Alessandra. "Wrought in Rhimes's Image: Viola Davis Plays Shonda Rhimes's Latest Tough Heroine." *The New York Times*, September 18, 2014. www.nytimes .com/.

Staples, Brent. "Barack Obama, John McCain and the Language of Race." *The New York Times*, September 22, 2008.

Steyn, Mark. "Mrs. Obama's America." *National Review*, April 21, 2008.

"Storm in a handbag: Oprah Winfrey accuses Zurich boutique of racism." *Swiss Info*, August 9, 2013. www.swissinfo.ch/.

Sue, Derald Wing. *Microaggressions in Everyday Life: Race, Gender, and Sexual Orientation.* Hoboken, NJ: Wiley, 2010.

———. *Race Talk and the Conspiracy of Silence: Understanding and Facilitating Difficult Dialogues on Race.* Hoboken, NJ: Wiley & Sons, 2016.

Sullivan, Margaret. "An Article on Shonda Rhimes Rightly Causes a Furor." *The New York Times*, Public Editor's Journal, September 22, 2014. http://publiceditor.blogs .nytimes.com/.

Swarns, Rachel. "In First Lady's Roots, a Complex Path from Slavery." *New York Times,* October 7, 2009.

"Swiss racism upsets Oprah." *Evening Times*, August 10, 2013. Accessed February 4, 2014. www.eveningtimes.co.uk/.

"Swiss sorry after Oprah snubbed in shop 'racism' row." *Belfest Telegraph,* August 10, 2013. Accessed February 4, 2014. www.belfasttelegraph.co.uk/.

Tasker, Yvonne, and Diane Negra, eds. *Interrogating Postfeminism: Gender and the Politics of Popular Culture.* Durham, N.C.: Duke University Press Books, 2007.

Thompson, Ethan, and Jason Mittell. "Introduction: An Owner's Manual for Television." In *How to Watch Television.* New York: New York University Press, 2013.

Thompson, Lisa B. *Beyond the Black Lady: Sexuality and the New African American Middle Class.* Urbana, IL: University of Illinois Press, 2012.

Thompson, Paul. "Education is why we need this bailout says First Lady." *The Evening Standard,* February 2, 2009.

TMZ. "Passive Aggressive Oprah—Gives BS Apology for Switzerland Racist Flap." *TMZ.com,* August 13, 2013. www.tmz.com/.

Trebay, Guy. "She Dresses to Win." *New York Times*, June 18, 2008. Accessed January 24, 2010. www.nytimes.com/.

U.S. Breast Cancer Statistics. *Breastcancer.org,* September 30, 2016. www.breastcancer .org/.

Uppity. *Urban dictionary.* Accessed January 7, 2014. www.urbandictionary.com/.

Vats, Anjali. "Racechange is the New Black: Racial Accessorizing and Racial Tourism in High Fashion as Constraints on Rhetorical Agency." Communication, Culture & Critique 7 (2017): 112-135. doi:10.1111/cccr.12037.

Vavrus, Mary D. *Postfeminist news: Political women in media culture.* Albany, NY: State University of New York Press, 2002.

Verica, Tom. "The Lawn Chair." *Scandal* (March 5, 2015). Hollywood, CA: ABC Studios.

Wall, Cheryl A. "Review of Carole Boyce Davies, *Black Women, Writing and Identity: Migrations of the Subject.*" *Criticism* xxxix, no. 3 (1997): 456–58.

Walley-Jean, J. Celeste. "Debunking the Myth of the 'Angry Black Woman': An Exploration of Anger in Young African American Women." *Black Women, Gender & Families* 3, no. 2 (2009): 68–86. doi:10.1353/bwg.0.0011.

Warner, Kristen J. "A Black Cast Doesn't Make a Black Show: City of Angels and the Plausible Deniability of Color-Blindness." In *Watching While Black: Centering the Television of Black Audiences*, 49–62. Edited by Beretta E. Smith-Shomade. New Brunswick, NJ: Rutgers University Press, 2012.

———. *The Cultural Politics of Colorblind TV Casting.* Transformations in Race and Media. New York: Routledge, 2015.

———. "The Racial Logic of *Grey's Anatomy*: Shonda Rhimes and Her 'Post-Civil Rights, Post-Feminist' Series." *Television & New Media* 16, no. 7 (2015): 631–647.

Watkins, Mel. *On the Real Side: A History of African American Comedy.* Chicago: Chicago Review Press, 1999.

Watts, Eric King. "The (Nearly) Apocalyptic Politics of 'Postracial' America: Or 'This is Now the United States of Zombieland.'" *Journal of Communication Theory* 34, no. 3 (2010): 214–222.

Weber, Brenda R. *Makeover TV: Selfhood, Citizenship, and Celebrity.* Durham, NC: Duke University.

Weheliye, Alexander G. *Habeas Viscus: Racializing Assemblages, Biopolitics, and Black Feminist Theories of the Human.* Durham, NC: Duke University Press, 2014.

White, Cindy L., and Catherine A. Dobris. "The Nobility of Womanhood: 'Womanhood' in the Rhetoric of 19th Century Black Club Women." In *Centering Ourselves: African American Feminist and Womanist Studies of Discourse*, 171–185. Edited by Marsha Houston and Olga Idriss Davis. Cresskill, NJ: Hampton Press, Inc., 2001.

White, Deborah Gray. *Aren't I a Woman? Female Slaves in the Plantation South.* New York: W.W. Norton, 1999.

Williams, Jesse. "2016 BET Humanitarian Award Acceptance Speech." *BET Awards*, Los Angeles, CA. June 26, 2016. www.youtube.com/watch?v=HeRIUPlxlv4.

Williams, Patricia J. *The Alchemy of Race and Rights.* Cambridge: Harvard University Press, 1991.

Williams, Verna L. "The First (black) Lady." *Denver University Law Review* 86 (2009): 833–850.

"Winfrey regrets storm stirred by racism story." *Pretoria News*, August 14, 2013.

"Winfrey sorry for 'racism' furore; Panorama around the world in 10 stories Switzerland." *Independent Print*, August 14, 2013.

Wolfe, Alexandra. "The TV Producer on Her Hit Shows, Finding Balance and Her One-Year Plan to Conquer Her Fears." *Wall Street Journal*, October 30, 2015. www.wsj.com/.

Wood, Helen. *Talking with Television: Women, Talk Shows, and Modern Self-Reflexivity.* Urbana, IL: University of Illinois Press, 2009.

Wright, Stephen C., and Donald M. Taylor. "Responding to Tokenism: Individual Action in the Face of Collective Injustice." *European Journal of Social Psychology* 28, no. 4 (1998): 647–67. doi:10.1002/(SICI)1099–0992(199807/08)28:4<647:: AID-EJSP887>3.0.CO;2–0.

Yu, Jessica. "Blown Away." *Scandal* (December 13, 2012). Hollywood, CA: ABC Studios.

Zook, Kristal Brent. *Color by Fox: The Fox Network and the Revolution in Black Television.* New York: Oxford University Press, 1999.

INDEX

Page references in italics indicate an illustration.

Bush, George W., 11–12
Bush, Laura, 31
Butler, Judith, 19, 39
Byrd, Ayana D., 156

Caldwell, John Thornton, 88, 116, 161, 163
Camp, Stephanie M. H., 22
Carter, Jimmy, 12
Catanese, Brandi, 93
CBS network, 174
Ceccarelli, Leah, 15–17, 41, 205–6n47
celebrity: good role model vs. bad black
    stereotype, 24. *See also* Obama,
    Michelle; Rhimes, Shonda; Winfrey,
    Oprah; *and other individual celebrities*
Celeste, Manoucheka, 4, 159
Center for Contemporary Cultural Stud-
    ies (CCCS; University of Birming-
    ham), 218n1
Charles, Camille Z., 76, 212n57
Chartier, Roger, 204n39
circuit of culture, 17, 161, 218n1
civil rights, 4, 10–11, 34–35, 37–38, 40–41
class: and Blackness, 158; and respectabil-
    ity politics, 142; Winfrey as transcend-
    ing, 58
Clinton, Bill, 11
Clinton, Hillary, 35, 41, 47, 50
Cloud, Dana, 45
code: coded postracial resistance, 67;
    coded racism, 185–87, 197; code-
    switching, 12, 15, 151–54; encoding/
    decoding model, 114–15, 161; Michelle
    Obama's use of, 35, 38, 41, 43–44, 49,
    53, 55, 57, 209n17
collectivity vs. individualism, 43–44
Collier, Aldore, 95
Collins, Patricia Hill, x, 22, 34, 40
colorblindness: vs. assimilation, 10; vs.
    celebrating diversity, 180; and the
    civil rights movement, 10–11; of *Grey's
    Anatomy's* casting/scripting, 4, 25, 84,
    89, 90, 91–94; objections to colorblind

casting, 93–94; pervasiveness of ideol-
    ogy of, 89; and police violence against
    Black people, 104; Rhimes's ideology
    of, 4, 91–92, 96, 98–101, 103–4; of
    Scandal's casting/scripting, 4; writings
    on, 10–11
colorism, 145–51, 154
Combahee River Collective, 39–40
Cooper, Brittney, 31
Cosby, Bill, 84–85, 174
Cosby, Camille, 174
The Cosby Show, 157, 214n34
Cosby Workshop (Guy Hanks and Mar-
    vin Miller Writing Program, USC), 174
Crenshaw, Kimberlé Williams, 10, 36, 38
Crossroads, 83
Crowe, Russell, 98
"crying racism" trope, 69, 71, 73, 82
CSI, 89
Cullors, Patrisse, 6
culture of performance, 164
Cussaux, Michelle, 6

Davies, Carole Boyce, 17, 44, 67–68
Davis, Adrienne, 42–43
DeAngelis, Michael, 21
Deen, Paula, 62
Derrida, Jacques, 10, 36
Desperate Housewives, 89
DiAngelo, Robin, 40–41, 137–38
Dickerson, Vanessa D., 88
differential consciousness, 53
disidentification, 19
Disney, 174
Diversity Initiative for Writers, 174
Dobris, Catherine A., 22–23
Douglas, Kirk, 98
Dubrofsky, Rachel, 144
duCille, Ann, 208n4
Durham, Aisha S., 113
Durkheim, Émile, 173
DuVernay, Ava, 82
Dyson, Michael Eric, 9

racism: coded, 185–87, 197; colorblind, 73; difficulties identifying, 192; and diversity rhetoric, 188; in exclusive spaces, 81; in Hollywood (*see* Black women television workers); and inclusion (claiming a seat at the table), 3, 86, 195–98; as lack of equal opportunities, 187–88; prejudice, 150–51; social isolation resulting from, 188–92; use of "n-word," 62–63, 65–67, 181; use of "uppity," 76, 212n57, 212n60; white supremacy, 150–51

Radway, Janice, 115, 215n15

Ralph J. Bunche Center for African American Studies (UCLA), 164

reading simultaneity, 36, 209n19

reading strategies, changing, 28–29

Real Housewives of Atlanta, 106

reality TV. *See under* television; *and specific shows*

reception studies. *See* audiences

reflexionism, 204n39

Republican National Convention (RNC; 2008), 46

Republican patriotism, 45–47

Repulsa, Rita (cartoon character), 74, 212n43

resistance: by Black feminists, 21–23, 86–87; by Black women television workers, 179, 193; everyday, 22; individual, 13; for liberation/survival, 207n82; postracial, coded, 67; postracial, in media culture, 13, 21, 34, 40–41; silence as, 23; via strategic ambiguity, 2–4, 10, 13–14, 17, 21, 29, 197; by Winfrey, 24, 64

respectability politics, 13, 133–60; and Black authenticity, 136; and Black feminist resistance, 86–87; and the "Black lady" performance, 22–23; in the #BlackLivesMatter era, 104; and class, 142; via colorism, 145–51, 154; of Cosby, 84–85; culture of dissemblance created by, 23; and the culture of

poverty, 85; definition/history of, 84; of *Grey's Anatomy*, 91; and individual resistance, 13; and race hazing, 157; racial uplift via, 84–85, 141–42; rejection of, 140–45, 160; of Rhimes, 25–26, 84–85, 88, 95–96, 103–4, 106–7; and stereotypes as pornography, 134–35; and stereotypes of women of color by White women, 136–37; and White women's fear of Black women's anger, 137–41; and women's hair, 155–56

Retman, Sonnet, 99

Rhimes, Shonda, 5, 83–107, *95*; as Angry Black Woman, 100–101, *102*; on backlash against diverse shows, 165–66, *166*; Black womanhood represented by, 106; burden of representation carried by, 103; colorblind casting/ideology of, 4, 91–92, 96, 98–101, 103–4; criticism of, 104–5; as groundbreaker/role model, 195; on the Magic Negro, 87; as making a difference, 189–92; on meritocracy, 94; *New York Times* racist attack on, 100–101, *102*, 104; as pleasant and an asset to her race, 94–95; popularity/success of, 83–84, 105–6, 190–91; on race, 98–100; racial critiques by, 20; on racialized sexism, 84, 101, 104; respectability politics of, 25–26, 84–85, 88, 95–96, 103–4, 106–7; Shondaland, 83, 97–99, 104; on stereotyping, 95; strategic ambiguity avoided by, 165–66, *166*; strategic ambiguity used by, 84–88, 91–92, 94–96, 99–107, 191–92, 195; Winfrey's interview of, 83–84, 91–93, *93*, 103. See also *Grey's Anatomy*; *How to Get Away with Murder*; *Private Practice*; *Scandal*

Rhodes, Jane, xi, 141, 217n13

Rice, Condoleezza, 44

Rice, Tamir, 6, 87

Rihanna, 119

Roberts, Robin, 1

strategic ambiguity (*cont.*)
power of screens as enabling, 19–20; as race hazing, 134; respectability politics expressed via (*see* respectability politics); vs. silence, 86; vs. strategic essentialism, 16–17; by television workers (*see* Black women television workers)
structuralism, 36
Sue, Derald Wing, x, 64, 129
Sullivan, Margaret, 101
Swiss xenophobia, 73
symbolic annihilation, 138, 139

Talley, André Leon, 37
Taylor, Donald M., 128
television: access to/consumption of, 121–26; audience demographics, 123–24; Black dating shows, 124, 134–35, 142–45; Black sitcoms, 140, 167–68, 171–73, 182–83; communal watching of, 125; enculturation via, 18; hate-watching of, 110, 114, 124–26, 131–32, 140–41, 151, 215n4; new technologies in, 19–20; racial disproportionality on, 89; reality shows, 16, 77, 124–26, 131, 133, 142–44, 159 (see also *America's Next Top Model*); "White shows," 131. *See also* Black women television workers
textual analysis, 4, 14, 24, 115–16, 161, 197, 204n39
Tharps, Lori L., 156
Thompson, Ethan, 117, 123
Thompson, Kathleen, 22
Thompson, Lisa B., 22–23, 84
TMZ, 71–72, 72
tokenism, 126–31, 216–17n37
Tometi, Opal, 6
Touré, 9–10
True Match makeup, 4
Trump, Donald, 7, 56, 197–98
Turner, Sarah E., 10–11
Turner, Tina, 75

UPN network, 167–68
Urban Dictionary, 212n57

Vats, Anjali, 11
Vavrus, Mary D., 208n5
Vergara, Sofia, 188
VH1 network, 124, 144
Vick, Michael, 119–20
The View, 24, 33, 47–52, 48, 55, 57

Wall Street Journal, 105–6
Walters, Barbara, 48
Ward, Janie Victoria, 207n82
Warner, Kristen J., 93–94, 104–5
Washington, Kerry, 1–3, 2, 87, 97, 195–96, 198
Watkins, Mel, 173
WB network, 167
weapons of mass destruction (WMDs), 15, 205n43
Weber, Brenda, 37
Weheliye, Alexander, 210–11n7
WGA (Writers Guild of America), 92, 164, 177
White, Cindy L., 22–23
White, Deborah Gray, 21–22, 78
Whites: fragility of Whiteness, 40–41, 137–38; hypersexual stereotype of White women, 128–29; as raceless, 12; white as normal, 98–99; White womanhood, 40–41, 78–79; White women's fear of Black women's anger, 137–41; White women's stereotyping of women of color, 136–37
Williams, Jesse, 87, 214n15
Williams, Patricia J., 81, 213n76
Williams, Verna, 55
Wilson, Midge, 150
Winant, Howard, 39–40
Winfrey, Oprah, 5, 7, 58–82; as Angry Black Woman, 25; "Black don't crack" used by, 60; in *The Butler*, 62; conspicuous consumption by, 59, 74; as

"crying racism," 69, 71, 72, 82, 211n17; discrimination against, 20; *Entertainment Tonight* interview with, 60–68, 63, 76, 80; as groundbreaker/role model, 195; as iconic/religious figure, 58–59, 82; in media culture, 80–81; *Oprah Winfrey Show*, 59, 61; OWN cable channel of, 61, 82; popularity/success of, 24–25, 58–59; postracial resistance by, 24, 64; racial coding used by, 59–60; Rhimes interviewed by, 83–84, 91–93, 93, 103; strategic ambiguity used by, 58–61, 63–64, 67, 73, 82, 87, 93, 195; as transcending race/gender/class, 4, 58–60, 73, 81–82; on true racism, 62–66; wealth of, 74–76, swiss incident, 60–62; crying racism, 13, 60–61, 65, 69–73, 72; and the limits of strategic ambiguity, 80–82; media

response to crying racism, 60–61, 69–76, 72, 79–81, 211n17; Oprah's apology, 70–72, 72; Oprah viewed as Angry Black Woman, 61, 70, 76–79, 78; Oprah viewed as uppity, 61, 70, 75, 76; shop owner's denial, 79, 80; Twitter responses to, 68–69, 69, 77, 211n14

wink, textual, 67

women of color theory, 34–36, 39–41, 46, 57

Wood, Helen, 135

Wright, Stephen C., 128

Writers Guild of America (WGA), 92, 164, 177

Writers Mentoring Program, 174

Written By, 91–92

Zimmerman, George, 62, 214n35

Zook, Kristal Brent, 173

ABOUT THE AUTHOR

Ralina L. Joseph is Associate Professor of Communication at the University of Washington, Seattle, and the founding director of the Center for Communication, Difference, and Equity. Ralina's first book, *Transcending Blackness: From the New Millennium Mulatta to the Exceptional Multiracial*, came out in 2013.